A Pocket Guide to Opera

Rupert Christiansen was born in London and educated at King's College, Cambridge. After further study as a Fulbright scholar at Columbia University, he has written several books including *Prima Donna*, *Romantic Affinities*, *Paris Babylon*, *The Visitors* and *Arthur Hugh Clough*. In 1997, he was elected a Fellow of the Royal Society of Literature.

He is currently opera critic of the London *Daily Telegraph* and a member of the editorial board of *Opera* magazine. He has contributed to many newspapers and magazines, including *The Spectator*, *TLS*, *Harpers & Queen*, *Los Angeles Times*, *Vanity Fair*, *New Yorker* and *Talk*.

A POCKET GUIDE TO
Opera

Rupert Christiansen

faber and faber

First published in 2002
by Faber and Faber Limited
3 Queen Square, London WC1N 3AU

Published in the United States by Faber and Faber Inc.
an affiliate of Farrar, Strauss and Giroux LLC, New York

Typeset by Faber and Faber in Janson
Printed in England by Bookmarque Ltd, Croydon

A CIP record for this book
is available from the British Library

ISBN 0–571–20900–9

10 9 8 7 6 5 4 3 2 1

For Katherine and Benjamin Dempsey,
in the hope that one day they will see the point

Contents

Contents

Introduction

Whether you are a first-timer at *La Bohème* or a seasoned Wagnerian, every opera-goer can benefit from a little background information. This book aims to provide just that, setting out concise, friendly and accessible introductions to the most frequently performed works in the repertory, discussed without confusing detail or abstruse technical terms.

Now that translated text titles, projected on to either a screen or the backs of seats, are so widely in use, only a minimal synopsis seems necessary. In any case, it is my firm belief that the human brain finds the intricacies and absurdities of opera plots impossible to grasp for more than the nanosecond they take to enter one ear and exit the other. I have preferred instead to sketch in a few points of musical interest and some reference to outstanding productions and lines of dramatic interpretation, as well as recommending a widely available recording, and identifying one or two of its outstanding performers and the conductor.

I hope that the result is easily digestible and immediately useful, and if what I have written stimulates some conversation in the interval or at dinner afterwards, I shall have done the job I set out to do. Those who want to take their study a stage further can be encouraged to consult either *Kobbé's Complete Opera Book* (edited by Lord Harewood) or *The New Penguin Opera Guide* (edited by Amanda Holden), both of them more scholarly and comprehensive than I can hope to be.

Within the dimensions of a pocket guide, it is impossible to do justice to the entire operatic corpus. I have excluded the work of any composer born after 1950, which means that new operas which I guess to have a fair chance of surviving their novelty – such as Mark Anthony Turnage's *Greek* – do not feature. Among a senior generation, I particularly regret that more room could not be found for dealing with operas by Stockhausen, Berio, Henze, Ligeti, Ruders and Messiaen.

Nor do Rameau, Massenet, Rimsky-Korsakov or Prokofiev receive their due – my apologies to their shades, but I can only blame the size of the average pocket.

I owe debts to a range of sources, among them ENO's excellent series of Opera Guides, edited by the late Nicholas John, the epic and authoritative *Grove Dictionary of Opera*, Tom Sutcliffe's survey of operatic production *Believing in Opera*, back numbers of the unbeatable *Opera* magazine, and most of all, my vast and mercifully well-catalogued collection of programmes, chronicles of over thirty years of opera-going and evocative documents of some of the most wonderful experiences of my life.

My thanks to Sarah Hulbert for her expert copy-editing, to Belinda Matthews, a most sympathetic and supportive commissioning editor, and to Gerald Martin Moore, who has contributed vital expertise in matters relating to the human voice.

Rupert Christiansen, 2002

Notes

Because translators make such different interpretations, aria titles are presented in their original language.

Arpeggio a chord in which the notes are sounded sequentially rather than simultaneously

Cabaletta a fast section of music which brings formal arias in pre-1850 Italian opera to a conclusion

Cadenza the concluding flourish of an aria

Coloratura fast, florid passages of an aria

Da capo see pp. 4–5

Motif, leitmotiv melodic phrase attached to a character or an emotion

Obbligato solo instrument accompanying the voice in an aria

Opera buffa see p. 5

Opera seria see pp. 4–5

Ostinato a persistent melodic figure, usually repeated as a bass line in the orchestra

Pentatonic a five-note scale, common in folk music

Recitative musically pitched but unmelodic setting of speech, accompanied by harpsichord, piano or orchestra

Singspiel see p. 64

Trill very fast repetition of two alternated notes.

Châtelet Théâtre du Châtelet, opera house in Paris

Covent Garden commonly used name for the Royal Opera House, London

ENO English National Opera, based at the Coliseum in London

Met commonly used abbreviation for the Metropolitan Opera in New York

WNO Welsh National Opera, based in Cardiff.

PART ONE

Baroque and Classical Opera

Music has always formed an integral part of drama – the purely spoken play is a nineteenth-century aberration – and even infants seem to understand instinctively the idea that a song can tell a story or express an emotion. So why has opera developed a reputation as a difficult and exclusive art-form?

Perhaps because it grew from roots that were both aristocratic and academic. Surviving evidence suggests that throughout the Middle Ages music was used in various ways for plays both religious and secular, but these had no direct influence on the development of opera, and it was only in the High Renaissance period that the seeds found the cultural conditions in which to flourish. During the sixteenth century, the French and Italian royal and ducal courts lavished expense and ingenuity on mounting splendid entertainments as part of the celebrations surrounding weddings, christenings, birthdays and political treaties. These often focused on a play or masque, in which the spoken episodes would be broken up by musical interludes, also known as *intermedii*. In each *intermedio*, a madrigal choir would recite a little mythical story – comic, pastoral or romantically poignant – which costumed dancers simultaneously acted out in mime.

Towards the end of the sixteenth century, two groups of scholars and composers, known as the '*camerata*', met in Florence to discuss their research into classical drama. Fascinated by the idea that the Ancient Greeks had sung their plays throughout, they developed a theory of what they called '*stile rappresentativo*', 'representative style', in which solo (as opposed to choral) voices sang a form of musical speech, now known as 'recitative' or '*arioso*', accompanied by a small band of instruments.

Modern scholars still dispute what should rank as the very first opera, and in fact the term 'opera' (a Latin word, meaning literally 'works') did not come into general use until the end of the seventeenth century. Before then, the sung plays which evolved out of the *intermedii* and the writings of the *camerata* were generally called '*dramma per musica*', 'drama through music'.

The first great composer to exploit the possibilities of sung drama was Claudio Monteverdi. His *Orfeo*, the earliest opera to maintain a regular place in the modern repertory, was written in 1607 for a private court performance in Mantua; later in his career, he moved to Venice, where he produced several works for the first opera houses, built to admit a paying public.

In the second half of the seventeenth century, opera became more elaborate, both vocally and scenically – audiences demanded spectacle, excitement and novelty, as well as comic relief from the high-flown emotions of mythological heroes and heroines. An important development was the idea of pausing the narrative for an aria, a song which allowed the singer to show off his or her prowess, and which stood out from the recitative or *arioso* passages which carried the story forward: one pioneer here was another Venetian composer, Francesco Cavalli. Opera also spread to France, where the *tragédies en musique* ('tragedies in music') of Jean-Baptiste Lully and Jean-Philippe Rameau emphasized the role of the chorus and introduced elaborate ballet sequences. In England, John Blow and Henry Purcell wrote both musical interludes for plays and short operas drawing on the French model.

In the early years of the eighteenth century, the young German-born composer George Frideric Handel travelled to Italy, where he imbibed the innovations developed by composers such as Alessandro Scarlatti: these included the use of a larger, more varied orchestra and an extended form of aria. The latter became the building block for a style which would dominate the genre for the best part of a hundred years – '*opera seria*', meaning not 'serious opera', as is often thought, but opera based on arias illustrating a series of stock emotions (unfulfilled desire, vengeful anger, painful remorse and so forth). These almost always follow the tripartite *da capo* (or 'from the beginning') form, in which a first melody is followed by a second melody of contrasting mood and pace, with a final return to the first melody, embellished with 'ornaments' or 'decorations', added according to the singer's fancy.

In 1710, Handel came to London and for the next thirty years produced an astonishing succession of operas based on this principle. The *da capo* aria requires singers of great technical stamina and precision, especially female sopranos and castrati. These were men, almost all of them Italian, whose seminal cords had been severed in pubescence, resulting in a hormonal development which gave them large pigeon chests (allowing vast intake of breath) and a hauntingly beautiful, other-worldly timbre. Today the roles written for castrati are taken by either female mezzo-sopranos or male counter-tenors, who can only approximate the freakish feats of the castrati.

The Venetian composer Antonio Vivaldi also wrote over forty operas in the *opera seria* mode; they are not easily distinguishable.

In the 1760s, in a preface written to the score of *Alceste*, Christoph Willibald von Gluck attacked the domination of the virtuoso singer and the ever more formulaic convention of the *da capo* aria, proposing a return to a musical simplicity which could be more directly expressive of real emotions: 'I have striven to restrict music to its true office of serving poetry by means of expression,' he wrote, 'and I have avoided making displays of difficulty at the expense of clarity.' His example would prove enormously influential on the next generation of composers.

Meanwhile, as another antidote to the tragic, tangled and mythological plots of *opera seria*, there developed a genre of short and sharp comic opera, generally known as *opera buffa*. Avoiding both the exoticism of the castrato and the excess of the *da capo* aria, *opera buffa* presented contemporary characters in some light-hearted marital or amorous intrigue, usually involving a master and servant, or a mistress and a maid, either disguised or mistakenly identified: Giovanni-Battista

Pergolesi's *La Serva Padrona* (*The Maid who is Mistress*, 1733) and Domenico Cimarosa's *Il Matrimonio Segreto* (*The Secret Marriage*, 1766) are outstanding examples of this.

Joseph Haydn wrote several operas on both the *seria* and *buffa* models, but their occasional modern revivals have fallen flat. The work of Haydn's young friend Wolfgang Amadeus Mozart, on the other hand, has remained universally popular, and in the second half of the twentieth century he is ranked among the supreme opera composers. Without setting out to be so, he proved a revolutionary, embracing the traditions of *seria* (in *Idomeneo*) and *buffa* (*Le Nozze di Figaro*) as well as the reforms of Gluck, but introducing a fresh urgency, vitality, flexibility and subtlety of dramatic tone in mature masterpieces such as *Don Giovanni* and *Così fan tutte*. Perhaps his greatest innovation was his sophisticated use of the contrapuntal ensemble, in which three or more characters simultaneously express various feelings within one musical number.

Claudio Monteverdi (1567–1643)
Orfeo (*L'Orfeo*)

**Prologue and five acts. First performed Mantua, 1607.
Libretto by Alessandro Striggio**

'It should be most unusual as all the actors are to sing their
parts.' Thus wrote Francesco Gonzaga, son of the Duke of
Mantua, to his brother Ferdinando on the subject of an
entertainment which he had asked the court composer
Monteverdi to prepare for the carnival of 1607. Opera was
still an experimental novelty at this point, although Monteverdi
plainly knew of another musical staging of the Orpheus
legend, performed in Florence five years previously.

The Mantuan performance took place in the private apartments of the duke's sister. There would have been little or no
scenery, and there is evidence that the opera was played without an interval. The cast consisted of singers permanently
employed by the court, with four of the female roles taken by
castrati – only the Orfeo, also a castrato, was borrowed from
the Grand Duke of Tuscany. Copies of the libretto were
handed to the small private audience of courtiers, and the
performance was so successful ('women wept because nothing like this had been heard before', reported the court
chronicle) that it was repeated a few days later.

ᴥ Plot

Orfeo (Orpheus), the renowned Thracian singer, rejoices in
his love for his wife Euridice. When a messenger brings news
that she has died of a snake bite, he is so grief-stricken that he
resolves to venture into Hades and plead with Pluto to
restore her to life. Using all his musical powers, he lulls
Charon, who ferries the dead across the river Styx, to sleep
and makes his way into Pluto's domain. When he presents his
case, Pluto's wife Proserpina is so moved that she persuades

her husband to break the immutable law of death and restore Euridice to life. Out of love for Proserpina, Pluto agrees, on condition that Orfeo does not turn to look at Euridice on the journey back. But Orfeo, always ruled by emotion rather than reason, cannot resist the temptation, and Euridice is lost to him again. Disconsolate, he returns to Thrace. The god Apollo intervenes, and turns both Orfeo and Euridice into stars in the night sky.

ᴄᴠ What to listen for

As in early Greek tragedy, the chorus plays the dominant role, framing the soloists' monologues and dialogues with a series of madrigals and dances.

Two episodes exemplify aspects of Monteverdi's dramatic genius. The Messenger (mezzo-soprano) who brings Orfeo news of Euridice's death recounts the incident in extraordinarily varied music which vividly evokes the scene and the emotions which the tragedy provokes. The plea that Orfeo (tenor) makes to Charon, 'Possente spirto', doesn't have a story to tell, but is charged with a high pitch of intensity, and decorated with the vocal ornaments and flourishes that mark this phase of baroque music – one of the most obvious being the 'goat trill', in which the same note is repeatedly hammered at the end of a phrase.

For singers, the major challenge presented by Monteverdi is that of drawing out the emotional nuances while keeping the line classically clean and clear. In *Tosca* or *Madama Butterfly*, an effect can be made by sobbing, rasping, shrieking or holding a note longer than the score indicates, but such tricks don't work in an opera like *Orfeo*. Monteverdi's operas require lighter, sweeter, more flexible voices than those of Puccini, and although they make no great demands in terms of physical range or volume, they provide an acid test of the capacity to sustain a vocal line through smooth breath control.

Although musicologists disagree about the precise balance of instruments and the details of what and how they should play, the opera's orchestration can broadly speaking be said to consist of keyboards (chamber organ or harpsichord) and both bowed (violins, violas and cellos) and plucked (lutes and harp) strings, with recorders and brass instruments such as cornets and sackbutts being added for dances, fanfares and processions. On first hearing, the carpet of sound can seem rather threadbare and monochrome, but familiarity will reveal the richness of the palette. Every syllable of the text should be immediately audible.

∾ In performance

This opera appears to have been occasionally performed in Italy until the mid-seventeenth century, but its first full-scale modern revival took place in Paris in 1911. Since then, the sketchy indications of instrumentation and harmonization in the score published in 1609 have allowed free play of interpretation. Broadly speaking, the fashion for modern composers (Orff, Hindemith, Dallapiccola, Berio and Henze among them) fleshing Monteverdi's bare bones out with music composed in their own idioms has passed, and the trend now is for scholar-conductors (Nikolaus Harnoncourt, Roger Norrington and John Eliot Gardiner among them) to aim at the maximum degree of historical 'authenticity', using reconstructions of baroque instruments and following original performance practice – though the surviving evidence for this is often so ambiguous and scanty that what constitutes this 'authenticity' remains hotly contested and conjectural.

Most productions aim to recreate either the splendours of seventeenth-century baroque or the simplicity of Ancient Greece, but the most successful recent staging is probably that of David Freeman at ENO, which presents the opera as if it was being enacted by a community of Balkan peasants. They appear to devise the performance before the audience's eyes, dancing as well as singing, with the soloists also part of the chorus. The action gains in spontaneity and emotional immediacy whatever it loses in 'authentic' courtly formality.

❧ Recording

CD: John Mark Ainsley (Orfeo); Philip Pickett (cond.).
L'Oiseau Lyre 433 545 2

Il Ritorno d'Ulisse in Patria
(*The Return of Ulysses to his Homeland*)

**Prologue and three acts. First performed Venice, 1640.
Libretto by Giacomo Badoaro**

Unlike the courtly and dignified *Orfeo*, this is an opera
composed for a sophisticated public of merchants and entre-
preneurs. By the late 1630s, opera had become a popular
form of commercial entertainment in the wealthy republic of
Venice, and its paying audiences demanded something other
than the ethical seriousness of the earliest operas – hence the
introduction of elements of spectacle and knockabout
humour.

The plot is drawn from books 13 to 23 of Homer's *Odyssey*.
The score survives in one anonymous manuscript, discovered
in Vienna, and only informed guesswork ascribes it to
Monteverdi.

❧ Plot

Faithful Penelope, Queen of Ithaca laments the twenty-year
absence of Ulysses, whose return from the Trojan War has
been delayed by long years of wandering on the sea and the
hostility of its god, Neptune. Penelope has had no news of
him, but bravely resists the aggressive foreign suitors who
bully her to admit that he is dead and that she must now
remarry. Meanwhile, Ulysses has finally returned to Ithaca,
watched over by his tutelary goddess, Minerva. She advises
him to disguise himself as a beggar and only to reveal his true
identity when the time is ripe. He is secretly reunited with his

servant Eumaeus and his son Telemachus, who returns from exile in Sparta at Minerva's behest.

Using her divine powers, Minerva prompts the unwitting Penelope to announce an archery contest with a coveted prize – whoever can string Ulysses's bow may marry her. The suitors all fail the test, but Ulysses, still disguised as the old beggar, succeeds. He renounces the prize, but turns the restrung bow on the suitors and shoots them dead. Penelope remains reluctant to believe that the beggar is Ulysses. Only when he shows her a familiar scar on his shoulder and describes the cover of their marriage bed does she recognize him, and the opera ends with the joyful reunion of husband and wife.

◑ What to listen for

The chorus is no longer the central force that it was in *Orfeo* – the soloists have assumed increasing prominence, both musically and dramatically, and the opera divides more clearly into passages of speechlike recitative and songlike aria. The role of Penelope (mezzo-soprano) is notable for the short and jagged phrases which are used to indicate her emotional upheaval; only in the beautiful final duet with Ulysses (baritone) does her music ease and expand lyrically.

◑ In performance

This is a long opera with several sub-plots and it is not easy to stage: the challenge is to find a way of recreating the lavish scene-changes and spectacular effects (Neptune emerging from the sea, Minerva flying through the air in a chariot, etc.) which Venetian opera houses were purpose-built to provide. Successful modern solutions were achieved by Peter Hall's production at Glyndebourne and Adrian Noble's at Aix-en-Provence.

◑ Recording

CD: Sven Olof Eliasson (Ulisse); Nikolaus Harnoncourt (cond.). Teldec 229 2424962

L'Incoronazione di Poppea
(The Coronation of Poppea)

**Prologue and three acts. First performed Venice, 1643.
Libretto by Giovanni Busenello**

This is believed to be the first opera to be based on a historical rather than mythological source (its plot and characters
are drawn from Tacitus and Suetonius) and its tone is a
remarkable mixture of emotional moods – comic and tragic,
romantic and cynical, high- and low-minded. Two versions of
the score and ten of the libretto survive from Monteverdi's
time: the differences between them have fomented scholarly
controversy, and there is a widespread view that the music for
Ottone and the final duet between Nero and Poppea are not
by Monteverdi at all.

∾ Plot

In a Prologue, the figures of Fortune, Virtue and Love argue
as to which of them has the most power over humanity. Love
claims the victory – as the story which unfolds will justify.

Ottone returns from the wars to find that the beautiful but
schemingly ambitious Poppea has left him for the tyrannical
emperor Nerone (Nero). Despite the wise counsel of the
philosopher Seneca, Nerone resolves to rid himself of his
wife Ottavia and make Poppea his empress. Nero sentences
Seneca to death. Ottone plots with Drusilla, a lady of the
court who is in love with him, to kill Poppea. When their
scheme is foiled, Nerone sends them into exile, along with
Ottavia. Nerone crowns Poppea empress, and they celebrate
their love.

∾ What to listen for

More lightly orchestrated than *Orfeo* or *Il Ritorno d'Ulisse*,
this opera is close to the ideal of a 'sung play', in which the
drama is continuous and each character sharply drawn.

Nevertheless, there are some exquisite lyrical passages, such as the lullaby with which the nurse Arnalta calms Poppea or the madrigal in which Seneca (bass) is implored by his friends not to kill himself. Ottavia has two great solo scenes, 'Disprezzata Regina' and her farewell to Rome, 'Addio, Roma', which demonstrate Monteverdi's power of expressing the gamut of tragic emotions. In casting this opera, it is important to select voices which balance and contrast in colour: to achieve this, the role of Nerone may be sung by either a counter-tenor or a mezzo-soprano.

ᴥ In performance

Today's directors tend to interpret *Poppea* as a cynical sex comedy, and several productions have presented the opera in an ambience reminiscent of Fellini's *La Dolce Vita* or *Satyricon*, playing up the sleazy erotic decadence of Nero's court: a good example of this is David Alden's version, seen both at WNO and in Munich. The more sensitive approach taken by directors like Luc Bondy (in Brussels) and Klaus-Michael Gruber (in Vienna and Aix-en-Provence) suggests a moral maze of motive and emotion, questioning our assumption that love is always a force for good in the world. Either way, *Poppea* remains an extraordinarily modern and adult opera that hits audiences hard.

ᴥ Recording

CD: Elisabeth Söderström (Nerone); Nikolaus Harnoncourt (cond.). Teldec 835247

Francesco Cavalli (1602–76)
La Calisto

**Prologue and three acts. First performed Venice, 1651.
Libretto by Giovanni Faustini**

One of eleven operas that the hugely prolific Cavalli wrote in
collaboration with Faustini, this is a typical product of the
Venetian baroque style, alternating pathos and romance with
saucy comedy and containing several opportunities for
magical stage effects and changes of scene.

∿ Plot

The earth is barren in the aftermath of war. Jupiter descends
to earth to restore fertility, but his attention is immediately
caught by Calisto, a high-minded nymph who attends adoringly on the chaste Diana. She rebuffs his coarse advances.
Mercury cunningly suggests that in order to endear himself
to Calisto, Jupiter should transform himself into the sem-
blance of Diana. The trick seems to work. When Calisto later
mistakes the real Diana for Jupiter–Diana and attempts to
renew the love-play, the real Diana is appalled at her lesbian
indecency. The situation is further complicated by the real
Diana's secret passion for the shepherd Endimion, Pan's lust
for the real Diana and the finger-wagging of a withered old
killjoy nymph, Linfea.

Juno comes down to earth in search of her erring husband
Jupiter. What she hears from the innocent Calisto confirms
her worst suspicions. Meanwhile, Endimion mistakes the real
Diana for Jupiter–Diana and is seized and tortured by the
henchmen of the jealous Pan. Eventually the complications
unravel: Linfea is humiliated, Diana and Endimion are united,
and Juno arranges for Calisto to be transformed into a little
bear. Finally, Jupiter is restored to his original shape. He
commands that Calisto be elevated to the heavens in the form
of the night-star Ursa Minor (the little bear).

ᜆ What to listen for

A delightful farcical fantasy which may never plumb the emotional depths reached by Monteverdi, but which is rich in melodic charm and grace. The score is distinguished by the separation of passages of recitative from aria – the latter marked by opportunities for melismatic flourishes which can be added according to the abilities and whim of the singer, as well as the limitation of the roles of chorus and orchestra. All these portend the more static and elaborate form of *opera seria* which would develop by the end of the seventeenth century.

ᜆ In performance

The first modern revival took place in 1970 at Glyndebourne, where Peter Hall produced a memorable pseudo-baroque staging, on a steeply raked and long-receding platform with *trompe l'oeil* changes of scene. The scholar–conductor Raymond Leppard shamelessly assembled his own edition of the opera, interpolating passages from other works by Cavalli and creating inauthentically sumptuous orchestral textures. Later productions have taken a rather more rigorous line.

ᜆ Recording

CD: Janet Baker (Jove/Diana); Raymond Leppard (cond.). Decca 436 216 2

George Frideric Handel (1685–1759)
Giulio Cesare in Egitto
(*Julius Caesar in Egypt*)

Three acts. First performed London, 1724.
Libretto by Nicola Haym

Highly successful throughout Europe during Handel's lifetime, the composer revised the score several times, adding arias tailored to the capacity of specific singers. The action is grounded in Julius Caesar's historically documented visit to Egypt in 48 BC, although the intrigues of the plot are pure fiction.

✎ Plot

Cesare has defeated his rival Pompeo and arrives in Egypt, demanding homage. In an attempt to ingratiate himself with Cesare, Tolomeo (Ptolemy), King of Egypt, kills Pompeo. But Cesare is appalled by his treachery. Pompeo's widow Cornelia rejects both Roman and Egyptian suitors, and Sesto, son of Pompeo and Cornelia, vows vengeance on Tolomeo.

Tolomeo and his beautiful sister Cleopatra scheme against each other. Cleopatra disguises herself as 'Lidia' and uses her feminine wiles to enlist Cesare's support. Cornelia and Sesto are arrested after a foiled attempt on Tolomeo's life, but Sesto escapes from prison.

Tolomeo falsely believes himself to have triumphed over Cesare in battle. He attempts to force his attentions on Cornelia, but Sesto surprises him in the act and kills him. Cesare and Cleopatra are united. Under Cesare's guidance, Egypt is promised peace and liberty.

✎ What to listen for

Among the richest and most lavishly orchestrated of Handel's operas, *Giulio Cesare* is also very long. Whichever of the various surviving versions of the score is used, modern staged performances are almost always cut to some degree – in deference to both the audience's and the singers' endurance. Whether to excise parts of arias, entire arias or entire characters is a knotty question.

Outstanding features of Act I include Cesare's 'Va tacito', with its horn accompaniment suggesting that Cesare is closing in like a huntsman on Tolomeo, and Sesto's intense 'Cara speme'. In the opening scene of Act II, Cleopatra attempts to seduce Cesare with the sensuous 'V'adoro pupille'; as the act closes, she vows in 'Si pietà di me non senti' to die if Cesare is killed in battle. Act III finds her lamenting in 'Piangerò la sorte mia' and rejoicing in the brilliant 'Da tempeste il legno infranto'. Cesare expresses his grief at the temporary loss of Cleopatra in the heart-rending 'Aure, deh, per pietà'.

A 'double' orchestra is used in the scene at the beginning of Act II. Nine instruments on stage assist Cleopatra in her seduction of Cesare, combining and contrasting with the orchestra in the pit.

✿ In performance

The most frequently performed and popular of Handel's Italian operas, first revived in modern times in 1922. At first, the roles originally ascribed to castrati – Giulio Cesare, Nireno and Tolomeo – were transposed to suit baritones and basses; over the last thirty years or so, it has been considered important to preserve at least approximately Handel's own vocal pitches, and counter-tenors or, in the case of Cesare, mezzo-sopranos have taken them over. Cleopatra has provided a brilliant showcase for the coloratura virtuosity of sopranos such as Joan Sutherland, Beverly Sills and Kathleen Battle, while Janet Baker, Ann Murray and Anne-Sofie von Otter are among the mezzo-sopranos to have made swaggering and convincing Cesares. The role of Sesto was originally written for a mezzo-soprano, though Handel later rewrote it for a tenor. Today, it is customarily taken by a mezzo-soprano, unless an outstanding counter-tenor like David Daniels is available. Incidentally, some of the more purist 'authentic' performances are tuned by the conductor to Handel's original pitch, a good semitone lower than modern standard orchestral pitch. This makes life a lot easier for the singers.

A controversial 1985 production by the American director Peter Sellars updated the scenario to show Cesare as an American president visiting a Hilton hotel in some modern terrorist-infested Middle East capital and indulging in some very dirty power-games. This bold and often amusing production emphasized the sly satire in the libretto and prompted several further burlesque updatings. Zaniest of all was probably Richard Jones's 1994 production in Munich, dominated by a crumbling model of a Tyrannosaurus rex and a bald Cesare in kilt and Doc Martens boots.

ᙯᙚ Recordings

CD: Janet Baker (Caesar); Charles Mackerras (cond.). EMI 769 760 2. Sung in English, with modern instruments.

Jennifer Larmore (Cesare); René Jacobs (cond.). HMC 90 1385–7. For a more authentic approach and a complete score, based on the 1724 edition.

Rodelinda

Three acts. First performed London 1725.
Libretto by Nicola Haym

An instant success when first performed this opera also led the modern revival of interest in Handel's stage works – the production at the University of Göttingen in 1920 was the first any of his operas had received since 1754! Its plot, drawn from a play by the seventeenth-century French tragedian Corneille, reflects a contemporary fascination with the figure of a beleaguered solitary woman who remains firm in her virtue. Although the plot is convoluted and confusing, the characters of Eduige and Grimoaldo stand out in the generally black or white moral world of Handelian opera as characters of considerable psychological complexity and mixed motives. In other respects, it follows the 'A loves B who loves C' trail commonly taken in baroque opera.

ᴄᴠ Plot

When the old King of Lombardy dies, a war of succession ensues between Bertarido and Grimoaldo. Grimoaldo appears to have triumphed and Bertarido is supposed dead. His wife Rodelinda mourns him, and rejects Grimoaldo's offer of marriage, even though it would restore her to the throne. Bertarido's ambitious sister Eduige is in love with Grimoaldo, but, to her fury, he refuses to honour a promise to marry her. Eduige intrigues with the Duke of Turin, Garibaldo, who pretends to be in league with Grimoaldo but craves power himself.

Bertarido is not dead. He has returned in disguise and, hiding in a grove which contains his own memorial, erected by Grimoaldo, he witnesses an unpleasant scene: by taking Bertarido's and Rodelinda's son as hostage, Garibaldo forces Rodelinda to consent to marry Grimoaldo.

Now that Rodelinda has agreed to wed Grimoaldo, Garibaldo persuades Eduige to marry him instead. Rodelinda asks Grimoaldo either to execute her son or Garibaldo – for she cannot be both mother of the legitimate heir to the throne and wife to its usurping tyrant. Grimoaldo recoils.

Bertarido reveals himself to his sister Eduige. He tells her that he no longer wants the throne, only his wife and son. Sensing that this facilitates her own ambitions, Eduige agrees to help Bertarido to find Rodelinda. As husband and wife are joyfully reunited, Grimoaldo appears and arrests Bertarido.

Grimoaldo is now tormented by his crimes and yearns for a simpler life. While he is asleep, Garibaldo attempts to murder him, but Bertarido, who has escaped from prison, foils the attack and kills Garibaldo. In gratitude, Grimoaldo yields the throne to Bertarido and renews his vows to Eduige.

❧ What to listen for

As always in Handel's operas, what should matter to an audience is not so much every twist and turn of the plot, but an awareness of the emotional states which each aria represents.

Rodelinda's music offers a soprano a wide range of contrasting emotions, but it is Bertarido (originally a castrato role, now given to counter-tenors) who sings the single most beautiful and celebrated number in the opera, 'Dove sei?', as he stands by his own memorial lamenting the absence of his beloved wife. The Victorians loved this melody, and made it famous out of its operatic context as a consolatory sacred aria, with a new text and title, 'Art thou troubled?'.

Unusually among Handel's operas, there is in Grimoaldo an important role for a tenor. It was specially written for Francesco Borosini, a popular Italian singer for whose voice Handel also adjusted the mezzo-soprano part of Sesto in *Giulio Cesare*.

❧ In performance

The opera is set in seventh-century Milan – not a period easy to represent convincingly on stage. In an attempt to escape the usual Louis XIV or XV solution, the 1998 Glyndebourne production, directed by Jean-Marie Villégier, set the opera in a vaguely Fascistic environment, doubtless inspired by the tyrannical tendencies of Grimoaldo and Garibaldo, and suggested that the opera was a satire on the psychotic folly of those who stalk the corridors of power. But *Rodelinda* contains none of the comedy obviously intended in *Giulio Cesare* and perhaps it is an opera best taken seriously, at its own face value.

❧ Recording

Video: Andreas Scholl (Bertarido); William Christie (cond.). Glyndebourne production. Warner 398 423 0243

Ariodante

Three acts. First performed London, 1735.
Anonymous libretto

In 1734, after losing his base at the King's Theatre, Haymarket, Handel moved to the Covent Garden Theatre (on the site of today's Royal Opera House) and proceeded to brave the competition with *Ariodante* and *Alcina*, two spectacular operas with prominent ballet sequences in each act, designed to show off the charms and ankles of the French dancer Marie Sallé.

Based on a story-line in Ariosto's verse epic *Orlando Furioso*, *Ariodante* is set in Edinburgh, though there is no local Scottish colour in the opera to ratify the location. The plot contains parallels to the intrigues surrounding Claudio and Hero in Shakespeare's *Much Ado About Nothing*, though it is highly unlikely that either Handel or his librettist were aware of them.

❧ Plot

Ginevra, daughter of the King of Scotland, is happily betrothed to the wandering knight Ariodante. But Polinesso, Duke of Albany, is determined that he shall be the one to marry Ginevra and ascend the throne. He enlists the help of her infatuated lady-in-waiting Dalinda in a scheme designed to disillusion Ariodante, persuading Dalinda to dress up as Ginevra and enter his bedroom. Ariodante witnesses this apparent adultery and leaves the court in despair. The king rejects his daughter as a harlot, and Ginevra faints away at the news that Ariodante has killed himself.

But Ariodante secretly returns to the court and rescues Dalinda from assassins sent by Polinesso, who wishes to be rid of her. A grateful Dalinda explains the deception to Ariodante, who presents himself before the king to fight for Ginevra's honour. Polinesso is killed, and the lovers are reunited.

✎ What to listen for

Originally written for a castrato, the title role has over the last thirty years become a great vehicle for star mezzo-sopranos such as Janet Baker, Tatyana Troyanos, Ann Murray, Anne-Sofie von Otter and Lorraine Hunt Lieberson. Alongside coloratura showpieces such as 'Con l'ali di costanza' and 'Dopo notte' with its two-octave scale, the part also contains one of Handel's most intense and moving inspirations, 'Scherza, infida', sung in Act II as Ariodante reflects on Ginevra's apparent betrayal. Here is an aria which not only tests a singer's ability to sustain a smooth line, but also offers a wonderful opportunity to show how, by colouring and decoration, the repeated melodic material can be made to chart an emotional journey.

✎ In performance

A relatively simple plot, without subsidiary strands, makes this one of the most immediately enjoyable of Handel operas. ENO's production, directed by David Alden and designed by Ian MacNeil, presented the piece in a decaying baroque palace. At the back sat a small picture-frame space within which the characters' inner thoughts were dramatized; the flamboyant costumes mixed Renaissance and baroque styles.

✎ Recordings

CD: Anne-Sofie von Otter (Ariodante); Marc Minkowski (cond.). Archiv 4572712
DVD: Ann Murray (Ariodante); Ivor Bolton (cond.). ENO production. Arthaus 064

Alcina

Three acts. First performed London, 1735.
Anonymous libretto

Handel's second opera for Covent Garden, like its predecessor *Ariodante*, is a lavish affair, drawn from an episode of
Ariosto's *Orlando Furioso* and rich in opportunities for both
spectacular stage effects and dance sequences. The latter
were provided as a vehicle for Covent Garden's star attraction, the French ballerina Marie Sallé. But her appearance
as Cupid in *Alcina* was disastrous – her male admirers did
not care to see her dressed as a boy, and their booing and
hissing forced her to leave Covent Garden for ever. For a
later revival of the opera, Handel cut the dance music and
today it is rarely included at length. Those who find the
second and third acts somewhat long-winded will be interested to know that Handel also sanctioned cuts in these
acts.

A contemporary review held *Alcina* to be 'a beautiful and
instructive allegory', designed to prove that 'neither the
Council of Friends, nor the example of others . . . can stop the
giddy head-strong Youth from the Chase of imaginary or
fleeting Pleasures'.

✥ Plot

The enchantress Alcina lures men to her beautiful magic
island and its magnificent palace. Once she wearies of her victims' amorous attentions, she transforms them into rocks,
trees or animals. As the opera opens, she has fallen in love
with the knight Ruggiero, who under her spell has become
equally infatuated and forgotten his betrothed Bradamante.
Disguised as Ricciardo, Bradamante arrives on the island in
the company of her wise old tutor Melisso with the aim of
rescuing Ruggiero from Alcina's spell.

Alcina's sister Morgana encounters Bradamante–Ricciardo
and falls in love with 'him'. Morgana's lover Oronte, the commander of Alcina's army, is appalled, and in revenge tells
Ruggiero about Alcina's sorcery, fabricating a story that she is
now in love with 'Ricciardo'. Bradamante reveals her true
identity to Ruggiero, but he does not believe her, assuming
this is a ploy by 'Ricciardo' to hide his love for Alcina.

But Melisso enlightens Ruggiero as to the extent of Alcina's trickery, and Ruggiero prepares to flee the island with Bradamante, whose true identity he now acknowledges. Morgana reports back to Alcina, who jealously summons her evil spirits to thwart Ruggiero's escape, but they refuse to obey her and she mourns the loss of her magical powers.

Alcina confronts Ruggiero, and pleads with him to return to her; when he refuses, she vows revenge. But Morgana is rejected by Oronte, who joins forces with Ruggiero and Bradamante to defeat Alcina, smashing the urn which holds the source of her magical power.

Alcina and Morgana vanish and her enchanted lovers are transformed back to human shape amid general rejoicing.

∾ What to listen for

Alcina is both heroine and anti-heroine of this opera – a woman gripped by hopeless love and a ruthless sorceress who will stop at nothing to get what she wants. Handel seems more than half in love with her himself: at least, he provided her with some of his most rapturously and lushly beautiful soprano arias – in Act I, the gently seductive 'Sì, son quella'; in Act II, the lament 'Ah! mio cor' and 'Mi restano le lagrime', as well as the nervously intense 'Ombre pallide', a dramatic invocation of infernal powers which do not respond. Some interpreters of the role, Joan Sutherland included, have also appropriated Morgana's 'Tornami a vagheggiar', a coloratura showstopper (with a melody taken from an earlier cantata) which ends Act I. There is justification for this inasmuch as Handel himself allocated Alcina the aria in a revival which recast Morgana as a mezzo-soprano. The role of Alcina lies extremely high, and most sopranos today prefer to sing it at the original lower baroque pitch.

The role of Ruggiero was written for Giovanni Carestini, the castrato who sang Ariodante, and their arias are similar in several respects. 'Verdi prati', an aria in Act II in which Ruggiero celebrates the beauties of Alcina's island, shows Handel at his most warmly lyrical – Carestini complained that it failed to show off his virtuosity, much to the composer's disgust. As if to compensate, 'Stà nell'Ircana' is rousingly brilliant, with duetting horns providing a whooping accompaniment. Today, the role is sung by a mezzo-soprano.

Handel inserted the minor role of Oberto into the opera at a late stage of rehearsal as a way of incorporating the talents of a boy treble called William Savage. Today, Oberto is sung by a soprano, or cut altogether.

∾ In performance

Franco Zeffirelli's 1960 staging of *Alcina* – primarily mounted as a vehicle for the vocal talents of Joan Sutherland in the title role – was much criticized for the fussy splendour of its *faux*-baroque sets and costumes as well as the cuts, transpositions and alterations freely made by the conductor Richard Bonynge. But Zeffirelli's approach was true to the extravagance of the original 1735 performances, and for all its inauthenticity, the subsequent Sutherland and Bonynge recording brought the great beauties of the score to wider public notice. More recent productions, such as Robert Carsen's at the Paris Opéra (with Renée Fleming in the title role) and Jossi Wieler's and Sergio Morabito's at the Stuttgart State Opera, have interpreted the story in terms of modern sexual obsessions, bringing a surrealist flavour to the fantasy in the plot.

At ENO, David McVicar's staging appeared to pick up on a remark made by one of Handel's lady friends after she watched him conducting a rehearsal of this opera; 'whilst Mr Handel was playing his part, I could not help thinking him a necromancer in the midst of his own enchantments'. At ENO, Alcina's magic was not controlled by a wand but her singing voice, and the urn which contained her power was represented by a bust of Handel.

∾ Recording

CD: Renée Fleming (Alcina); William Christie (cond.). Erato 857 802 33 2

Serse (Xerxes)

Three acts. First performed London, 1738.
Anonymous libretto

Handel came close to mental and physical breakdown in 1737, the result of overwork and the stress of keeping the Covent Garden Opera alive against competition from the King's Theatre, Haymarket. *Serse* is the result of his convalescence, and responds to the vogue for satirizing the excesses of the Italian opera style, provoked by John Gay's *The Beggar's Opera* and John Lampe's pantomime *The Dragon of Wantley*: *Serse* is shorter and more wryly comic than the operas Handel was writing three years previously.

Yet despite the presence in the title role of the sensational castrato Gaetano Caffarelli, *Serse* was unsuccessful. Perhaps audiences wanted opera to be either outright burlesque or the traditional recipe, and the tone of *Serse* is more subtle than that.

In the twentieth century, however, *Serse* has become one of Handel's most popular and frequently performed operas – partly because it is relatively easy to cast and sing, and partly because of 'Ombra mai fù', sung by Serse at the opening of the opera and commonly featured on lists of the World's Best Tunes as 'Handel's Largo'. The manuscript score is actually marked 'Larghetto', indicating that Handel did not wish the melody to proceed at the funereal pace at which church organists customarily play it.

The libretto is very loosely based on an episode of Herodotus' *Histories*, as elaborated by other contemporary Italian opera librettos.

✎ Plot

Serse, the flamboyant and tyrannical King of Persia, loves Romilda, daughter of Ariodate, commander of the Persian army. Serse asks his brother Arsamene to inform Romilda of his infatuation, but Arsamene is in love with Romilda himself and refuses to help. The situation is complicated by

Romilda's sister Atalanta, who is in love with Arsamene. Atalanta resolves to clear the field by encouraging Arsamene's suit, but Serse banishes him.

A foreign princess, Amastre, is betrothed to Serse. Unable to bear separation from him, she disguises herself as a soldier and fights in Ariodate's army. When she discovers Serse's passion for Romilda, she, too, vows revenge.

Atalanta schemes to persuade Romilda that Arsamene is unfaithful, but Romilda remains steadfast. Serse inspects a new bridge across the Hellespont which will allow him to invade Europe, but its collapse in a violent storm humiliates him. He persuades Romilda's father Ariodate to agree that she should be married to a royal prince and orders Arsamene's execution. Arsamene believes Romilda to have betrayed him, but Ariodate, misreading the identity of the 'royal prince', marries Romilda to Arsamene. Serse is furious when he discovers this, but when Amastre steps forward and reveals herself, he has no alternative but to marry her instead.

∾ What to listen for

This is one of Handel's most concise operas, marking a move away from the full-scale heroic *da capo* aria and the introduction of shorter, more simple strophic arias. Although the score is high-spirited and inventive, it contains several 'borrowings', if not outright plagiarisms, from other composers – evidence that Handel's energies were low at the time of composition. The castrato role of Serse is sung today by mezzo-sopranos, although no modern singers can match the incredible feats of breath control that the castrati could achieve and some notes have to be eliminated in order to give an ordinary mortal the chance to inhale. On the other hand, the role of Arsamene, originally taken by a female soprano, is now usually assigned to a counter-tenor in order to widen the spectrum of vocal colour.

Characterization in the opera is sharp, and even the scheming Atalanta is allowed a poignant aria, 'Voi me dite', which suggests her vulnerability.

❧ In performance

Nicholas Hytner's production for ENO, designed by David Fielding, is rated as one of the great modern stagings of Handel. Set in an eighteenth-century pleasure garden, it suggested that the opera was a satire on sophisticated London of the 1730s, without ever allowing the witty visual jokes and allusions (including a hilarious miniature version of the bridge across the Hellespont) to swamp the characters or their emotional dilemmas.

❧ Recordings

Video and DVD: Ann Murray (Xerxes); Charles Mackerras (cond.). ENO production. Universal 02792933 (video) and Arthaus Musik 076 (DVD)

Semele

Three acts. First performed London, 1744.
Libretto by William Congreve

The master of Restoration comedy William Congreve wrote the libretto in 1705 for an opera in English composed by John Eccles, but because of the sudden fashion for imported Italian opera, this version was not performed until 1972. In 1743, however, Handel adapted Congreve's libretto, turning it into something closer in form to the English oratorios (like *Messiah* and *Samson*) he was writing at the time than to the Italian operas of the 1720s and 1730s which had now gone out of fashion. The first performance of *Semele* was presented in concert form, without scenery or costumes, but because it had a saucy mythological plot rather than the sacred biblical subject common to oratorio, it seems to have baffled the audience, and it is only in the last thirty ears that its charms have been widely appreciated.

Ꮽ Plot

Cadmus, King of Thebes prepares to marry his dazzling daughter Semele to Prince Athamas. But Semele is hesitant, as she is secretly in love with Jupiter, king of the gods, who has visited her in mortal disguise, and it is Semele's sister Ino who truly loves Athamas. Semele is carried off to Olympus by Jupiter disguised as an eagle and is set up as his mistress, much to the disgust of Jupiter's vengeful wife Juno, who enlists the help of Somnus, god of sleep.

Armed with Somnus's magic, Juno disguises herself as Ino and presents Semele with a mirror which tricks Semele into falling in love with her own beauty. Juno–Ino then advises Semele to have Jupiter make love to her in godlike form rather than his mortal disguise – a sight which will confer immortality on whoever witnesses it. Semele thinks this is a fine idea, and when Jupiter returns, she rejects his amorous advances until he promises to give her whatever she demands. He agrees, and she asks him to take her in his godlike form. Jupiter is horrified, but she refuses to accept anything less, and Semele is duly destroyed by the burning radiance of Jupiter's true form. Juno is delighted.

Ino and Athamas marry with Jupiter's blessing, and Apollo announces that Bacchus, the god of wine and pleasure, will rise from Semele's ashes.

Ꮽ What to listen for

Because *Semele* owes so much to the form of the oratorio, the chorus plays a much larger role here than in any other Handel opera. But it is Semele who dominates the show – it is a dream role for every first-rate light soprano with good looks and the ability to act flirtatious (Kathleen Battle, Valerie Masterson, Ruth Ann Swenson and Rosemary Joshua among them). The arias become more difficult as the opera progresses, the trickiest being the 'Mirror' aria, 'Myself I shall adore': this contains sequences of rising triplets which only the most technically adept manage to execute in perfectly even rhythm. The final 'No, no, I'll take no less' involves some fiendishly long runs, some of them lying very low in an otherwise bright and high role – sopranos often use their freedom to ornament to take the music to a more comfortable area further up the stave!

The role of Jupiter demands a tenor who can provide both an effortlessly sweet legato for 'Where'er you walk' and vigorous coloratura for his other arias – most singers tend to be markedly better at one or the other. The roles of Juno and Ino are often doubled by the same mezzo-soprano: Juno's 'Iris, hence away' is a show-stopper.

☙ In performance

John Copley's 1982 production at Covent Garden is one of many which presents this opera in lavish baroque style, with designs that echo the great murals and frescos of Tiepolo or Boucher; Robert Carsen's 1996 production, first seen in Aix-en-Provence, treats it more as a cynical modern sex comedy, with Semele as a vain little gold-digger who gets her come-uppance at the hands of a vicious suburban housewife.

☙ Recording

CD: Kathleen Battle (Semele); John Nelson (cond.).
DG 4357822

Christoph Willibald von Gluck (1714–87)
Orfeo ed Euridice (*Orpheus and Eurydice*)

Three acts. Italian version first performed Vienna, 1762.
Libretto by Ranieri de Calzabigi.
French version first performed Paris, 1774.
Libretto by Pierre-Louis Moline

The first of Gluck's so-called 'Reform' operas, in which a classical simplicity and nobility, of both music and plot, replace the extravagance and complexities of *opera seria*. It exists in various forms. The first version, with an Italian libretto, was written for the contralto castrato Gaetano Guadagni; this was revised for a soprano castrato in 1769. In 1774, Gluck revised the opera again for a French text, transposing the title role for a *haut-contre* tenor, roughly comparable to a modern counter-tenor, and adding new material which included extended ballet sequences. Further minor adaptations were made after Gluck's death, and in 1859 Berlioz made a full-scale consolidation of the best of the French and Italian versions, rewriting the title role for the mezzo-soprano Pauline Viardot but keeping the French text.

Another important edition, conflating the Italian versions, which became standard until the 1970s, was made by the publishers Ricordi in 1889: it conflates the Italian versions. The majority of modern performances are of the Italian version, but Berlioz's edition has lately come back into fashion. Both counter-tenors and mezzo-sopranos covet the role of Orfeo–Orphée, and baritones such as Dietrich Fischer-Dieskau have attempted it too.

❧ Plot
Orfeo (Orpheus) and his friends mourn the death of his wife

Euridice. When he resolves to descend into Hades to seek her out, the god Amor tells him that if he can calm the spirits of the dead with his lyre, he will be able to return to the living world with Euridice – on condition that he does not look at her on the journey back.

Orfeo braves the horrors of Hades, and wins over the Furies who guard its portals with his music. He finds Euridice in the Elysian Fields. As he leads her back to earth, she becomes increasingly agitated by his refusal to look at her. Eventually, Orfeo can resist her imprecations no longer – he turns round, and Euridice dies.

Orfeo resolves to kill himself, until Amor appears to inform him that the gods think that Orfeo has given proof enough of his fidelity. Euridice is restored to life, and the opera concludes with rejoicing.

✏ What to listen for

What makes *Orfeo* so radical and so important to the development of the art-form is (a) its elimination of harpsichord-accompanied recitative in favour of a stronger and more expressive dramatic declamation, reinforced by the orchestra; (b) the abandonment of the heavily ornamented *da capo* aria which dominated the Italian *opera seria* of Handel, Vivaldi and others; and (c) the prominence of the chorus.

Nobody is certain whether Gluck wrote Orfeo's heroically virtuoso aria at the end of Act I or not, though he certainly sanctioned its inclusion in the French version. It represents a throwback to the *opera seria* style, and purists consider it to be out of keeping with the rest of the opera, but it undoubtedly makes a strong climax to the scene and it is hard not to prefer it to the cursory and unmemorable ending of the original Italian version.

The most famous number in the score is 'Che farò senza Euridice?' or 'J'ai perdu mon Eurydice' (translated as 'What is life to me without thee?' in the version recorded by Kathleen Ferrier) – a miraculously simple tune in a major key which conveys the full force of Orfeo's loss without rhetorical exaggeration. Equally remarkable is Orfeo's impassioned dialogue with the Furies at the beginning of Act II – a passage typical of Gluck's delight in alternating solo and choral voices – and Orfeo's rapturous aria 'Che puro ciel'/'Quel nouveau ciel', in which the warmth and radiance of the Elysian Fields shines through the vocal line with its sun-dappled oboe accompaniment.

✍ In performance

Orfeo provides a great role for mezzo-sopranos from Kathleen Ferrier to Shirley Verrett, Janet Baker and Anne-Sofie von Otter as well as counter-tenors such as Jochen Kowalski and David Daniels – the challenge being not so much any vocal hurdle as the realization of the character's emotional journey. Kowalski was famous for playing the role as a burnt-out rock star, his harp a guitar, in a hard hitting production by Harry Kupfer.

✍ Recording

CD: Anne-Sofie von Otter (Orfeo); John Eliot Gardiner (cond.). EMI 49834 2

Alceste

Three acts. Italian version first performed Vienna, 1767.
Libretto by Ranieri de Calzabigi.
French version first performed Paris, 1776.
Libretto by Marie-François Roullet

The second of Gluck's 'Reform' operas, *Alceste* also exists, like *Orfeo ed Euridice*, in substantially differing versions. The first, written to an Italian text, has now been almost entirely supplanted by the 1776 French version which has the advantage of presenting the figures of Alceste and Admete in depth and focus, and the disadvantage of the tiresome figure of Hercules, whose 'comic' intrusion at the climax of the tragedy seems to modern audiences both implausible and inappropriate. The Italian version contains longer, grander choruses and a simpler happy ending, effected by the appearance of Apollo, restoring Alceste to life.

The libretto is drawn from the tragedy by Euripides.

✎ Plot

Admete, King of Thessaly lies gravely ill, and through his oracle the god Apollo makes it known that he must die unless he can find someone else to die in his place. His wife Alceste resolves to make this terrible sacrifice.

Admete recovers, but is appalled to hear what Alceste has promised without his consent. Alceste will not relent. She bids farewell to her beloved children. Admete begs the gods to take him instead. In vain – Alceste crosses into the realms of death. The tragedy is unexpectedly resolved by the bluff strong-man Hercules, who is passing through Thessaly. When he hears what has happened, he uses his superhuman strength to bring Alceste back from Hades, reuniting her with Admete. The people of Thessaly rejoice.

✎ What to listen for

One of the most moving of all eighteenth-century operas, *Alceste* is coloured by a pall of doom and despair which doesn't lift until Hercules makes his incongruous appearance. Its style has a solemn purity, devoid of all extraneous ornament or effect. Compared to Handel's operas, *Alceste* moves with seamless continuity and clarity, charged with dramatic recitative (accompanied by the full orchestra, rather than a harpsichord or cello) out of which grow powerful arias ('Divinités du Styx', sung by Alceste at the end of Act I, being the most celebrated) and an overwhelming emotional intensity.

✎ In performance

Alceste can't be messed about with – its drama is too austere for fanciful directorial interpretation to add anything of value, and most productions opt for a conventional neo-classical setting of temples and togas. Robert Wilson's staging – seen in

Chicago and Paris – aimed at a more radical stylization, with abstract settings and the singers, austerely clad in black, confined to a minimal choreography of gesture and movement. Despite these restrictions, both Jessye Norman and Anne-Sofie von Otter have given memorable performances in the title role. Among other great interpreters of Alceste are Kirsten Flagstad, Maria Callas, Julia Varady and Janet Baker.

∾ Recording

DVD: Anne-Sofie von Otter (Alceste); John Eliot Gardiner (cond.). Arthaus 160.

Iphigénie en Tauride

Four acts. First performed Paris, 1779.
Libretto by Nicolas-François Guillard

Drawn, like *Alceste*, from a tragedy by Euripides, *Iphigénie en Tauride* is widely considered Gluck's masterpiece. It followed five years after *Iphigénie en Aulide*, which treats of an earlier episode in the character's mythological life and revolves, like *Alceste*, around the question of a human sacrifice demanded by the Gods. *Iphigénie en Tauride* is even more concentrated, eliminating the long *ballets-divertissements* that were a great feature of the French style of the time and integrating both dancers and chorus into the main action. There are no obvious set-pieces in *Iphigénie en Tauride* – for sheer dramatic fluency and depth of characterization, there are few operas to match it.

∾ Plot

Iphigénie is a Greek priestess, daughter of Agamemnon and Clytemnestre, sent by the goddess Diana to the island of Tauris, where she is forced to sacrifice human beings on her altar. Unknown to her, her brother Oreste has killed their mother Clytemnestre in revenge for her murder of Agamemnon.

As the opera opens, Iphigénie beg the gods to calm a terrible storm. She despairs – in a dream, she has seen herself about to kill her brother Oreste. Thoas, King of the Scythians, is terrified by an oracle which commands him to sacrifice any stranger who lands on the island or to face death himself. Oreste and his friend Pylade are washed up on the island by the storm and Thoas duly condemns them to death.

Oreste is consumed with guilt, both on account of his murder of Clytemnestre and for the plight in which he has put the loyal Pylade. The Furies hound Oreste. Iphigénie confronts Oreste, but they do not recognize each other. Oreste tells her the story of the deaths of Agamemnon and Clytemnestre and pretends that the assassin Oreste then killed himself.

Iphigénie cannot understand the pity she feels for the nameless man. She resolves to release him and sacrifice only Pylade. But Oreste begs to die in Pylade's place; reluctantly, Iphigénie agrees and Pylade is set free.

As Iphigénie is about to slit Oreste's throat, he accidentally reveals his true identity. Iphigénie throws down the sacrificial knife and embraces her long-lost brother. But Thoas appears in fury at Iphigénie's evasions: as he is about to kill Oreste himself, Pylade returns with soldiers and in the ensuing battle, Thoas is killed.

Only the intervention of the goddess Diana stops the bloodshed: she decrees that Oreste and Iphigénie will return to reign in Greece.

✎ What to listen for

A score so taut and continuously coherent that one cannot talk of its 'highlights'. Note, however, the economy of orchestration (trombones accompanying the arrival of the Furies, the oboe echoing and enhancing the wretchedness of Iphigénie's aria, 'O malheureuse Iphigénie', in Act II) and the use of poundingly insistent rhythmic pulsion to indicate situations of dramatic terror and urgency.

Mozart's *Don Giovanni*, Berlioz's *Les Troyens* and Wagner's *Lohengrin* are only three of the many operas to emulate *Iphigénie*'s solemn tragic grandeur and sense of the sublime.

∾ In performance

A famous and much-travelled production, conceived in 1974 by the choreographer Pina Bausch for the Tanztheater Wuppertal, used Gluck's 1781 German version of the opera: the action was entirely danced, with the singers performing off-stage. For WNO, Patrice Caurier and Moshe Leiser created a memorably grim, vaguely modern setting, with Tauris interpreted as a bombed-out war zone, stricken by fear and deprivation. *Iphigénie en Tauride* is too austere and serious to be widely popular, but no true opera lover should miss a chance of experiencing the tremendous impact it exerts in a good performance.

∾ Recording

CD: Diana Montague (Iphigénie); John Eliot Gardiner (cond.). Philips 416 148

Wolfgang Amadeus Mozart
(1756–91)
Idomeneo, Re di Creta
(*Idomeneo, King of Crete*)

Three acts. First performed Munich, 1781.
Libretto by Giovanni Varesco

The young Mozart became tired of writing aria-dominated opera in the style of Italian *opera seria*. *Idomeneo*, written when he was twenty-five to a commission from the Elector of Bavaria for the court opera house in Munich, shows him experimenting with the reforms being proposed at the time by Gluck. Mozart's letters to his father in Salzburg suggest the difficulties he had persuading the librettist and a cast of varying abilities and egocentricities to sacrifice easy applause in the interest of brevity and dramatic credibility. During rehearsal, Mozart made many cuts and alterations, leaving today's productions with a number of options – including the omission of the Act III arias for Idomeneo and Elettra.

After the first performance, Mozart pondered writing another, less compromised version of the opera in German, giving the role of Idomeneo to a bass and bringing the whole opera closer to the Gluckian model. In the event, he made only minor revisions when the opera was revived in Vienna in 1786, transposing the role of Idamante from soprano castrato to tenor (it is now often sung by a mezzo-soprano), abbreviating the secondary role of the High Priest Arbace, and moderating the showiness of Idomeneo's big aria 'Fuor del mar'.

The libretto is adapted from a long-forgotten French opera of 1712, reduced from five acts to three, shorn of its prologue and provided with a happy ending which accords with the moral optimism of the Enlightenment.

∾ Plot

King Idomeneo, returning from the Trojan War to his home-land, Crete, is caught on the sea in a terrible storm. He prays to the god Neptune to allow him to live, promising that when he reaches the shore he will make a sacrifice of the first human being he sees. Neptune agrees to the cruel bargain, but Idomeneo is aghast when it is his son Idamante who awaits him as he emerges from the shipwreck.

The Trojan princess Ilia has already been sent back to Crete as a prisoner of war. Idamante hopes to marry her, and forge a peaceful alliance between their peoples. Although he is a member of the enemy, Ilia is slowly won over by his sincerity. But Princess Elettra, a refugee from Argos, loves Idamante and is determined that he shall not marry Ilia. Idomeneo's adviser Arbace suggests to Idomeneo that he secretly send Idamante with Elettra back to Argos, as a way of avoiding the sacrifice. But as they are about to leave, a massive storm breaks out and a monster emerges from the waves, raised by Neptune in fury at the attempt to deceive him.

Idamante prepares to battle with the sea monster which has ravaged Crete with the plague. As he and Ilia declare their love, Elettra rushes in mad with jealousy, accompanied by Idomeneo, who reveals for the first time the truth about the vow he made to Neptune. Idamante kills the monster and then nobly offers to be sacrificed, as does Ilia. But Neptune now commands that Idomeneo abdicates the throne, and that Idamante rules in his place, with Ilia as his wife. Elettra storms off in fury, but Idomeneo is happy to stand down and restore peace to Crete.

∾ What to listen for

Clearly influenced by the solemnity and majesty of Gluck, *Idomeneo* is perhaps Mozart's most purely beautiful opera, even if it lacks the wit, sparkle and variety of pace which mark his later Italian works. *Idomeneo* can seem slow on first encounter, but repeated hearings will prove ever more deeply rewarding. The Act II quartet 'Andrò, ramingo e solo' in which Idomeneo, Idamante, Ilia and Elettra simultaneously voice contrasting feelings is a turning-point in the history of opera – the first moment when an ensemble, rather than a solo aria, functions as the central form of emotional and dramatic expression.

The title role attracts tenors not normally associated with Mozart, including Domingo, Pavarotti and Heppner. The big bravura aria 'Fuor del mar' in Act I presents difficulties for such voices because of its fast coloratura, but Mozart also wrote a less strenuous version which can be substituted. The other problematic role is Elettra – like Donna Anna in *Don Giovanni*, this requires a dramatic soprano with spitfire energy and heft for 'D'Oreste, d'Ajace', but also high-lying soft singing for the exquisite solo 'Soave zeffiri' which interrupts the chorus 'Placido è il mar' and sounds as though it should be sung by the gentle-hearted Ilia.

ᦉ In performance

Idomeneo is a difficult opera to stage: elaborate baroque productions such as Jean-Pierre Ponnelle's at the Met tend to weigh the drama down; more recently, directors such as Trevor Nunn (at Glyndebourne) and David McVicar (Scottish Opera and Antwerp) have opted for a visually minimalist approach and concentrated on the emotional interaction between the four principal characters. More ambitious productions have attempted to explore Cretan society and the nature of Idomeneo's regime, as well as the horrors of the plague that is visited upon it, but such things really have little place in Mozart's music or Varesco's text.

ᦉ Recording

CD: Anthony Rolfe Johnson (Idomeneo); John Eliot Gardiner (cond.). Archiv 431 674 2

Die Entführung aus dem Serail
(The Abduction from the Seraglio)

Three acts. First performed Vienna, 1782.
Libretto by Gottlieb Stephanie

Weber once wrote that *Entführung* marked 'the victory of youth in all its freshness': it is certainly an opera full of exuberance, written at the time of Mozart's courtship of Constanze Weber. Constanze's cantankerous mother put considerable difficulties in the way of their marriage, and it is surely not fanciful to believe that the traditional theme of young lovers escaping from tyranny had a pressing personal relevance to the composer – not least because of the neat coincidence of a heroine called Constanze in the libretto on which the opera is based.

Turkey and the Islamic Middle East was a fashionable terrain for eighteenth-century literature and drama, and the figure of the Noble Infidel showing up the lily-livered Christians would have been familiar to Mozart's audiences. The opera was a big instant hit, performed all over Europe, but because of the absence of copyright law, Mozart only ever made his original fee of 100 ducats out of its success.

There is a probably apocryphal story that the Emperor Joseph II greeted the composer after the first performance with the effete judgment, 'Too beautiful for our ears, and far too many notes, my dear Mozart.' To which the indomitable Mozart smartly retorted, 'As many as are needed, Your Majesty.'

ᦉ Plot

The young Spanish nobleman Belmonte has come to Turkey to rescue his beloved Constanze, who has been sold into the harem of Bassa Selim after her ship was captured by pirates. Belmonte plots with his quick-witted manservant Pedrillo to gain admittance to Bassa (Pasha) Selim's palace by pretending to be an architect.

Bassa Selim craves Constanze's love, threatening to torture her unless she complies. She remains fiercely loyal to Belmonte. Meanwhile the lecherous Osmin, overseer of the harem, has designs on Constanze's pert English maid Blonde, who is enamoured of Pedrillo. Belmonte and Pedrillo ply the susceptible Osmin with alcohol laced with a sleeping potion, and after he collapses in a stupor, they meet up with Constanze and Blonde. The men doubt that the women have been faithful to them – a charge the women furiously repudiate.

At dead of night, Belmonte and Pedrillo return with a ladder, but the wakened Osmin catches the foursome in the act of escaping and brings them before Bassa Selim. When Belmonte reveals his true identity, it emerges that he is the son of Bassa Selim's worst enemy, a man who has done him a terrible wrong. Fearing his wrathful judgment, the foursome ask only to die together. But Bassa Selim shows them clemency, scorning to repay evil with evil, in the hopes that Europeans will follow his example. To Osmin's disgruntlement, he sets the lovers free.

✃ What to listen for

This is an opera written in conscious opposition to the high-flown rigour of Italian *opera seria* – like *Die Zauberflöte*, it falls into the genre of *Singspiel*, or sung play, advancing the plot by spoken dialogue rather than harpsichord-accompanied recitative, and mixing elements of the Italian style (Constanze's long and elaborate concertolike aria, 'Martern aller Arten') with knockabout farce (the farcical duet for Pedrillo and Osmin, 'Vivat Bacchus!') and the purely Mozartian inspiration of the Act II finale, in which the four lovers meet, quarrel and then kiss and make up in the course of one magnificent quartet.

The role of Constanze is probably the most difficult of any in Mozart's *œuvre*, and few singers have made any real mark in it. It was written for the great coloratura soprano of the day, Caterina Cavalieri, and Mozart seems to have made her music – to an almost vindictive degree – a challenge to

Cavalieri's abilities to execute fast runs, roulades and high notes. The result is that it lies too high for the sort of singer who may be comfortable with the soprano roles in *Così fan tutte* or *Don Giovanni*, but is too heavy and demanding for the sort of high-register light soprano who sings the Queen of the Night in *Die Zauberflöte* or Constanze's maid Blonde. The prevalent views about 'authenticity' and honouring the letter of Mozart's score means that the nineteenth-century solution – transposing the arias to a lower key – is no longer considered acceptable.

For a tenor, Belmonte is another demanding role, benefiting only from the common practice of omitting one or other of his arias. Nor is Osmin much fun for a bass: his music requires numerous trills, triplets, and several bottom Ds – the lowest notes Mozart ever wrote for a human voice – and his aria 'Ha! Wie will ich triumphieren' extends over the wide range of two octaves. Even Blonde has her nasty moments, notably the three staccato top Es in her first aria which floor all but the most fearlessly accomplished soubrettes. Only Bassa Selim escapes the musical minefield – his role is entirely spoken.

∾ In performance

The fact that so many singers shy away from the technical difficulties of this opera contributes to the relative rarity of performance. Straightforwardly decorative productions like those of Elijah Moshinsky at Covent Garden and John Dexter at the Met provide an attractive setting, but avoid the plot's curious erotic, racial and religious implications. In contrast, a famous production in Frankfurt, directed by Ruth Berghaus, was set mostly within a cage, suspended in a white box full of trapdoors. It emphasized the sexual politics of Constanze's situation and the idea of smug Europeans confronting the superior moral delicacy of the Muslim world. At the end of the opera, the lovers did not escape to happiness, but remained lost in a maze of their own making.

∾ Recordings

CD: Luba Organosova (Constanze); John Eliot Gardiner (cond.). Archiv 4358572
Video: Edita Gruberova (Constanze); Karl Böhm (cond.). Bavarian State Opera production. DG 0724083

Le Nozze di Figaro
(The Marriage of Figaro)

Four acts. First performed Vienna, 1786.
Libretto by Lorenzo da Ponte

Perhaps the first opera to use a contemporary theatrical hit as its libretto – Beaumarchais's *Les Noces de Figaro* had been given its première barely two years before Mozart and da Ponte's adaptation. It caused an immediate sensation, and was banned in several countries on the grounds that it presented the aristocracy in such a poor light and the servant class as cheeky, ambitious and ready to fight back. Later, it would be regarded as a crucial harbinger of the French Revolution.

In fact, the libretto largely ignores the dangerous political gauntlet that Beaumarchais's Figaro throws down against *ancien-régime* privilege, as well as omitting a long trial scene; instead, it finds greater poignancy in the loneliness of the Countess's situation in contrast to the general erotic exuberance of the intrigue.

∾ Plot

Figaro and Susanna, servants to the Count and Countess Almaviva, are happily preparing for their wedding. But there are two shadows over their happiness – one being the Count's obvious sexual interest in Susanna and his feudal right as her master to take her virginity; the other being Figaro's promise to marry the middle-aged governess Marcellina if he does not repay the money he owes her. Marcellina conspires with Dr

Bartolo, who has his own reasons for wanting revenge on Figaro. The Count's priapic page Cherubino is another problem – he is infatuated with the Countess and knows all about the Count's designs on Susanna, as does the creepy music master Don Basilio. But the Count has discovered that Cherubino has been misbehaving with the gardener's daughter Barbarina, and he uses this as an excuse to send Cherubino off to join his regiment.

Later that morning, the Countess sits in her boudoir lamenting the loss of her husband's affections. Together with Figaro, Susanna and Cherubino, she devises a plan to expose his philandering: Susanna will propose a rendezvous with the Count, but it will be Cherubino, dressed as Susanna, who will take her place. The Count bursts in on their discussions, suspecting Cherubino's presence. But Cherubino has jumped out of the window to escape, and the Countess pretends that only Susanna was with her. Later, the gardener Antonio appears, complaining of smashed glass and broken flower-pots below the Countess's window and brandishing Cherubino's army commission which dropped from his pocket. Figaro helps to cover up, but he has lost track of the intrigue and is confused and suspicious too.

Marcellina is becoming more insistent that Figaro pays back the money he owes her, but he forestalls her by refusing to marry without his parents' consent. When he reveals a birthmark on his arm, it emerges that Marcellina is his long-lost mother, and the embarrassed Dr Bartolo his father. Susanna appears to find Figaro embracing Marcellina, and misinterprets the gesture. Explanations are made, all is forgiven and Bartolo and Marcellina, as well as Figaro and Susanna, are married before the Count and Countess. Cherubino is forgiven too and allowed to marry Barbarina, as the Count realizes that he cannot afford to make an enemy of him. During the ceremony, Susanna hands the Count a seductive letter specifying a time and place for their meeting – to confirm the assignation, she asks that he returns her the pin which seals the envelope: Barbarina will act as go-between.

That same evening in the garden, Barbarina searches for the pin, which she cannot find in the darkness. Figaro finds her, and the girl unwittingly reveals that she is carrying a message from the Count to Susanna. Figaro is furious, suspecting that Susanna is double-crossing him. The Count appears to meet Susanna, but the woman who awaits him is the Countess. After a further round of comically mistaken identities, Susanna reveals the whole story to Figaro and the humiliated Count begs forgiveness of the Countess. Everybody decides to learn from the experience of the day and resolves to enjoy the fun of the wedding party.

✎ What to listen for

With its charm, energy, pace, humour, incomparably vivid characterization, wonderful melodies and profoundly sympathetic understanding of human emotions and behaviour, *Le Nozze di Figaro* is justly rated as one of the greatest and most popular of operas. Only half its numbers are arias for solo voice, and the score is equally notable for the vivacity of its recitatives and its duets, trios and ensembles, in particular the masterfully constructed finale to Act II and the comic sextet in Act III. Both of these episodes serve to carry the plot forward with effortless fluency.

Many of the shorter arias seem to flow out of the dramatic moment too: Susanna's 'Venite, inginocchiatevi', sung as she helps Cherubino to dress as a girl; Cherubino's outburst of undirected erotic fervour, 'Non so più'; or Barbarina's lament for the lost pin, 'L'ho perduta'.

So much of the joy of *Figaro* lies in the detail – and in a good performance, the exchange of recitative should be as lively and expressive as the arias. Only the last garden scene is slightly problematic: if Basilio's and Marcellina's arias are omitted (which they sometimes are), the scene seems too short; if they are included, their stately minuet pace and formality drags it down.

Susanna is a wonderful role for a lively lyric soprano, but a long one, demanding considerable stamina – the big aria, 'Deh vieni non tardar', comes at the end of a long evening when the singer will be tired, not only from singing but also from running round the stage. The Countess is blessed with two sublimely beautiful arias, but both are taxing. Her very first utterance, 'Porgi amor', is a severe test of nerve: without any recitative or chance to warm the voice into focus, it demands a soft and perfectly steady legato. 'Dove sono', in Act III, lies in a notoriously problematic area of the soprano voice, which is why its climax, although not stratospherically high, is often negotiated with a sense of strain. In the interests of contrasting the timbres of the female singers, Cherubino is usually assigned to a mezzo, but the arias lie much more easily in the soprano voice. The men have an easier time of it. Figaro can be sung by either a bass or a baritone with a strong lower register; the Count is written one step higher – most singers have difficulty articulating the run of triplets at the end of the Act III aria.

There is some scholarly controversy over the 'authentic' order of the numbers in Act III, and to make the plot run more smoothly, some performances put 'Dove sono' before rather than after the sextet. In 1997, Cecilia Bartoli caused controversy at the Met by replacing Susanna's 'Venite inginocchiatevi' and 'Deh vieni non tardar' with two arias which Mozart substituted for a revival of the opera in 1789 – a valid experiment, even if one that few could wish to become established as the norm.

⌘ In performance

Until the 1960s, productions were inspired by the paintings of Fragonard and Boucher, making the opera seem deceptively frilly, pink, well-upholstered and blandly pretty. In the 1970s, there was a vogue for productions like those of Giorgio Strehler and Jonathan Miller which played up the political edge to the situation and went for a more grittily realistic look. Recent stagings, such as those by Graham Vick at ENO and Glyndebourne, have adopted a more abstract setting, highlighting the interaction of character but eliminating much sense of social context. Peter Sellars amusingly relocated the entire opera to modern-day plutocratic Manhattan – but such violent updating makes nonsense of the class tensions on which the opera is based.

The translator Jeremy Sams rightly pointed out that *Figaro's Wedding* is the more correct and telling English rendition of the Italian title, and that is what Graham Vick's production at ENO has always been called.

The plot is intricate, though in performance it is easy to follow its gist. On being told by a courtier that she would be seeing a performance of *Le Nozze di Figaro* during a foreign tour, Her Majesty Queen Elizabeth II is famous for asking drily, 'Is that the one with the pin in it?'

∿ Recordings

CD: Cesare Siepi (Figaro); Erich Kleiber (cond.). Decca 417 315 2DM3

   Carol Vaness (Countess); Charles Mackerras (cond.) Telarc 80449

DVD: Renée Fleming (Countess); Bernard Haitink (cond.). Glyndebourne production. Warner 0630 14013 2

Don Giovanni

Two acts. First performed Prague, 1787.
Libretto by Lorenzo da Ponte

The tale of Don Juan has its ultimate source in a seventeenth-century Spanish black farce by Tirso da Molina. The story was subsequently told many times, in different ways, notably in plays by Goldoni, Shadwell and Molière, but da Ponte seems to have drawn most closely on the libretto for an obscure one-act operatic version which was produced in Venice in 1787.

After its first production in Prague, Mozart revised the score for Vienna to accommodate the abilities and demands of a new cast of singers. He added a duet for Zerlina and

Leporello (a weak number, very rarely heard today) and a major aria for Elvira, 'Mi tradì', as well as replacing Ottavio's 'Il mio tesoro' with the easier 'Dalla sua pace' and deleting the final scene after Giovanni has been dragged down to hell. Productions today generally include 'Mi tradì' and both of Ottavio's arias, but otherwise follow the Prague version.

❦ Plot

In Seville, Don Giovanni, a charming but amoral and sexually compulsive nobleman, attempts to rape Donna Anna. She evades him, but in the ensuing fracas her father the Commendatore is killed by Giovanni. Anna and her fiancé Don Ottavio swear to take revenge on her attacker, although Anna is not sure of his identity.

Giovanni and his cowardly servant Leporello encounter the hysterical Donna Elvira, a lady from Burgos whom Giovanni seduced and then abandoned. She is determined on revenge; Leporello explains that he is unstoppably promiscuous, showing her the list of his international conquests recorded in a book – fat ones, thin ones, young and old, blonde and brunette, 1,003 in Spain alone.

Giovanni now begins a heavy flirtation with the gullible peasant girl Zerlina, as she celebrates her betrothal to Masetto. He woos her with false promises, until Elvira interrupts him. Anna decides that Giovanni is her attacker, and she and Ottavio join forces with Elvira against him.

Giovanni throws a riotous party at his mansion: Zerlina, Masetto and friends are much impressed by his apparent munificence. Three uninvited guests appear in masks – Elvira, Anna, and Ottavio. With his customary bravado, Giovanni bids them welcome and then renews his assault on Zerlina. As his dishonourable intentions become plain, the masked trio confront Giovanni. But he passes the blame on to Leporello, and in the confusion manages to escape.

Leporello threatens to leave Giovanni's service, but is won back with money. Giovanni and Leporello swap clothes so that Giovanni can pursue Elvira's maid and put his pursuers off the scent. Giovanni beats up Masetto, and the other characters triumphantly corner the person they believe to be Giovanni – only to discover that he is actually Leporello.

Giovanni and Leporello take refuge in a graveyard. As they fool around, the statue of Anna's father the Commendatore suddenly speaks, solemnly inviting himself to dinner at Giovanni's house. Despite Leporello's terror, Giovanni is delighted at the prospect of such an amusing guest. Anna tells Ottavio that her grief for her father is such that she cannot marry him yet.

The dinner finds Giovanni in sparkling form. Elvira rushes in to beg him to repent, but he brushes her off with contempt. As she leaves, she encounters the awesome statue of the Commendatore, which enters Giovanni's house announcing that he cannot partake of mortal food and asking Giovanni to come to dine with him. Giovanni accepts with alacrity, but when he grasps the statue's proffered hand, he finds its grip is ice-cold. Unrepentant to the last, Giovanni is dragged down to Hell by demons. As the dust settles, the other characters appear. They review the situation, resolve to get on with their lives and point the obvious moral of Giovanni's fate.

✎ What to listen for

Musically, the darkest-toned of Mozart's operas. The Gothic spookiness of the opening bars of the Overture sets the mood, with its rising chromatic scales and blasts of trombone (an instrument exclusively associated with the vengeful majesty of the Commendatore), and elsewhere in the score there is always an undercurrent of unease and ambiguity to the harmony. Giovanni himself sings neither high nor low, and the role can be taken by either bass or baritone, so long as he can communicate both energy and charm: he has no long major aria, but his brief explosion of exuberance in Act I, 'Fin ch'han dal vino', tests the ability to sing notes precisely at great speed – sometimes one is left with a sense of singer and conductor racing to the finishing line. In Act II,

Giovanni's mandolin-accompanied serenade requires a seductive legato and smoothness of tone which is testing in another respect, and basses generally have difficulty lightening their tone for the number.

The role of Donna Anna lies high for any soprano, and her first aria, 'Or sai chi l'onore', demands drama, heft and the ability to sustain some top As; the remainder of the role is much more lyrical, with some coloratura in the second aria 'Non mi dir' – a passage which Berlioz considered grossly out of character and a great blot on the score. The best of recent Donna Annas was probably the young Carol Vaness, who was also superlative in the similar role of Elettra in *Idomeneo*. Zerlina may appear pretty and straightforward to sing, but her Act I aria, 'Batti, Batti', lies at just the point (E–F, at the top of the stave) at which most sopranos' voices tire or 'break'. Her duet with Don Giovanni, 'Là ci darem la mano', is invariably a favourite with the audience.

The two arias for Ottavio are both very grateful to a lyric tenor, but it's almost impossible to make such a passive character seem credible, let alone sympathetic.

◌ In performance

A great deal of intellectual effort has been spent on analysing the figure of Giovanni and determining his moral status: is he a Byronic rebel, nobly fighting fate and convention in the name of romantic individuality, a sexually compulsive psychotic, or perhaps just an irresistible pantomime rogue? Maybe he isn't a hero, but his defiance as the Commendatore exerts his icy grip is certainly admirable, and it's hard to doubt that Mozart has a sneaking sympathy for him – don't we all?

The voice of morality is certainly much less appealing. Anna seems frigidly repressed and self-centred (the German writer E. T. A. Hoffmann famously claimed that she was secretly in love with Giovanni); Elvira is hysterical and hopeless; Ottavio is locked into his role as the gentleman, who claims that he would like to do something to help, but ends up walking politely one step behind the ladies. The lower classes – Zerlina,

Masetto and Leporello – don't have much to offer either: they are presented as merely gullible and venal.

Like *Hamlet*, there is something about *Don Giovanni* that doesn't quite add up, and this is perhaps why there are so few satisfying productions of the opera: almost every director has had a go at it, but those who are successful at exploring one aspect of the piece – such as the sexual seaminess – invariably seem to have neglected another, such as Giovanni's deceptive veneer of aristocratic nobility.

✎ Recordings

CD: Joan Sutherland (Donna Anna); Carlo Maria Giulini (cond.). EMI 5556232 2

Peter Mattei (Don Giovanni); Daniel Harding (cond.). VC 5454242

Video: Ruggero Raimondi (Don Giovanni); Lorin Maazel (cond.). Directed by Joseph Losey. ARTOP 2

Così fan tutte
(*Women all do the same*)

Two acts. First performed Vienna, 1790.
Libretto by Lorenzo da Ponte

The secret test of lovers' constancy is an old literary theme, but da Ponte's twist on it is quite original. Almost nothing is known about the work's origins, gestation or reception, though it is amusing to speculate on the irony of da Ponte's mistress being cast as the first Fiordiligi, while her sister sang Dorabella. It has also been suggested that Mozart's unresolved feelings about his wife's sister Aloysia may explain – unconsciously, at least – his attraction to such a plot.

Nineteenth-century audiences were shocked at what they saw as *Così*'s cynicism, and the libretto was frequently rewritten, usually so as to suggest that Fiordiligi and Dorabella were simply pretending to fall for Alfonso's ruse. This embarrassment prevented the sheer sensual beauty of the score from being fully appreciated, and only since the 1960s, with the opening-up of the debate about sexual behaviour and the morality which attempts to govern it has the opera assumed its rightful place in the standard repertory.

✤ Plot

Fashionable Naples, in the late eighteenth century. The cynical Don Alfonso is weary of hearing his young officer friends Ferrando and Guglielmo extolling the virtues of their lovers, the sisters Fiordiligi and Dorabella. Alfonso strikes a wager with Ferrando and Guglielmo, aimed at testing the strength of the ladies' feelings. Ferrando and Guglielmo are to pretend that they have been called to the wars. The ladies bid them a sad goodbye and sink into a state of romantic agitation. Ferrando and Guglielmo then secretly return at once, disguised as two visiting Albanians. Without explaining who the Albanians really are, Alfonso enlists the help of the ladies' maid Despina in the scheme.

At first, Fiordiligi and Dorabella profess themselves heartbroken and shun the Albanians' extravagant amorous attentions. Then the Albanians pretend to collapse in front of them, claiming that such is their despair that they have swallowed poison. They are revived by Despina, masquerading as a doctor. The ladies are so relieved by the miraculous recovery that their antipathy begins to wane and, egged on by Despina, they decide to indulge in what they think is only an innocent flirtation with their new admirers. But things swiftly become more serious, as real feelings begin to emerge. Dorabella, the more relaxed of the two sisters, exchanges lockets with Fiordiligi's amour, Guglielmo; Fiordiligi holds out a little longer, resolving to don male clothing and follow Guglielmo to the wars. But when Ferrando appears and perhaps sincerely begs her not to go, she too succumbs. Alfonso meets up with the disillusioned Guglielmo and Ferrando, and advises them not to take the ladies' change of heart too hard: all women do the same, *così fan tutte*.

The sisters agree to marry the Albanians, and after Despina, now masquerading as a notary, draws up the contract, the wedding feast begins. Don Alfonso then announces that Ferrando and Guglielmo have unexpectedly returned home from the wars. The Albanians vanish, and Ferrando and Guglielmo re-emerge, feigning shock at the sight of the wedding contract and vowing to kill the Albanians. The ladies are mortified – at which point, Alfonso reveals the entire intrigue. He has won his wager. It is not clear whether the ladies return to their original partners or remain with their Albanian incarnations, but all join to point the moral: happy is the man who is guided by reason through the trials of life.

ᦥ What to listen for

It is interesting to note that Mozart indicated that all the female roles in *Così* (as well as in *Le Nozze di Figaro* and *La Clemenza di Tito*) should be sung by a soprano. But what is important in performance is that the three women characters blend and contrast in timbre, so the most common solution is to assign Fiordiligi to a full lyric soprano, Despina to a light soubrette and Dorabella to a mezzo-soprano – even though Fiordiligi occasionally descends lower than her sister and Despina sings below her in the ensembles! So Dorabella may also be sung by a soprano, Despina by a mezzo. Cecilia Bartoli, who refuses to categorize herself as either a mezzo-soprano or a soprano, has at different times successfully sung all three roles.

Così is a long opera, and Ferrando's high-lying Act II aria, 'Ah, lo veggio', is usually cut, much to the relief of most of the tenors who sing the role. Fiordiligi's two arias are markedly different in mood and style – the first, 'Come scoglio', is a parody of the formal arias of old-fashioned *opera seria*, with its exaggeratedly heroic sentiments and cruelly wide leaps; the second, 'Per pietà', is a ravishing rondo, introspective in mood, with a melancholy horn obbligato.

As in the case of *Figaro*, the ensembles in *Così* are as vivacious and inventive as the arias, particularly in Act I, with its rapturous trio, 'Soave sia il vento', sung as the ladies wave farewell to the 'departing' officers, and its brilliantly amusing comic finale. In a weak performance, the second act can seem a slight anticlimax, hanging fire both dramatically and musically – hence the desirability of a smart cut or two.

ᴥ In performance

For most of the twentieth century, *Così* was staged as a pretty rococo fantasy of a sort often depicted on the top of chocolate boxes; in the 1970s, it became more like a drily witty satire comparable to a novel by Jane Austen. Latterly, it has been seen as harshly contemporary: one rarely encounters the opera costumed in late eighteenth-century style, and it has often been staged as the sort of modern sexual comedy familiar to fans of television series such as *Friends*: one famous version, directed by David Freeman for Opera Factory, set the opera on the beach of an Italian resort; while Peter Sellars saw it all as a muddle suffered by some teenagers hanging out in Despina's Diner.

Producers have also become obsessed with the scenario's darker implications: is the opera anti-feminist, or are the women simply innocent victims of male bullying and condescension? Is Don Alfonso a ruthless behavioural scientist or a Sadean manipulator, with deeply questionable motives? Is the ending a happy one, or do all four of the lovers retire bitter and hurt? Does it matter who gets who in the end, or does nobody get anybody? What has anyone learned from their embarrassing experience?

This opera is no longer regarded as a laughing matter. But it shouldn't be forgotten that *Così* was conceived as a comedy, written for the sophisticated audience of the Viennese court in the style made fashionable by French playwrights such as Marivaux, who depicted highly cultivated people playing with the subtleties and contradictions of erotic love in the spirit of a game.

ᴥ Recordings

CD: Montserrat Caballé (Fiordiligi); Colin Davis (cond.). Philips LRC 1044

Hillevi Martinpelto (Fiordiligi); Simon Rattle (cond.).
EMI 5556170 2
DVD: Cecilia Bartoli (Fiordiligi); Nikolaus Harnoncourt
(cond.). Zurich Opera production. Arthaus 012

La Clemenza di Tito
(The Clemency of Titus)

Two acts. First performed Prague, 1791.
Libretto by Caterino Mazzolà

Written in haste to mark the coronation of Leopold II of
Bohemia, with a brief to honour the occasion with something
conservative and conventional in form, this opera marks a
stylistic retreat from both Gluckian principles and the free
spirit which informs Così fan tutte and Don Giovanni to the
rigidity and decorum of opera seria. The première was a disaster, not least because the non-arrival of the royal party
delayed the start by three hours!

Although popular during the years following Mozart's death
– in 1806, it became the first of his operas to be performed in
London – its critical reputation sank dramatically thereafter.
Wagner thought it 'stiff and dry', while the great Mozart
scholar of the 1920s, Edward J. Dent, wrote it off as 'pompous
and frigid'. It is only in the last thirty years or so, with the
renewed interest in early eighteenth-century opera, that the
merits and beauties of the score have been recognized.

The libretto was swiftly adapted from an existing text written in 1734 by Pietro Metastasio. The plot revolves around
one of those tiresome 'A loves B loves C' scenarios so common to Handelian opera. On paper, the motivations of the
central characters may seem implausible – Sesto, one feels,
could not be such an idiot, nor Tito so impolitic – but
Mozart's music dramatizes their emotions with great force
and conviction.

ᏉᏉ Plot

Rome, first century AD. The ambitious Vitellia is jealous that the Emperor Tito (Titus) plans to marry the foreign princess Berenice and plots to assassinate him. Tito's friend Sesto (Sextus), infatuated with Vitellia, agrees to help her, against his better judgment.

Meanwhile, out of a sense of duty to Rome, Tito has sent Berenice away. Instead, he asks to marry Servilia, but when he learns that she loves Annio, he honourably surrenders his suit and reverts to the plan of marrying Vitellia. A message sent to summon her to the palace arrives too late – Vitellia has already dispatched Sesto on his murderous mission.

Sesto sets fire to the Capitol, but in the ensuing confusion, Tito escapes unharmed. Sesto is arrested and condemned to death. Tito cannot believe that his friend would betray him. Under interrogation, Sesto stands firm and refuses to reveal the identity of the other conspirators. Then Vitellia has a change of heart. She admits her guilt to Tito, pleading with him on Sesto's behalf. The merciful Tito relents, and all parties are reconciled, praising his virtuous rule.

ᏉᏉ What to listen for

Despite its traditional frame, *Clemenza* only contains four big set-piece arias (two for Sesto, one each for Vitellia and Tito). Between them, Mozart sneaks in all sorts of smaller-scale delights – Servilia's 'S'altro che lagrime', and her duet with Annio, 'Deh prendi un dolce amplesso', for example. Perhaps the highlight of the score, however, is the superb first-act finale, which inexorably gathers pace and intensity as the voices of soloists and chorus accumulate, only to avoid the expected fortissimo climax and die away in a sigh of grief at the conspirators' treachery. Here, at least, Mozart's genius is working at white heat.

Vitellia is almost as difficult a role as Constanze in *Entführung*. It ranges between a contralto's low G and a top D (a note occurring in the trio in Act I and considered so perilous that many singers leave it out altogether). The castrato role of Sesto is now given to a mezzo-soprano; the rather lifeless and unrewarding role of Tito goes to a tenor. Servilia and Annio have some of the most glowingly charming music in the opera and, for relatively little effort, often walk away with the warmest applause.

Mozart did not write the recitatives: he assigned them to his pupil Süssmayr, who later completed the *Requiem* which Mozart left unfinished at his death. They are dull and even clumsy at times, and attempts have been made to rewrite them.

∾ In performance

Many productions have opted for a baroque setting, inspired by the paintings of Tiepolo. More imagination was shown at Glyndebourne, where Nicholas Hytner, with the help of brilliant design by David Fielding, found a stylized way of suggesting the setting of Imperial Rome without resorting to either archaeological pedantry or Hollywood kitsch. Other directors have seemed bored with the surface of the piece and use it as a vehicle for extreme deconstructive interpretation – for example, the Salzburg production by Karl-Ernst and Ursel Herrmann in which all sorts of obscure (if not downright pretentious) symbolism involving water-melon and Cinderella's stray slipper was introduced in order to suggest neuroses and contradictions behind the libretto's confidently black-and-white moral façade.

∾ Recordings

CD: Janet Baker (Vitellia); Colin Davis (cond.). Philips 422 544²

Julia Varady (Vitellia); John Eliot Gardiner (cond.). Archiv 431 806 2AH2. Period instruments

Video: Philip Langridge (Tito); Andrew Davis (cond.). Glyndebourne production. Warner 0792013

Die Zauberflöte (The Magic Flute)

Two acts. First performed Vienna, 1791.
Libretto by Emanuel Schikaneder

Composed not for an opera house but for Schikaneder's popular suburban vaudeville theatre, this is one of Mozart's very
last works, written at a time when he was desperate for
money. Its libretto, drawn from a bewildering variety of
sources, mixes elements of pantomime, farce, spoken dialogue and 'special effect' scenes with the mystical Masonic
philosophy to which Mozart subscribed, and, starting with
the three solemn chords which open the Overture, the opera
contains many references to the rituals and symbolism of the
sect, as well as the contemporary debate among its members
over the admission of women.

It has been suggested that the Queen of the Night represents the reactionary Empress Maria Theresa and Tamino
her more enlightened son Josef II, but the plot remains a
splendid muddle which defies all attempts to interpret it as a
coherent allegory. One theory is that, for some reason, the
moral natures of Sarastro and the Queen of the Night were
reversed half-way through the writing of the libretto – how
else can one explain that it is the evil Queen of the Night who
controls the benevolent magic of the flute and the Three
Boys, or Sarastro's employment of a rogue like Monostatos?

ᴓ Plot

Prince Tamino, wandering far from home, is rescued from a
monster by Three Ladies, though the comically cowardly
birdcatcher Papageno tries to take the credit. Their mistress,
the Queen of the Night, asks Tamino to rescue her beautiful
daughter Pamina from the clutches of her rival Sarastro. To
help him in his quest, Tamino is given a magic flute. Three
Boys, also possessed of supernatural powers, show him the
way, and he sets off together with Papageno, who is given
some magic bells.

In Sarastro's domain, Pamina suffers from the lascivious attentions of her guard, the moor Monostatos. Papageno sneaks in and assures her that help is on its way. Meanwhile, Tamino encounters a priest at the gateway to the temple. Tamino questions him, and discovers that Sarastro is far from the wicked tyrant described by the Queen of the Night: in fact, he is the leader of a new order dedicated to the virtues of Wisdom, Reason and Nature. It is the Queen of the Night who is the villain, and Sarastro is only protecting Pamina from her evil intentions. Tamino enters the temple, playing the magic flute. As they run away from Monostatos, Papageno and Pamina are drawn to the sound. Papageno's magic bells set everyone dancing. Tamino and Pamina fall instantly in love, and are brought before Sarastro. Sarastro orders Monostatos to be punished and invites Tamino and Pamina to submit to the ceremonial trials which precede initiation into his order.

Tamino and Papageno are taken away in preparation for the trials. They resist the wiles of the Three Ladies, who appear in their cell and attempt to lure them back to the Queen of the Night's cause. Meanwhile, Pamina is visited by her mother, who commands her to kill Sarastro. Monostatos continues to threaten Pamina, until Sarastro banishes him.

As part of their trial, Tamino and Papageno are told to keep silent. Papageno, an incorrigible chatterbox, finds the injunction impossible to keep. An old hag appears and claims to be his sweetheart. At first he mocks her, but is thrilled when she is transformed into the lovely Papagena, the mate he has always longed for. As part of his trial, she is then whisked away from him.

Driven mad by Tamino's refusal to speak to her, Pamina contemplates suicide. But the Three Boys lead her to Tamino and, with the help of the magic flute, they endure the trial by fire and water together, emerging from it triumphant. Now it is Papageno's turn to despair: he will hang himself if he cannot have his Papagena. As he is about to fasten the noose, the Three Boys intervene and Papageno is finally united with

Papagena. The power of the Queen of the Night is defeated, and Pamina and Tamino are welcomed into Sarastro's order.

∾ What to listen for

A score of extraordinary contrasts, embracing Papageno's immediately catchy hit-tunes and the solemn dignity of Tamino's Gluck-influenced dialogue with the old priest who guards the temple entrance. Yet aside from the flamboyantly operatic nature of the music for the Three Ladies and the Queen of the Night, it is its quality of simplicity which is most striking (compare the sophistication of *Così fan tutte* or the grandeur of *La Clemenza di Tito*, both of them close in date of composition). This can partly be explained by the fact that *Zauberflöte* was written for a theatre, not an opera house, and Mozart tailored the music to the modest vocal abilities of some of the original cast – Schikaneder, who played Papageno, was an actor by profession rather than a singer, hence the musical simplicity of the role; Pamina was the seventeen-year-old Anna Gottlieb, who had also sung Barbarina in the first performance of *Le Nozze di Figaro*. It is also worth noting that the tenor who sang Tamino was an accomplished flute player (nowadays his music is usually played from the pit, where Papageno's magic bells are also rendered by a glockenspiel).

Pamina's Act II aria, 'Ach, ich fühl's', is a test of both singer and conductor, inasmuch as its very slow tempo can easily drag beyond the point at which the soprano can maintain sufficient breath to phrase it. The role of the Queen of the Night, with its dazzling coloratura and celebrated top Fs, is strongly contrasted with that of her antagonist Sarastro, whose calmly authoritative and godlike arias feature low Fs. Not all the music is of the highest quality, and there are miscalculations, particularly towards the end of the opera, where there's too much of Papageno, the music for flute, brass and timpani which accompanies Tamino and Pamina's final ordeal scarcely suggests anything very terrifying, and the closing chorus seems like a perfunctory full stop rather than a genuine climax. But this is a bran-tub of an opera, with something for everyone, generous in its spirit and irresistible in its charm.

❧ In performance

For all its fun and innocence, *Die Zauberflöte* is not easy to stage convincingly. As a *Singspiel*, it contains long stretches of spoken dialogue, something which opera singers are not generally accomplished at delivering. Some productions cut this element drastically; others have attempted to liven it up with racily idiomatic modern translation and opportunities for Papageno to ad lib. But balancing the pantomime gags with the sublime seriousness of Sarastro's temple and Tamino's quest for truth is tricky. One version which managed to generate both childlike wonder and dramatic tension is Ingmar Bergman's 1975 film, which begins in a theatre full of attentive children but gradually moves out into darker, more adult territory. Staged productions which have succeeded more conventionally include Nicholas Hytner's at ENO and John Cox's, designed by David Hockney, and seen at Glyndebourne and the Met.

Several directors, notably Peter Sellars in his controversial Glyndebourne production (set on and under a Los Angeles freeway), have presented Sarastro as a figure every bit as sinister as the Queen of the Night, implying that his devotees are a zombie-like cadre of people mesmerized by his tyranny, rather than the votaries of a new order of Wisdom, Reason and Nature. The parallel with modern religious sects such as the Moonies is obvious – perhaps excessively so.

❧ Recordings

CD: Ruth Ziesak (Pamina); Georg Solti (cond.). Decca 433 210 2

Rosa Mannion (Pamina); William Christie (cond.). Erato 0630 12705 2. Period instruments

Video: Lucia Popp (Pamina); Karl Böhm (cond.). Bavarian State Opera production. Philips 0704053

PART TWO

German Opera

German opera in the early nineteenth century struggled to liberate itself from the domination of sternly regulated royal or ducal theatres and a preference for the proprieties of Italian *opera seria*. As part of the revolution in the arts known as Romanticism, composers reached for a freer, more demotic range of subject-matter, drawn from the history and legends of the German peoples rather than regal personages and classical mythology. The crucial work of this period was Carl Maria von Weber's *Der Freischütz* (1821), an opera embodying the fascination with sinister aspects of the natural world and the mists of the medieval past which also colours contemporary cultural phenomena such as Schubert's *Lieder*, Grimm's fairy-tales and Caspar David Friedrich's paintings. The use of spoken dialogue, customary in the genre of eighteenth-century German comic opera known as *Singspiel*, is another remarkable feature of *Freischütz*, as are its episodes of light relief.

Robert Schumann, Heinrich Marschner, Albert Lortzing and Otto von Nicolai were among the many composers who fell under Weber's influence, but it was Richard Wagner who decisively broke through the folkloric parameters to themes of broader significance. In early operas like *Das Liebesverbot* (*The Ban on Love*, based on *Measure for Measure*) and *Rienzi* (about a revolutionary uprising in fourteenth-century Rome), he drew on elements of Italian and French fashion. Gradually, however, his own voice grew in power and confidence. Essays written in 1849–51 outline his rejection of the trivialities and excesses of operas written only for profit or effect and point the way forward to the *Gesamtkunstwerk*, 'the complete work of art'.

What this implied was a return to the ideals of Greek drama: opera, Wagner believed, presented an opportunity to combine all the arts into a uniquely powerful unity. It should deal with themes of fundamental importance and embrace all members of society rather than just a wealthy bourgeoisie. Shakespeare, Beethoven, and a variety of religious philosophies are invoked, and although Wagner's thinking was increasingly twisted by violently irrational racial hatreds, there can be no question of his high intellect and erudition.

Wagner went on to realize his ideas in the great operas of his maturity, *Lohengrin* to *Parsifal*, as well as building at Bayreuth an opera house which replaced the conventional horseshoe arrangement, and its tiers of boxes and galleries, with a more egalitarian amphitheatre layout, masking the orchestra beneath a hood. Here, the lights were extinguished during a performance and the usual hum of chatter and casual coming-and-going silenced. Wagner's critics may have deplored his pretensions and branded Bayreuth as more a temple than a place of entertainment, but his impact was soon to prove revolutionary, not least in his eschewal of spoken dialogue or recitative and his weaving of a continuous *durchkomponiert* ('through-composed') musical fabric, coloured by the practice of attaching a melodic theme (or leitmotiv) to a particular character or dramatic emotion.

Among Wagner's immediate disciples were Engelbert Humperdinck and Richard Strauss. The latter composed operas between 1894 and 1942, and during that half-century his technically brilliant essays in Wagnerian grandiosity were later balanced by excursions back to the more gentle and intimate musical worlds of Mozart and operetta. Throughout, Strauss remained fundamentally backward-looking, a romantic conservative, and it was left to Alban Berg to incorporate the more radical changes in musical language proposed in Vienna by his teacher Arnold Schoenberg, whose own mightily impressive but dauntingly austere biblical opera *Moses und Aron* was left unfinished at his death in 1951.

Other composers who produced significant work through the terrible upheavals of the First World War, the Weimar Republic and Hitler's rise to power include Erich Korngold, whose Straussian expressionist fantasy, *Die Tote Stadt* (*The*

Dead City), was enormously successful in the 1920s, and Paul Hindemith, who backed away from the extremes of romanticism and modernism in *Cardillac* and *Mathis der Maler* (*Matthias the Painter*). More lastingly popular has been Kurt Weill, a composer with a great sense of theatre, as well as a punchy energy and simplicity of means which owes much to J. S. Bach. Following his collaboration with Brecht in Berlin on operas with a socialist bent, Weill emigrated to America and became a prolific composer of Broadway musicals.

Of post-war German composers, only the traditionally crafted neo-romantic operas of Hans Werner Henze have penetrated internationally, though Gottfried von Einem and Aribert Reimann have made their mark between Berlin and Vienna. Bernd Alois Zimmermann's *Die Soldaten* was a sensation of the 1960s. Exploring the horrors which fall out from war, it uses a collage of eighteenth- and twentieth-century narratives, incorporating film, jazz and electronic elements. Karlheinz Stockhausen's even more daring experiments along these lines, manifested in a cycle of seven long operas (one for each day of the week) called *Licht*, make Wagner's pretensions look modest. But neither composer has to date found favour with a wide public.

Ludwig van Beethoven (1770–1827)
Fidelio

Two acts. First performed Vienna, 1814.
Libretto by Joseph von Sonnleithner and Georg von Treitschke

Beethoven's only opera has a complicated history. Drawing on a libretto by Jean-Christophe Bouilly which had already served for three composers, he began work on a three-act version in 1804. After problems with the censors (Vienna had just fallen under Napoleonic occupation), this was given a handful of unsuccessful performances in 1805. To avoid confusion with its predecessors, it was entitled *Fidelio* – Beethoven would have preferred *Leonore*. In 1806, the score was revised and reduced to two acts for a further Viennese production.

In 1814, Beethoven returned to the opera again, making even more extensive revisions to the score, providing new finales to both acts and substantially altering Leonore's and Florestan's arias. With the help of Georg von Treitschke, the libretto was drastically rewritten too. It is this version which has been performed ever since, though the earlier versions have occasionally been revived and even recorded. The protracted and hopelessly stilted passages of spoken dialogue are now almost invariably abbreviated.

Further confusion is caused by the existence of four overtures relating to the opera. *Leonore No. 2* was written for the 1805 production, *Leonore No. 3* for 1806, *Leonore No. 1* for an 1807 production in Prague which never materialized. The overture known as '*Fidelio*' was composed for the 1814 version. Until quite recently, it was the practice to play the *Fidelio* overture at the beginning of the opera, with *Leonore No. 3* as an entr'acte after the dungeon scene. But the latter is now considered to be dramatically inappropriate, and it has become a show-piece for the concert hall rather than the opera house.

The story is supposedly based on an actual incident during the French Revolution.

ᴕ Plot

Near Seville, sometime in the mid-eighteenth century, Leonore has disguised herself as a boy named Fidelio, with the aim of rescuing her husband Florestan from unjust imprisonment, ordered by the tyrannical Don Pizarro. She has taken a job with the jailer Rocco, whose daughter Marzelline has lost interest in her humble suitor Jacquino and fallen in love with 'Fidelio' instead. The materialistic, opportunistic Rocco admires the hard-working 'Fidelio', but insists that marriage has to be based on a sound financial footing.

'Fidelio' begs to be allowed to accompany Rocco on his visit to a cell in which a secret prisoner is kept – she suspects, rightly, that he must be Florestan. Keen for some help, Rocco agrees, even though it contravenes Pizarro's orders. Overheard by Leonore, Pizarro instructs Rocco to kill Florestan and bury him in his cell before the Minister Don Fernando comes to inspect the prison. Realizing that the testing moment has come, Leonore steels her courage. Rocco allows some prisoners to be briefly let out into the courtyard – much to Pizarro's fury.

Locked and chained in a dark subterranean cell, Florestan struggles to keep hope alive. Rocco and 'Fidelio' enter, and dig Florestan's grave. As Pizarro is about to stab Florestan, 'Fidelio' brandishes a pistol and reveals her true identity. As the three men stand frozen in amazement, a distant trumpet call is heard, signalling the arrival of the minister Don Fernando. Pizarro is arrested. The other prisoners are released and reunited with their families. Florestan is publicly reunited with Leonore, and all join to praise her wifely courage and constancy.

ᴕ What to listen for

Despite its awkward, melodramatic plot, two-dimensional characterization and the uneven inspiration of the long first act, Beethoven's music can make *Fidelio* an overwhelming experience.

The early domestic scenes have a certain charm, even if Beethoven lacks the Mozartian lightness of touch. Another composer might have made more of Rocco's aria preaching the virtues of a positive bank balance – it's as dull as befits its subject. But the canonic quartet 'Mir ist so wunderbar' for Leonore, Marzelline, Jacquino and Fidelio and the chorus for the prisoners as they are led from their cells into the sunlight both show Beethoven's genius at its most sublime and intense.

There's a whiff of cloak-and-dagger ham to Pizarro's aria 'Ha! welch' ein Augenblick', but it can be very exciting if the bass-baritone doesn't rush over the top and simply shout it. Leonore's 'Abscheulicher!' is much more than an aria – within its outwardly conventional three-part structure, it charts the character's spiritual journey, from fear and revulsion to hope to defiant resolution. Beethoven did not write with realistic ideas of human vocal capacity – tenors suffer from more than their chains as Florestan and even the most powerful of dramatic sopranos find the climax of this aria, with its prolonged ascent to a top B, almost unsingable. Because Leonore has to soar over a couple of loud ensembles, hefty Wagnerians are often cast in the role – but it is the smaller-voiced, more flexible lyric sopranos who find this aria, and much else in the score, easier to negotiate.

It is in Act II that Beethoven's imagination seems to become fully engaged. Here the drama proceeds in one great arc, from the tenor Florestan's anguished cry of 'Gott! welch Dunkel hier', followed by an aria which echoes Leonore's 'Abscheulicher!'; a tense trio as the grave is being dug; the thrilling climactic quartet 'Er sterbe', broken by the distant trumpet call (evoking the Last Judgement); and the culminating release of the ecstatic duet between the reunited Florestan and Leonore. The final scene constitutes one of Beethoven's great essays in epic choral writing, alongside the last movement of the Ninth Symphony and the *Missa Solemnis*.

∾ In performance

Fidelio is often said to be 'dramatic' rather than 'theatrical', and the heavy-handedness of the libretto and plot does make it difficult to stage convincingly, not least because Leonore's male disguise is rarely plausible. One soprano who could look convincingly boyish, the tall, slim Anja Silja, used to fling off her cap at the moment of revelation and let her long hair cascade down her shoulders. Electrifying in the theatre, but a gesture which rather begs the question as to why Leonore didn't cut it off in the first place!

Post-war productions by German directors such as Joachim Herz and Harry Kupfer have emphasized parallels between Pizarro's prison and the concentration camps of modern totalitarianism, but Leonore's disguise is much more credible in an eighteenth-century context (successfully portrayed in naturalistic detail by Peter Hall at Glyndebourne). Herbert Wernicke (at Salzburg), Andrei Serban (at Covent Garden) and Jürgen Flimm (at the Met) have interpreted the opera in more universal terms, as a tale of the constant struggle between goodness and evil, darkness and light. What one makes of Rocco, the decent man executing someone else's evil orders, is another matter.

In our cynical, pampered age, we may find it hard to connect with the simple heroism and black-and-white morality at the heart of *Fidelio*. But those who lived under the shadow of war found the opera profoundly moving, and the power of great singers like Lotte Lehmann and Jon Vickers in the roles of Leonore and Florestan is still remembered with awe.

∾ Recordings

CD: Christa Ludwig (Leonore); Otto Klemperer (cond.). EMI 55170 2

Charlotte Margiono (Leonore); Nikolaus Harnoncourt (cond.). Teldec 94560 2

Carl Maria von Weber (1786–1826)
Der Freischütz (*The Sharp-shooter*)

Three acts. First performed Berlin, 1821.
Libretto by Johann Friedrich Kind

After the Napoleonic occupation, German culture was concerned to re-establish its national roots, rejecting both the elegance and symmetry of neo-classicism and the French-dominated rationalist philosophy of the Enlightenment. In their place came a fascination with more distant episodes of German history, the landscape of river and forest, and ghoulish peasant folklore – this was the age of Caspar David Friedrich's paintings, the researches of the Brothers Grimm and the nightmarish imaginings of 'Romantic' fantasists such as E. T. A. Hoffmann. Weber's opera is another product of this movement: a bold experiment with the *Singspiel* form, first performed on the anniversary of the Battle of Waterloo, it cleverly took a specific historical setting (Bohemia, just after the Thirty Years' War), used catchy folk-style melodies for the choruses, and for the climactic Wolf's Glen scene travelled into a world of devil-raising black magic which also gave theatrical technicians a chance to show off a battery of special effects and frighten audiences deliciously out of their wits. Such was *Der Freischütz*'s instant and lasting success that it can be said, without exaggeration, to have set the agenda for the next fifty years of German opera.

∾ Plot

The young forester Max plans to marry the lovely Agathe, but her father Cuno insists that he must first prove himself as a crack marksman in the presence of the Prince. When the opera opens, Max has just lost out in a competition: he feels dogged by bad luck. A veteran of the Thirty Years' War called Kaspar tells Max that his rifle is cursed and that only magic bullets can break the spell on it. After Kaspar helps him to shoot down a high-flying eagle, Max agrees to meet Kaspar at midnight in the Wolf's Glen, where such bullets are forged. What Max does not know is that Kaspar has himself been spurned by Agathe and is planning revenge.

At the same moment that Max shoots the eagle, a painting mysteriously falls off the wall in Cuno's hunting lodge, injuring Agathe. Her cousin Aennchen attempts to cheer her up, but she is further worried by a warning of impending evil she has received from an elderly hermit. Agathe fails to deter the overwrought Max from visiting the sinister Wolf's Glen.

Kaspar has made a devilish bargain with Samiel, the Black Huntsman. In return for three years of life, he promises to deliver Samiel three human victims – Max, Agathe and Cuno. Samiel agrees to let Kaspar forge seven magic bullets: six will hit whatever target their marksman aims at; the seventh is Samiel's. Max appears, terrified by the spookiness of the place. Despite visions of his dead mother and Agathe drowning herself, he watches Kaspar casting the magic bullets, attended by all manner of supernatural horrors.

Between them, Kaspar and Max fire six of the bullets, leaving Max the seventh to shoot at his trial before the Prince – he does not know that it belongs to Samiel.

Nightmares have terrified Agathe, and Aennchen's further efforts to laugh off her forebodings are to no avail. The painting falls off the wall again, and a bridal box turns out to contain a funeral wreath. Agathe decides that at her wedding she will wear roses given to her by the Hermit instead.

Max's trial begins. The Prince tells him to shoot at a dove. Agathe begs him to hold back, crying out that she is the dove. Max shoots anyway, but Agathe is protected by the appearance of the mysterious Hermit and it is Kaspar who is felled by the seventh magic bullet. He dies cursing Samiel's trickery.

Max confesses his involvement in Samiel's sorcery, and the Prince angrily banishes him. The Hermit intervenes, however, persuading the Prince to soften the harsh sentence, and Max is finally allowed a year to prove himself, after which he may return and marry Agathe. The opera ends with a chorus affirming the wisdom of following God's commands.

✵ What to listen for

The superb overture is not so much a medley of the opera's tunes as a capitulation of the drama, stating several of the recurrent musical themes. Throughout the opera, the orchestration is notable for dark, rich colours, a startlingly original use of the clarinets and horns, and the tendency to use the lower register of the strings and wind. Agathe has two deliquescent arias; the second, an exquisite prayer which is placed at the start of Act III, 'Und ob die Wolke', is a show-piece for any lyric soprano, its slow tempo and long line mercilessly exposing any impurity of tone or unsteadiness of intonation. The third-act choruses are also of outstanding interest: the bridesmaids and huntsmen sound authentically rustic, even though the tunes are Weber's, while in the last scene the entire community rises to an almost Beethovenian solemnity and grandeur.

But it is in the sensational Wolf's Glen scene that the opera breaks all the rules and makes its greatest impact. The hell-ishness of the scene is depicted musically by the chord of the diminished seventh associated with Samiel, shuddering tremolos, screeching piccolos, and the use of a purely speak-ing voice for Samiel (today invariably further distorted by electronic amplification). Such is the startling power and energy of this scene that it seems to cast its pall over the rest of the opera – 'a metaphor', in the words of John Warrack, 'for how evil lurks within human beings and can rise up sud-denly to destroy' – leaving something unconvincing about the assertion of normal Christian values in the last scene.

✵ In performance

Directors like to see this opera as a fable symbolic of the German soul and its tragic descent into Nazism – in David Pountney's production for ENO, the apparitions in the Wolf's Glen were gas-masked First World War soldiers rising up out of the trenches. Kaspar is often portrayed as Max's *alter ego*.

For designers and the special effects department, the

Wolf's Glen scene offers tremendous opportunities, and even today, when the cinema has realized all our worst nightmares, the combination of evocatively horrible images with Weber's daemonic music can still send a frisson through the most jaded audiences.

∾ Recording

CD: Luba Organosova (Agathe); Nikolaus Harnoncourt (cond.). Teldec 97758 2

Richard Wagner (1813–83)
Der Fliegende Holländer
(*The Flying Dutchman*)

Three acts. First performed Dresden, 1843.
Libretto by the composer

Wagner liked to claim that his inspiration for this opera was his own experience of a stormy crossing of the North Sea, but the ghostly Flying Dutchman was also part of traditional nautical lore, and the tale had been retold several times in the early nineteenth century – notably by Heinrich Heine, who saw the situation in an almost comic light. Wagner's first idea was to set the opera in Scotland, but he was obliged to change the location to Norway to avoid accusations of plagiarizing a contemporary French operatic version.

❧ Plot

As a storm forces Daland's ship to seek shelter in a bay off the Norwegian coast, another ghostly ship looms up alongside. Its captain, the Dutchman, has been cursed. He is allowed on shore once every seven years to search for a woman who can lift the curse by swearing eternal fidelity. Without explaining this to Daland, he offers him riches in return for hospitality and asks to meet his daughter, Senta. Daland agrees, delighted at the prospect of marrying her off to a wealthy man, and a favourable wind allows both ships to sail to Daland's home port.

Senta has long been obsessed with the legend of the Flying Dutchman and believes herself to be the one destined to redeem him. Shunning Erik, the young man to whom she is betrothed, she is entranced when Daland introduces her to the mysterious stranger. Both of them feel they have met the fulfilment of their dreams, and Senta vows to be true to him unto death.

The Dutchman's ghostly ship terrifies the villagers. Erik pleads with Senta. The Dutchman overhears him, and decides to release Senta from her vow. He reveals his identity – which

Senta has guessed all along – boards his ship and prepares to sets sail. Senta despairingly flings herself into the sea, reasserting her fidelity. The Dutchman's ship immediately sinks, and a vision of the redeemed Dutchman embracing the transfigured Senta is seen floating above the waves.

ᦰᦰ What to listen for

Wagner wrote the opera in a single act, hoping to make it marketable as a curtain-raiser (!) to a ballet. Later, he separated it into three acts, and made various smaller-scale revisions. Both versions are regularly performed today, but the general feeling is that the opera works best if performed without a break (duration: about two and a half hours).

The storm-tossed overture is a showpiece of orchestral scene-painting. The influence of Weber's *Der Freischütz* is evident in the 'folk-tune' choruses for Senta's spinning friends and the rumbustious sailors, as well as the ballad in which Senta relates the legend of the Dutchman and the tense supernatural melodrama of the final fifteen minutes.

Wagner's mature style is foreshadowed in the long declamatory monologue for the Dutchman (bass-baritone) in the first scene, the extended duets for the Dutchman with both Daland (bass) and Senta (soprano), and the music associated with the idea of redemption through love.

ᦰᦰ In performance

Ever since its first performance, this opera has provided designers with opportunities to devise spectacular stage effects through which to depict the Dutchman's ship: today, film and laser projection often creates the necessary magic. Modern productions often emphasize the contrast between the narrow bourgeois materialism of Daland, Erik and the villagers and the higher spiritual plane inhabited by Senta and the Dutchman. Harry Kupfer at Bayreuth focused on the psychology of Senta's obsession, suggesting that the whole story was Senta's dream, a sort of fantasy rebellion against the pressures of a woman's narrow lot. Certainly nobody who saw the startlingly intense Julia Varady as Senta could doubt that it is she, rather than the gloomy Dutchman who is the opera's most interesting character.

∾ Recording

CD: Hildegard Behrens (Senta); Christoph von Dohnanyi (cond.). Decca 436 418 2

Tannhäuser, und der Sängerkrieg auf Wartburg
(Tannhäuser, and the Singers' Contest on the Wartburg)

Three acts. First performed Dresden, 1845.
Libretto by the composer

Wagner remained dissatisfied with this opera, and periodically made changes to the original score, most notably in 1860–1, when he sanctioned a French translation and expanded the first scene with Venus in the vain hope that it could be made palatable to the sophisticated Parisians (in the event, it was greeted by ruthless booing from members of the exclusive Jockey Club infuriated at Wagner's failure to provide a balletic interlude in its customary position half-way through the evening). Performances today generally follow the 1875 edition of the score.

The plot conflates two medieval legends – one, the story of the crusading knight Tannhäuser; the other, the song contest held in the Wartburg palace.

∾ Plot

Medieval Thuringia. Within the Venusberg mountain, the knight Tannhäuser lies in the arms of Venus, surrounded by orgiastic revelry. Tiring of such pagan pleasures, he wanders into a valley where he encounters a procession of pilgrims and is reminded of his beloved Elisabeth, niece to the Landgrave (Duke). Tannhäuser resolves to return to the Landgrave's palace in the Wartburg, where he is reunited with the rapturous Elisabeth, who knows nothing of his dalliance with Venus. The Landgrave announces a singing contest, for which the prize is Elisabeth's hand in marriage. The knight Wolfram sings of love in spiritual terms, but Tannhäuser is suddenly possessed, and bursts out in celebration of the carnal delight he enjoyed with Venus. The court is scandalized. Tannhäuser is immediately overcome with remorse, and Elisabeth dramatically intercedes to plead for mercy. But the furious Landgrave insists that Tannhäuser leave the Wartburg, join the pilgrimage to Rome and seek absolution from the Pope.

Months later, Elisabeth is still praying patiently for Tannhäuser's happy return from Rome. On the road home, Tannhäuser tells Wolfram that the Pope refused to pardon him, claiming that he could no more forgive him than his staff could sprout leaves. In despair, he plans to return to the Venusberg. As a vision of Venus appears, Wolfram reminds Tannhäuser of Elisabeth's devotion. Tannhäuser manages to resist the temptation and the vision evaporates. Elisabeth, however, has died. As her funeral procession passes, Tannhäuser collapses. The chorus of pilgrims tell of a miracle – the Pope's staff has burst into leaf, confirming that Tannhäuser's soul has been saved.

○ What to listen for

Few would claim that *Tannhäuser* is an immediately lovable piece. Of all Wagner's operas, it is the most badly dated, sinking into the quicksands of its own religiosity. It has dull and even inept patches (such as the overlong and relentless ensemble at the end of Act II) and an overall dramatic slackness which makes Act III an anticlimax. Wagner had still not altogether mastered the art of making dialogue musically engaging. Tannhäuser (tenor) himself is an unsympathetic character, both as sinner and penitent. But for the Victorians, this was

Wagner's most popular work and a good performance will still reward the listener with much unashamedly tuneful music, notably in Elisabeth's contrasting soprano arias, the jubilant 'Dich, teure Halle' at the beginning of Act II and the serene prayer to the Virgin Mary, 'Allmächt'ge Jungfrau', and the baritone Wolfram's showpiece, 'O du, mein holder Abendstern'. Other pleasures of the score include the lusciously sensual music for the mezzo-soprano Venus (a pre-echo of Act II of *Parsifal*) and the stirring fervour of the Pilgrims' chorus, both of which feature in the magnificent overture.

To make a dramatic point – they represent two sides of the same coin – Venus and Elisabeth are sometimes sung by the same soprano. This is not a vocally easy task, as the two roles are pitched and coloured so differently.

∾ In performance

A problem piece, which directors find hard to handle. Until the 1960s, the opera was seen as pivoting on a black-and-white conflict between the profane sensuality of Venus and the sacred purity of Elisabeth. In a controversial 1970s production at Bayreuth, however, Götz Friedrich suggested that the moral standards of the Wartburg were oppressive and coercive, and no better than the illusory fleshpots of Venusberg. For the rebellious outsider Tannhäuser, neither environment offered the opportunity for creative self-realization and his tragedy becomes that of a man who fails to find anything positive he can commit himself to. Younger directors have continued to question the opera's moral stance: in Chicago, Peter Sellars updated the action to the world of corrupt American tele-evangelists, with Tannhäuser as a preacher caught up in Venusberg sleaze; in Munich, David Alden saw the opera as a parable of sexual liberation, seen against the sinister background of German nationalism.

∾ Recording

CD: Rene Kollo (Tannhäuser); Georg Solti (cond.).
Decca 414 581-2

Lohengrin

Three acts. First performed Weimar, 1850.
Libretto by the composer

Wagner's previous operas had been composed piecemeal, in sections: *Lohengrin* was the first to be consecutively written, in draft form, starting at the beginning and ending at the end. This gives the opera a unity of style and dramatic continuity which had previously been lacking in his work.

The plot is based on an episode in Wolfram von Eschenbach's *Parzival*, a medieval poem to which Wagner would return for his last opera.

∾ Plot

Antwerp, in the tenth century. King Henry rallies the Brabantines to defend Germany against the encroaching Hungarians. Telramund accuses Elsa of murdering her vanished brother, Gottfried, heir to the dukedom. In league with his sorceress wife Ortrud, who has secretly used her powers to bewitch Gottfried, Telramund claims the succession for himself.

Elsa needs a champion to defend her honour. To answer her call, a mysterious knight appears in a boat drawn by a swan. This knight promises to defend Elsa, and then to marry her, on condition that she does not ask his name or origin. After she agrees, the knight defeats Telramund in a duel, but spares his life.

A furious Ortrud poisons Elsa's mind against the nameless knight. King Henry proclaims that Telramund has been banished and that the knight will marry Elsa and then march against the Hungarians. But Ortrud and Telramund disrupt the wedding procession with accusations that the knight defeated Telramund by sorcery. The knight still refuses to reveal his name.

In the bridal chamber, Elsa gives way to her burning curiosity and asks the knight the fatal question – at which point Telramund aggressively breaks in. The knight kills him and announces that he will answer Elsa's question by King Henry's judgment seat. There, in public view, he explains that he killed Telramund in self-defence and finally reveals his identity. He is Lohengrin, a knight of the Grail, son of Parzival, invincible only while anonymous. Now his secret has been revealed, he must return to Monsalvat, home of the Grail. The swan boat returns. Ortrud reveals that the swan is in fact Elsa's vanished bother Gottfried, transformed by her magic. Lohengrin kneels in prayer, and as a sacred dove descends, the spell is broken and the swan is turned back into Gottfried's human shape. Lohengrin names him Protector of Brabant and leaves in the boat, now drawn by the dove. Ortrud's magic is destroyed, but Elsa, heartbroken at Lohengrin's departure, collapses lifeless.

✎ What to listen for

In the way that particular characters, emotions or dramatic elements (such as the question forbidden to Elsa) are associated with specific melodic themes (often known as leitmotivs), *Lohengrin* may rank as Wagner's first mature opera. In many passages of the score (notably the highly charged duet between Ortrud and Telramund at the beginning of Act II), he seems to break away from conventional length and shape of phrase and make the characters 'speak in song', the rhythm and melody being moulded by the text and its implications rather than by any fixed tune: Elsa's 'Einsam in trüben Tagen' and Lohengrin's 'In fernem Land' are not so much arias as narrations. Both roles (for soprano and tenor) are among the most vocally gratifying in Wagnerian repertory, even if the loudest applause often goes to the mezzo-soprano singing Ortrud: her confessional rant in the final minutes brings an opera sometimes punningly described by its detractors as 'Slow and Grim' to an electrifying climax.

The famous bridal chorus occurs in Act II – in the opera, it is intended to convey a certain foreboding and hesitation on Elsa's part. Note also the contrast between the radiantly shimmering and diaphanous Prelude to Act I (the sound of which gave the poet Baudelaire the sensation of weightlessness and vision of white light that he otherwise obtained from hashish) and the brassily triumphant Prelude to Act III.

⨍ In performance

The clash between the Christian world of Lohengrin and the pagan world of Ortrud has fascinated many directors, but the most successful productions of this opera have been those which do not get too bogged down in interpretation. For Covent Garden, Elijah Moshinsky staged the piece within a gauzy white box, the costuming and props tastefully evoking the early medieval period, and its sheer unforced simplicity proved remarkably effective; Robert Wilson's even bleaker visual concept for the Met was less successful. One famous Bayreuth production, first seen in 1987, was staged by the film director Werner Herzog, who envisaged the opera in a landscape of snow-covered desolation and ruin, set against a black sky in the dead of winter.

Alas, the magic of theatre often seems to fluff the appearance of the swan-drawn boat and the descending dove – moments which are more likely to induce giggles than the rapture the composer intended.

⨍ Recordings

CD: Siegfried Jerusalem (Lohengrin); Claudio Abbado (cond.). DG 437 808 2
Video: Cheryl Studer (Elsa); Woldemar Nelsson (cond.). Bayreuth Festival production. Philips 070 411 3

Tristan und Isolde

Three acts. First performed Munich, 1865.
Libretto by the composer

In the score of *Tristan*, Wagner dissolves the rules of harmony and key which had prevailed for a hundred and fifty years, thus opening up a new series of possibilities for western music. The opera is based on the medieval poem by Gottfried von Strassburg, but also has its roots in Wagner's passionate affair with Mathilde, the wife of his patron Otto von Wesendonck, and in his reading of Buddhism and the philosophy of Artur Schopenhauer. Both of these led him to the idea, suggested in the meditations of Tristan and Isolde's Act II duet, that only by renouncing life and transcending worldly phenomena can one attain inner peace and wisdom.

Yet the score is also graphically sensual in its implication that physical sex is the way to nirvana, and the cautious, rational voices of Brangäne, Kurwenal and Marke are all given their due. Should we regard Tristan and Isolde as heroic witnesses to the ultimate truth, or a self-centred pair locked into suicidal folly? The greatness of the opera is that it allows both possibilities.

∾ Plot

A prisoner of war, Isolde is being brought from Ireland to Cornwall to marry Tristan's uncle, King Marke. On board Tristan's ship, she furiously tells her servant Brangäne how Tristan, disguised as Tantris, murdered her lover Morold and then came to her in search of balm to heal his wounds. Overcome by his pitiful pleas, she could not bring herself to kill him: but now she hands him what she believes to be a death potion which she too will swallow rather than marry King Marke. But Brangäne, fearing Isolde's suicidal impulses, substitutes a love potion, and when Tristan and Isolde have drunk it, they fall rapturously into each other's arms. The ship reaches Cornwall.

Isolde is forced to marry King Marke, but while he is out hunting one night, she resolves to meet Tristan. Brangäne, who repents of her substitution of the love potion, warns her against the machinations of the envious courtier Melot, but Isolde is oblivious and commands Brangäne to extinguish the torch at her door – the signal for Tristan to approach.

Through a long and ecstatic duet, Tristan and Isolde reflect on the meaning of their love and aspire to a dissolution of their individual identities at the ultimate level of sexual passion. As the music rises to an orgasmic pitch, King Marke returns from the hunt and is led to the lovers' lair by the treacherous Melot. Marke mourns his nephew Tristan's betrayal of his trust, but Tristan is oblivious. He asks Isolde to follow him into eternal night, and she assents. Tristan throws himself on Melot's sword.

Tristan is dying in disgrace in his castle in Brittany, attended by his bluff but loyal servant Kurwenal. He can think of nothing but the prospect of being reunited with Isolde and waits day and night for her ship to arrive. When it is finally sighted, he deliriously tears the bandages from the fatal wounds inflicted by Melot, and as Isolde rushes to his side, he dies.

Brangäne, Melot and King Marke follow in Isolde's wake. Kurwenal kills Melot, and then dies himself in the fray. Marke had nobly decided to yield Isolde to Tristan, but it is all too late – Isolde, in a trance, rejoices that she and Tristan will now be mystically united in death.

ॐ What to listen for

The whole opera seems to germinate out of the hauntingly bittersweet opening phrase of the Prelude – music which seems to hover outside any recognizable key, pulling itself upwards as if to describe the desperate yearnings of Tristan and Isolde. Act I belongs to Isolde, who immediately launches into a tirade of frustrated rage and later faces some killing fortissimo top Bs and Cs at the climax of the story she tells Brangäne of Morold and 'Tantris'. The temptation for any soprano is to get round the difficult notes and make an effect by shrieking – a tactic which will probably leave her no voice for the warmer and more lyrical music of the second and third acts.

Act II unites Tristan with Isolde in a half-hour duet (its first, frenzied section is sometimes cut) in which they move ever closer together, interrupted only by Brangäne's warning (a particularly beautiful melodic episode, which tests any mezzo-soprano's power to sustain a steady line) and followed by Marke's long slow bass monologue of rueful recrimination. Act III is dominated by Tristan's ravings as he waits for the shepherd's piping (on a cor anglais) which heralds Isolde's arrival. No tenor has ever communicated Tristan's mixture of sexual frustration, physical agony and hysterical impatience with more passion than Jon Vickers. But it was cruel of Wagner to expect an ordinary mortal tenor to have the vocal resources for these scenes at this late stage of a long evening.

The opera ends with Isolde's 'Liebestod' or love death – a nirvana in which all the frenzy of the opera reaches its consummation, all passion spent.

The opera is based on a web of melodic themes, embedded in harmonies so dense and evanescent that it is often impossible to identify the music's key. This is music which moves in a constant state of tension – never arriving at any real destination until the Liebestod.

ᖷ In performance

The most influential modern interpretation is that of Wieland Wagner, the composer's grandson. In 1952, his production at Bayreuth swept away all the trappings of Victorian symbolism and put the opera for the first time into a completely abstract setting which specified neither time nor place and focused attention entirely on the principal characters, often spotlighting them on a virtually bare stage – creating an impression on the vast Bayreuth stage of existential loneliness.

Ever since, the opera has usually been staged with varying degrees of minimalism – the much-admired 1993 Bayreuth production by Heiner Müller was described by one critic as taking place in 'an emotional compression chamber'. An interesting exception is David Alden's arresting production for ENO, set in what appears to be the backstage area of a bombed-out theatre.

❧ Recordings

CD: Kirsten Flagstad (Isolde); Wilhelm Furtwängler (cond.). EMI 7 47322 8

Birgit Nilsson (Isolde); Karl Böhm (cond.). Philips 449 772 2

Der Ring des Nibelungen
(The Ring of the Nibelung)

Das Rheingold, one act; *Die Walküre*, three acts; *Siegfried*, three acts; *Götterdämmerung*, three acts. First performed Bayreuth, 1876. Libretto by the composer

Broadly speaking, Wagner wrote the libretto for the *Ring* backwards, between 1848 and 1852. He then composed the music for *Das Rheingold* in 1853–4; *Die Walküre*, 1854–6; Acts I and II of *Siegfried*, 1856–7, Act III, 1869; and *Götterdämmerung*, 1869–72. In all, the cycle gestated over a quarter of a century, and Wagner then faced four more years of struggle in his campaign to build a theatre at Bayreuth capable of rehearsing and staging the four operas consecutively.

In all, the *Ring* contains over fourteen hours of music. It is an immense sprawling epic, loosely drawn from various German mythical sources (notably the medieval epic poem the *Nibelungenlied*), influenced in form and shape by Greek tragedy and reflecting the thought of various nineteenth-century philosophers (Schopenhauer, Hegel, Feuerbach, Proudhon) in its themes: the redemptive power of love, the moral poison of the struggle for political and material supremacy, the sterility of bourgeois marriage, the growth of individual self-awareness. But the *Ring* is also a wonderfully theatrical fairy-tale, rich in comedy, spectacle and adventure, as well as the natural beauty of forest and river.

∾ Plot

Das Rheingold

Three Rhinemaidens guard a magical lump of gold lying at the bottom of their river. They taunt the dwarf Alberich, telling him that whoever forges the Rhinegold into a Ring will gain power over all the world, if he also renounces love. Furious at the Rhinemaidens' emptily provocative flirtation, Alberich steals the gold and renounces love.

Wotan is currently king of the gods. High in the mountains, he and his strait-laced wife Fricka admire from afar the exterior of their new palace, Valhalla. It has just been built by the giants Fasolt and Fafner, who are now asking for the agreed payment – Freia, the beautiful Goddess of Youth. Wotan is reluctant to hand her over, and is advised by the cunning Loge, God of Fire, to steal the Rhinegold from Alberich instead. The giants agree to accept the gold in lieu, but hold Freia hostage meanwhile. In her absence, the gods age and wither.

Wotan and Loge descend into the Nibelheim, where Alberich, empowered by the Ring, tyrannizes slaves who mine him massive wealth. Wotan and Loge encourage Alberich to show off the power of the Tarnhelm, a helmet made from the Rhinegold which can transform the wearer into any shape he chooses. When Alberich changes himself into a toad, Wotan and Loge find it easy to seize both the Ring and the Tarnhelm, as well as the remainder of the Rhinegold. Alberich, reverted to his natural form, curses the Ring and all who own it.

Back in Valhalla, Wotan prepares to hand the gold over to Fasolt and Fafner, but attempts to keep the Ring back for himself – until the all-knowing earth-goddess Erda, whose divinity is more ancient than that of the current generation of gods, warns Wotan of the dangers. So the Ring is handed over to the giants, and at once Alberich's curse takes effect – Fafner kills Fasolt and makes off with the Ring, the Tarnhelm and the Rhinegold. Freia is released and the gods are rejuvenated. As they prepare to cross over the rainbow bridge and take up residence in magnificent Valhalla, Loge cynically comments from the sidelines that this collection of gods is dishonoured and that their downfall cannot be far away.

Die Walküre

Siegmund is one of several mortal children that Wotan has illegitimately fathered in his effort to breed mortal heroes who can break Alberich's curse on the Ring. He is driven by a storm to seek shelter in a forest hut, where he is welcomed to the hearth by Sieglinde, the sad and lonely wife of Hunding.

Although they have never met before, Siegmund and Sieglinde feel a mysterious bond, and when Hunding returns he is disturbed by the attraction between them, as well as their physical resemblance. Siegmund tells his story. He is a loner and a fugitive, whose mother was murdered and whose twin sister was abducted. Involved in a fight trying to save a woman, he killed some men. Hunding realizes that Siegmund's victims were his kinsmen and that he bears Siegmund a grudge. The laws of hospitality oblige him to offer Siegmund a night's shelter, but at dawn he will be obliged to challenge Siegmund to a duel.

Sieglinde drugs Hunding's drink. Returning to Siegmund in the middle of the night, she tells Siegmund how a strange man (unknown to her, the disguised Wotan) appeared at her wedding and thrust a sword into the tree-trunk that runs through the hut, declaring that only a hero would be able to extract it. Siegmund is entranced by her tale. The doors of the hut fly open, revealing a moonlit spring landscape which they greet rapturously. Siegmund pulls the sword, which he christens 'Nothung', from the tree, and Sieglinde ecstatically realizes that Siegmund is her long-lost twin-brother – a relationship which does not inhibit their sexual passion. As Hunding sleeps on, they run away into the forest.

Wotan orders Brünnhilde – favourite of his daughters by Erda, together known as the Valkyries, Amazonian virgins who gather up the bodies of slaughtered warriors and carry them on horseback to Valhalla – to defend Siegmund, who is being pursued by Hunding. But Wotan's wife Fricka, guardian of the sanctity of marriage, violently disapproves of incest and, after her tirade against immorality, Wotan is forced to withdraw his support of Siegmund, even though his heart cries out against the decision. He tells Brünnhilde the story of the Ring and the curse that lies on it, explaining that only a hero, acting of his own free will, can rescue the Ring from the clutches of Fafner and redeem the curse – even if that also means the end of the gods in Valhalla.

When Brünnhilde meets Siegmund, she is forced to warn him of his impending death. Yet she is filled with a new compassion when she observes his devotion to Sieglinde and their exhausted state. She decides to disobey her father's command and shield Siegmund in his duel with Hunding. Wotan, however, is obliged to shield Hunding, and Siegmund is struck dead. Brünnhilde flees with Sieglinde.

The Valkyries ride back to their lair, carrying the latest crop of fallen warriors. Brünnhilde follows, bearing not a soldier, but Sieglinde. She begs her sisters to protect her from Wotan's wrath, but they refuse. Brünnhilde hails the baby that stirs in Sieglinde's womb as the hero Siegfried and tells her that one day he will reforge the magic sword Nothung, shattered in the duel with Hunding. Heartened, Sieglinde escapes into the forest, carrying the remnants of Nothung.

Brünnhilde confronts Wotan's wrath. Because she has disobeyed his command, he sentences her to be exiled from Valhalla and locked into a magic sleep until the first mortal man who passes shall waken her. Brünnhilde pleads to be protected from an ignoble fate, and Wotan relents to the extent of surrounding her couch with Loge's magic fire which only the bravest will be able to penetrate. He bids a long, sad farewell to his noble beloved daughter.

Siegfried

In a cave, Alberich's former minion Mime is struggling to reforge the remnants of Nothung. He has reared Sieglinde's son Siegfried, entrusted to his care by Sieglinde when he found her dying in the forest. Mime knows that Siegfried could be the one to win him the Ring and its worldly powers. He hopes to arm Siegfried – a rough-edged, innocent and fearless boy – with Nothung and send him out to find and kill the Ring's owner, the giant Fafner, who has now transformed himself into a dragon, the better to guard his treasure. But Siegfried loathes and despises Mime, who tells him for the first time the truth about his parental origins.

Wotan appears in the disguise of a traveller (the Wanderer) and challenges Mime to a game of riddles, which Wotan wins. Mime forfeits his head, but, as he leaves, Wotan announces that he will let the fearless hero who wields Nothung take that prize.

Mime realizes that this hero must be Siegfried. He now plots to poison the boy after he has killed Fafner and recovered the Ring. Siegfried succeeds in reforging Nothung and sets out to search for Fafner.

Alberich still hopes to recover the Ring. He is lurking outside Fafner's cave when his old antagonist Wotan appears, still disguised as 'the Wanderer'. Wotan is friendly: he warns both Alberich and Fafner of Siegfried's arrival, but fails to persuade Fafner to give up the Ring.

Mime prowls in the shadows, tailing Siegfried and waiting for him to kill Fafner. But nothing goes according to Mime's plan: Siegfried does kill Fafner, but the dying dragon warns him of Mime's treachery, realizing that he is acting on Mime's orders. After accidentally tasting Fafner's blood, Siegfried is able to understand the helpful messages of a singing Woodbird – she advises him to take the Ring and the Tarnhelm from Fafner's cave.

Alberich and Mime quarrel over the treasure. When Siegfried emerges, Alberich scuttles off. Mime offers Siegfried the poisoned drink, but Siegfried turns on Mime and kills him without remorse. The Woodbird leads Siegfried towards Brünnhilde's fire-encircled rock.

Wotan summons the wise earth-goddess Erda, hoping to learn the future from her. She can tell him nothing. He tells her that he has renounced all his ambitions, and now wants nothing except an end to the curse of the Ring and the beginning of a new order. First, he must put his grandson Siegfried to the test by barring his way to the rock. Siegfried pours scorn on Wotan the Wanderer, unaware of his true identity. He shatters Wotan's spear with Nothung – a symbol of the end of Wotan's power – and Siegfried breaks through the magic fire and awakens Brünnhilde. Siegfried has never seen a woman before and believes Brünnhilde to be his mother. In fact, she is his aunt, a relationship which does not prevent the two from falling in love. Brünnhilde renounces her divinity and she and Siegfried vow to face the world together without fear.

Götterdämmerung

Erda's daughters, the Norns, weave the rope of destiny. They explain Wotan's past history and look forward to the day when Valhalla and its inhabitants will be consumed by fire, superseded by a new race of heroes. But when they come to talk of Alberich and the Ring, their rope snaps and they can see no further.

Siegfried and Brünnhilde emerge from consummating their love in ecstatic mood. Brünnhilde sends Siegfried off to pursue deeds of glorious adventure – as token of his fidelity, he gives her the Ring and sails off down the Rhine.

In the hall of the tribe of the Gibichung, its chieftain, the weak-minded Gunther asks his scheming half-brother Hagen what he can do to consolidate his power. Hagen is also Alberich's son, and is plotting to win back the Ring. Hagen replies that both he and his sister Gutrune should marry, telling them what he has heard about Brünnhilde and Siegfried.

Siegfried stops off on his journey down the Rhine. Gunther and Hagen welcome him, and he naïvely tells them about himself – including the vital information that he has given the Ring to Brünnhilde. Gutrune then gives Siegfried a drugged potion which causes him to forget his past. In this oblivious state, he falls for Gutrune and offers to marry her, and to fight on Gunther's behalf and find him a wife. Gunther suggests that Siegfried should use the Tarnhelm which hangs round his waist to disguise himself as Gunther and bring Brünnhilde back from the rock. The drugged Siegfried, who does not recall anything that has occurred between him and Brünnhilde, happily agrees. A ferocious oath of blood brotherhood is sworn – in which Hagen does not participate – and Siegfried sails back up the Rhine.

Meanwhile, Brünnhilde sits on her rock. She is visited by Waltraute, one of her Valkyrie sisters, who tells her that after his spear was smashed by Siegfried, Wotan returned to Valhalla, where he waits in passive resignation for the curse of the Ring to be broken and the end of the gods to ensue. Waltraute begs Brünnhilde to hasten this inevitable process by giving up the Ring: Brünnhilde adamantly refuses – for her, the Ring embodies her union with Siegfried. So her horror is all the more intense when Siegfried, disguised by the Tarnhelm as Gunther, arrives on the rock, pulls the Ring from her finger and informs her that she will now be his wife.

The ghost of Alberich appears to his son Hagen in a dream, urging him to recover the Ring. Brünnhilde is dragged in to the hall of the Gibichung, where she is appalled to see Siegfried, no longer disguised, in the arms of Gutrune and wearing the Ring on his finger. Siegfried, his memory still drugged by the potion, is baffled by her rage. Siegfried is married to Gutrune, and Brünnhilde joins forces with Hagen to revenge herself on Siegfried.

Siegfried rests on the banks of the Rhine, where the Rhinemaidens appear to warn him of the curse on the Ring, but this means nothing to him. He is joined by Hagen and Gunther, who gives him an antidote to the potion, and his memory slowly returns – as he begins to recall his encounter with Brünnhilde, Hagen stabs him in the back (his only vulnerable point, as Brünnhilde has revealed). A funeral procession takes his dead body back to the hall of the Gibichung.

Gutrune is horrified at the murder of her husband and the double-dealing of Hagen. In the ensuing fracas, Hagen kills

Gunther and attempts to seize the Ring from Siegfried's finger. But the dead man's hand resists him.

Brünnhilde now realizes how she has been duped by Hagen's treachery. She prepares a funeral pyre for Siegfried, takes the Ring from his finger and after a long peroration, rides her faithful horse Grane into the flames. In a cataclysmic climax, the hall of the Gibichung catches fire and the Rhine bursts its banks. The Rhinemaidens recover the Ring from Brünnhilde, and Hagen is drowned in a last desperate effort to seize it from them. In the distance, a vision of Wotan and the conflagration of Valhalla can be seen; the old order is finished, and the last chords of the cycle suggest hope and renewal.

◊ What to listen for

The *Ring* is constructed musically round a series of melodic themes or tags, known as 'leitmotivs' (or '*leitmotiven*'). This term is not used by Wagner, who preferred to talk of '*Grundthemen*', or 'fundamental themes', but it became current in his lifetime through the guides to his work published by Hans von Wolzogen. Each leitmotiv is attached to a particular dramatic theme, symbol or character. They recur, combined and contrasted, throughout the cycle.

Wagner has the reputation of being a very 'loud' composer, but he was generally considerate of singers and their needs. A good conductor should not allow his orchestra to play so loud that they are either drowned or exhausted by the effort of communicating the words or sustaining a phrase. The even greater challenge for a conductor of the *Ring* is to build its overall shape and development, so that the very first note of *Das Rheingold* seems inexorably tied to the last note of *Götterdämmerung*. The *Ring* is not a series of discrete numbers or arias, but a complex and continuous drama united by the leitmotivs.

Das Rheingold may, vocally, be the least lyrical and most expository of the four operas, but it contains several wonderfully imaginative orchestral passages, including the magical opening which seems to rise from the darkest primeval depths of the Rhine (orchestrated for double bass and bassoon) to its sun-dappled surface, where the Rhinemaidens splash and frolic in innocently sensual harmony; the thrilling descent into Nibelheim, with its relentlessly clanging anvils; and the glowing climax, with its ever so slightly ironic undertone, which accompanies the procession of the gods over the Rainbow Bridge entry into Valhalla.

The opera was unique at the time for its single-act span of 150 minutes (although Wagner did later sanction an interval) and absence of opportunities for prima-donna soprano or tenor. Singers of the antagonistic bass-baritone roles of Alberich and Wotan often resort to a sort of rough-edged barking to make a dramatic effect and hide their vocal shortcomings, but Wagner preferred his music to be sung with firm tone and clean line.

Die Walküre opens with a prelude which graphically depicts the storm through which the hunted Siegmund is running. Siegmund and Sieglinde, tenor and soprano, are two of the most human and sympathetic characters in all of Wagner's work, and the way Act I charts the growth of their feelings for each other is intensely moving – a process culminating in two lyrical outpourings which answer each other: Siegmund's 'Winterstürme' and Sieglinde's 'Du bist der Lenz', followed by the frenzied excitement of the recognition of their true sibling identities and the wresting of Nothung from the tree. This is one of the great scenes of German opera, and sopranos and tenors who lack the sheer physical resources and nerve to sustain the longer, bigger roles of Siegfried and Brünnhilde find it wonderfully gratifying to sing.

Act II introduces Brünnhilde with her war-whoop cry of 'Hojotoho' – the first of many vocal challenges that this vast role proposes. Only the very best sopranos sing the notes accurately; the rest just shriek them approximately. The ensuing long dialogue between Fricka and Wotan, followed by Wotan's monologue, together make this a stretch of the *Ring* which requires homework and concentration from the listener if it is not to seem dull. However, Brünnhilde's solemnly beautiful encounter with Siegmund, known as the 'Todesverkundigung' (the 'Announcement of Death') has an immediate emotional impact.

Act III opens with the familiar 'Ride of the Valkyries', after which Brünnhilde meets Sieglinde and the latter sings the ecstatically arching phrases of 'O hehrstes Wunder' – difficult to sing with requisite tonal radiance at the end of a long evening. The opera concludes with Wotan's overwhelming farewell to Brünnhilde, in which the bass-baritone singing the role must appear to drop his godhead and stand before the audience as a proud but grief-stricken father mourning his beloved daughter. This is some of the most poignantly noble vocal music ever written, capped by a depiction of the fire crackling round Brünnhilde's rock which embodies Wagner's brilliance as an orchestral colourist and scene-painter.

Siegfried is an opera often regarded as comparable to the lighter scherzo which forms the third movement of many classical symphonies, and is marked by Wagner's heftily Teutonic sense of humour, particularly evident in the scenes involving Mime (sung by a tenor whose voice must be deliberately grotesque without becoming tiresome). Siegfried too, is in many respects a comic figure – boisterously boyish and unfeeling in his banter with the self-pitying Mime, naïve in his dealings with Wotan, the Woodbird and Brünnhilde. Sadly, few tenors capable of singing the role have either the physique or acting skills to convey these facets of the role.

The opera is most delicately orchestrated and Act II is rich in representations of the glories of the natural world – music later adapted into a purely orchestral movement known as 'Forest Murmurs' – as well as the pantomime fun of the dragon Fafner. Half-way through the act, the voice of the Woodbird (sung by a light lyric soprano) reintroduces the sound of women after two hours of exclusively male singing.

Act III was written after a gap of eleven years (in between, both *Tristan* and most of *Die Meistersinger* were written) and the changes the interim period wrought in Wagner's musical style are noticeable – orchestral textures seem richer, deeper and warmer and the interplay of the leitmotivs seems more free, subtle and supple, with less obvious melodramatic 'sign-posting'. The opera concludes with the long scene between Brünnhilde and Siegfried, in the course of which both characters are born again in love. For the soprano Brünnhilde, the challenge of this thirty-minute duet is monumental. Starting cold, at a late stage in the performance, she hails the sun as she is awoken from her sleep, in stern declamatory phrases which lie low for a soprano and which are difficult to pitch and hold steadily. Slowly, the goddess thaws into an exuberant young woman and the opera ends in ecstatic jubilation. As one commentator puts it, 'it's like leaping out of bed and climbing a mountain very quickly without any breakfast', often hindered by a Siegfried who will be running out of stamina just as Brünnhilde is getting into her vocal stride. After her only performance of the *Siegfried* Brünnhilde, the renowned Australian soprano Dame Nellie Melba developed a node on her vocal cords and didn't sing a note for six months.

Götterdämmerung. After the grave recapitulatory scene for the Norns, Siegfried and Brünnhilde continue in jubilant duet, before Siegfried sets off down the Rhine – a journey through surging waters which Wagner depicts in another magnificent piece of scene-painting. The most moving music of the remainder of Act I (which lasts in total for over two hours) is contained in Waltraute's account of the decline of Valhalla. Act II is tensely dramatic, focused on Brünnhilde's humiliation and revenge, and featuring many elements common to nineteenth-century grand opera – a rousing chorus (of the Gibichung), a revenge trio, a wedding procession and some thrilling top notes for the prima donna. Act III opens in a more relaxed atmosphere – the Rhinemaidens' graceful bathing-beauties trio recalls the beginning of *Rheingold*, while Siegfried's lovely music as he recovers his memory of life in the forest and his discovery of Brünnhilde literally re-enacts

Act II of *Siegfried*. The black, explosive ferocity of the Funeral March offers opportunities for a conductor and a timpanist to show off the power of their downbeat.

Somehow, after fourteen hours of music, Wagner manages to bring the *Ring* to a conclusion that does not seem anticlimactic: Brünnhilde's immolation and the final orchestral postlude unite the leitmotivs in a tremendous musical apocalypse, which dies away to be replaced by a calm, clear light glowing with the promise of a new dawn.

✎ In performance

Before the Second World War, the *Ring* was staged in quasi-naturalistic style, faithfully if not pedantically following Wagner's elaborate stage directions. All that changed for ever in 1951, when Wagner's grandson Wieland directed a cycle at Bayreuth which eliminated much of the clutter (Fricka's chariot drawn by a pair of rams, for example) and reasserted the opera's roots in Greek tragedy. Sets, costumes and props were austere, and the design was dominated by a circular platform, symbolic of the Ring itself. Atmosphere was provided by evocative lighting. Wieland's approach proved enormously influential over the ensuing generation, even though his own second production, at Bayreuth in 1966, was more scenically graphic, making use of archetypal Jungian dream-images.

In 1976, Bayreuth celebrated the centenary of the first performance of the *Ring* with a radical new interpretation directed by a brilliant young Frenchman, Patrice Chéreau. In place of Wieland's emphasis on the timeless qualities of the opera, Chéreau gave each act a specific location (the Rhine itself became a hydro-electric dam), presenting the story in a real historical world, albeit one which seemed to span several periods. Chéreau was fascinated by George Bernard Shaw's idea that the *Ring* was an allegorical critique of modern capitalism, moving from Wotan's *ancien régime* in *Rheingold* to the distinctly Fascistic society of the Gibichung in *Götterdämmerung*. The acting style was vivid and credible, and the characters in this *Ring* emerged as real and even ordinary people.

This approach in turn inspired another generation of *Ring* productions, notably that of Nikolaus Lehnhoff in Munich and San Francisco. An even more subversive and extreme line was taken by Ruth Berghaus in Frankfurt and Richard Jones at Covent Garden, whose grotesque cartoon surrealism more conservative audiences found baffling and offensive. Meanwhile, in the 1980s, Peter Hall at Bayreuth and August Everding at the Met returned to a more traditional pre-Wieland approach, creating beautiful stage pictures and ignoring the darker political and psychological implications of the story in order to reassert the plot's roots in German folklore.

✎ Recordings

CD: Birgit Nilsson (Brünnhilde), Hans Hotter (Wotan); Georg Solti (cond.). Decca 414 100-2

Video and DVD: Gwyneth Jones (Brünnhilde), Donald McIntyre (Wotan); Pierre Boulez (cond.). Bayreuth Festival production. Philips 070 401-3 (*Rheingold*) / 402-3 (*Walküre*) / 403-3 (*Siegfried*) / 404-3 (*Götterdämmerung*) (video); 070 407 9 (DVD)

Die Meistersinger von Nürnberg
(*The Mastersingers of Nuremberg*)

Three acts. First performed Munich, 1868.
Libretto by the composer

Calling this opera a 'comedy' may set up the wrong expectations – only the figure of Beckmesser is liable to raise anything approaching a titter from a modern audience. But this is undoubtedly Wagner's most warmly genial and romantic work, full of a mellow wisdom about young love and middle age, as well as the relationship between traditions, rules and forms and the lonely development of an artist's creative vision.

The cobbler–poet Hans Sachs is a historical figure and the guild of Mastersingers actually existed: Wagner researched their history in some detail. Recent scholarship has argued that the opera's undoubtedly nationalistic ideology conceals an anti-Semitic element. But such a view remains highly contentious, and audiences may prefer to concentrate on the opera's wonderfully life-affirming qualities and belief in the virtues of the small democratic community.

✎ Plot

In a church in sixteenth-century Nuremberg, a wandering young knight Walther von Stolzing, exiled from his estates when his father died, tries to find out more about the lovely Eva, daughter to the goldsmith Veit Pogner. Her maidservant Magdalene explains that she is to be married to the winner of the city's annual song contest, to be held the following day.

Fired with passion for Eva, Walther is determined to enter the contest, and is instructed in all the Mastersingers' complicated rules of song composition by David, Magdalene's lover and apprentice to Nuremberg's most admired songwriter, the cobbler Hans Sachs. The panel of Mastersingers (local craftsmen who govern the city's cultural life) assemble for the auditions – among them is the pedantic town clerk, Sixtus Beckmesser, who is entering the contest himself in the hope of winning Eva and her handsome dowry.

Walther scores badly in his audition, his impassioned and beautiful but somewhat wild love-song marked down by Beckmesser for breaking the rules of composition. Hans Sachs is, however, much taken with Walther, recognizing in him a genuinely original poetic spirit.

It is Midsummer's Eve. Eva reciprocates Walther's interest in her, and asks Hans Sachs's advice. An attractive middle-aged widower, he is drawn to Eva himself, but kindly resolves to help the cause of young love. Beckmesser tries to serenade Eva, but Sachs ruins the music by hammering away at his cobbling. Eventually there is a general riot on the street, during which David cudgels Beckmesser under the impression that Magdalene is the object of the serenade.

The next morning, Midsummer's Day, Sachs sends David off on an errand and sits reflecting on the folly of humankind. He is visited by Walther. Sachs helps him mould his song. After they leave together, the cudgelled Beckmesser sneaks in and finds the manuscript of the song. He jumps to the conclusion that Sachs is entering the contest himself. Sachs returns and assures him that this is not the case and offers the song to Beckmesser, without telling him that the manuscript represents only its incomplete sketched-out form. Eva appears, on the pretext that a shoe Sachs has cobbled for her is hurting her foot. Sachs is overwhelmed by her beauty and Eva herself does not seem to know whether she loves Sachs or Walther more. With a supreme effort of renunciation, he reminds her of the tale of Tristan and Isolde, and what a fool King Marke made of himself, marrying a younger woman. Sachs promotes David to a journeyman cobbler and blesses his marriage to Magdalene; Walther completes his song and Eva is enraptured.

The song contest is held in a meadow, in front of the assembled townsfolk in party mood. Beckmesser sings his incomplete version of Walther's song and makes a complete mess of it – in his humiliation, he tries to blame Sachs, but Sachs calls upon Walther, who performs the same song with consummate artistry. Walther is unanimously acclaimed the winner, and Eva's hand is conferred upon him. At first, he refuses to join the guild of Mastersingers, but Sachs persuades him otherwise, pointing out that the guild is a bulwark of true German art and its noble traditions. The crowd acclaims Sachs's wisdom.

✎ What to listen for

The miracle of *Meistersinger* lies in the way that Wagner manages to marry his own mature style, with its flow of interacting motifs and chromatic ambiguities, to an imaginative evocation of the musical world of a sixteenth-century German town. The blazing assertions of the opera's prelude, with its dazzling counterpoint, is based in the primitive key of C major, and it modulates magically into a beautiful chorale (to a tune composed by Wagner, not J. S. Bach). The first act may have its longueurs – one may well feel that Wagner allows David too much time explaining the Mastersingers' rulebook, for instance – but the second and third have a warmth, grace and charm unmatched in his *œuvre*. Note Sachs's two monologues – one in Act II, one at the beginning of Act III – the spiritual heart of the opera, during which he ruminates on the loneliness of the artist in an enclosed bourgeois society and the evanescent folly and vanity of worldly aspirations. Act III also contains Eva's impassioned outburst, 'O Sachs, mein Freund', which often leaves one thinking that the girl would be far better marrying the cobbler than the wandering knight. This is followed by the radiant quintet – one of the few episodes in Wagner's mature work where solo voices sing in counterpoint. The final scene of the song contest itself starts as an exuberant parade of marches and dances, before focusing on the melody of Walther's Prize Song which has been slowly blossoming throughout the opera. One curiosity of the plot: where are the other contestants for Eva's hand? Surely Beckmesser and Walther can't be the only entrants for such a prestigious prize?

ᖗ In performance

Naturalistic representations of sixteenth-century Nuremberg tend to make the opera look kitsch and Toytown, but productions which insist on interpreting the story as a fable of the spirit of insular conformity which ultimately led Germany to Nazism have become even more tiresome and clichéd. Perhaps the most successful modern staging has been that of Herbert Wernicke, seen in Hamburg and Paris in the 1980s, which depicted an undercurrent of youthful riot and anarchy running counter to the rigid social demarcations that govern the vigilant and close-knit community of Nuremberg. How seriously to take Beckmesser's unpleasantness is a matter of great debate – there is evidence that Wagner intended the portrait to caricature the hostile critic Eduard Hanslick. Others have suggested that he is a Jewish bogeyman in disguise.

○◦ Recordings

CD: Elisabeth Grümmer (Eva); Rudolf Kempe (cond.).
EMI 64154-2
    Ben Heppner (Walther): Wolfgang Sawallisch (cond.)
EMI 555 142 2

Parsifal

Three acts. First performed Bayreuth, 1882.
Libretto by the composer

Wagner's last opera is based on the medieval epic poem by Wolfram von Eschenbach, a German offshoot of Arthurian mythology. Its symbolic import reflects elements of the philosophy of Schopenhauer (the idea of renunciation), Buddhism (Kundry's reincarnations, and Parsifal's pilgrimage towards enlightenment) and racist theory (the problem of regenerating a decadent culture).

The libretto was first drafted in the late 1850s, although the music was not written until 1878–82. Until the First World War, great efforts were made to prevent the work, 'a sacred stage festival play', from being performed anywhere outside Bayreuth, and only recently has applause been considered an appropriate response to the solemn Christian ritual which closes Act I.

○◦ Plot

The castle of Monsalvat is inhabited by an order of religious knights who guard the Grail of the Last Supper and the Spear which pierced Christ at the crucifixion. The order's leader, Amfortas, once set off with the Holy Spear to vanquish Klingsor, a wizard who had been denied membership to the order and then turned vengeful. Klingsor trapped Amfortas in his magic garden near Monsalvat and commanded his agent, the beautiful Kundry, to seduce him. Klingsor then seized the Holy Spear and stabbed the unmanned Amfortas with it. Amfortas returned to the Order of the Grail, but the wound inflicted by Klingsor refuses to heal and the Order of the Grail has fallen into terrible decline from which it can only be redeemed by 'a pure fool made wise by suffering'.

When the opera opens, the squires of the order, led by the elderly knight Gurnemanz, are preparing to bathe Amfortas's wound. Kundry, who schizophrenically embodies many aspects of womanhood, rushes in exhausted, dishevelled and hideous. She brings Arabian balsam, which she compassionately presents to soothe Amfortas's pain.

One of the sacred swans of the order is callously shot down by a wandering youth. When questioned by an angry Gurnemanz, he reveals that he knows nothing about himself – neither his name nor his origins. Gurnemanz believes that he may be the redeeming 'wise fool', and leads the nameless youth to witness the ceremonial unveiling of the Grail. The youth watches the solemnities without any sense of understanding, though a cry of pain from Amfortas shocks him. Gurnemanz hustles the youth out of the chapel.

From the tower of his magic castle, Klingsor orders Kundry – now transformed into his glamorous agent of evil – to ensnare the youth as he wanders away from Monsalvat. Klingsor's Flower Maidens lure him into the magic garden, and Kundry calls out his long-forgotten name – Parsifal. He listens entranced as she tells him how she once saw him as a baby at his mother's breast and how his mother had died of grief after he had wandered off and not returned. Parsifal's feelings of love for his mother are revived and confused by his carnal desire for Kundry. When she kisses him, however, he leaps up, suddenly seized by the memory of Amfortas's pain and an awareness of his suffering.

Kundry now begs Parsifal for help, explaining that she was eternally doomed centuries ago when she blasphemously laughed at Christ on the road to crucifixion. The purity of his love would bring her release. But Parsifal resists, knowing in some way that his responsibility lies with Amfortas. Kundry angrily turns back to Klingsor, who throws the Holy Spear at Parsifal. Parsifal catches it and makes the sign of the cross, at which Klingsor's castle and his magic is instantly destroyed.

Years pass. The Order of the Grail has continued to decline, and Gurnemanz lives in the forest as a hermit. One Good Friday, he discovers Kundry lying prostrate near his hut. She does not speak, except to beg that she be allowed to serve – in expiation for her sins. Then a mysterious knight appears – it is Parsifal, returned from long years of wandering during which he has matured spiritually. To Gurnemanz's joy, he carries the long-lost Holy Spear.

The knights are burying Amfortas's father Titurel, and Amfortas, exhausted by pain, begs them to put an end to his tormented life, too. But when Parsifal touches his wound with the Holy Spear, he is miraculously healed. Kundry dies, released from her spiritual torment, and as spring brings renewal to the natural world, so Parsifal brings redemption to the Order.

∾ What to listen for

Debussy famously said that the music of *Parsifal* was 'lit from behind' – an attempt to describe its uniquely translucent orchestral sound, often compared to the effect of Impressionist painting. Slow in pace but mesmerizingly tense, the drama moves with a trancelike fluidity that seems to float outside the normal limitations of time and space. The baritone role of Amfortas offers the most vocally gratifying music in the opera, while the schizophrenic character of Kundry – mother and lover, whore, witch and Magdalen penitent – offers its greatest challenge. Her lines lie high for a mezzo-soprano but low for a soprano, and the long lyrical stretches of Act II mount to a climax of fervent hysteria. Act III, however, presents her with only two almost-spoken words to sing: 'Dienen, dienen' ('to serve, to serve'). The rest is eloquent silence.

Parsifal's dissolution of harmonic definition was hugely

influential on the development of modern music, and works as different as Elgar's *The Dream of Gerontius* and Debussy's *Images* sought to emulate its dreamy intensity and radiant luminosity.

∾ In performance

Parsifal was the opera that reopened Bayreuth after the post-Nazi hiatus in 1951, in a production by Wagner's grandson Wieland that would set the tone for the next generation. Instead of the naturalistic presentation of the forest and temple of Monsalvat and Klingsor's castle and garden, complete with the spectacular transformation scenes characteristic of pre-war productions, came a concept that eliminated virtually all specific imagery and focused instead on varying degrees of light and darkness, which made the drama universal, timeless and archetypal.

In the 1980s, producers like Götz Friedrich became interested in the sociological implications of the plot, and new visual contexts evolved. The Knights of the Grail were seen less as Christian pilgrims than as members of a sinister secret society and the Flower Maidens were often dressed up (or down) to suggest the inhabitants of a brothel. In the 1990s, a much-travelled production by Klaus-Michael Gruber evoked a more complex and ambiguous atmosphere, using images drawn from surrealist painters like Paul Klee and Max Ernst. Others have chosen to underline, with varying degrees of sensitivity and crassness, the parallels between the racist élites of the Nazis and the 'brotherhood' of the Grail.

The opera continues to pose many problems to directors: how to avoid the bathos of the shot swan plopping down on to the stage, for example, how to suggest Kundry's multiple personalities, and how to avoid kitsch in the presentation of the Flower Maidens.

∾ Recording

CD: Jess Thomas (Parsifal); Hans Knappertsbusch (cond.). Philips 416 390 2

Engelbert Humperdinck (1854–1921)
Hänsel und Gretel

Three acts. First performed Weimar, 1893.
Libretto by Adelheid Wette

This delightful and surprisingly powerful opera began as a domestic entertainment, devised for the composer's sister and her children. When Richard Strauss received the complete score, he declared it 'a masterpiece of the highest quality', and it has remained a hugely popular Christmas show ever since. The plot is drawn from a tale by the Brothers Grimm.

◈ Plot

In the absence of their parents, little Hänsel and Gretel are playing when they should be working at household chores. The family is very poor and hungry, and when their harassed mother bursts in on their games, she is so angry that she sends them out into the forest to gather strawberries. Her husband cheerfully returns from work with a bag of food, but he is alarmed at the children's absence, remembering tales of a witch with a taste for children. Both parents rush into the forest to find Hänsel and Gretel.

The children are now thoroughly lost in the forest and fall asleep, watched over by the benign Sandman and Dew Fairy. The children are very hungry and begin to nibble at a strange hut made of gingerbread. Out of its front door jumps the Witch, who imprisons Hänsel in a cage and forces Gretel to help with the oven, announcing that she is fattening Hänsel up. But Gretel manages to free Hänsel and together the children push the witch into her own oven. The spells are broken, and children who have previously fallen victim to the witch's machinations are restored to life. Hänsel and Gretel's parents are relieved to find their children safe, and all ends happily.

∾ What to listen for

Hänsel und Gretel is rich in the simple folk-song and dance-tunes of Schubert and Weber's era, but its rich-textured orchestration and thematic intricacy evince the Wagnerian influence – Humperdinck actually assisted Wagner on *Parsifal*. Hänsel is generally sung by a mezzo-soprano and poses no problems; Gretel is trickier – although the composer evidently intended the role to be sung by a girlish soubrette soprano, the heavy orchestration tends to drown such voices. The aria for the Sandman is lushly beautiful, and on recordings is taken by sopranos of the calibre of Kiri Te Kanawa. Veteran mezzo-sopranos enjoy hamming it up as the Witch – a role also taken on occasion by character tenors.

∾ In performance

Many productions are specifically geared to children and will be staged in traditional pantomime style, but *Hänsel und Gretel* is a good enough opera to stand up to 'adult' treatment. At ENO, David Pountney's staging set the opera on a suburban estate, and doubled the role of the mother with that of the Witch, suggesting parallels with modern fears of 'child abuse'. For WNO, Richard Jones presented the piece as a dark fantasy of a child's relationship with food, hunger and greed, depicting the Witch's kitchen as a vast steel-lined industrial plant geared to mass catering.

∾ Recording

CD: Ann Murray (Hänsel), Edita Gruberova (Gretel); Colin Davis (cond.). Philips 438 013 2

Richard Strauss (1864–1949)
Salome

One act. First performed Dresden, 1905.
Libretto by Oscar Wilde, translated by Hedwig Lachmann

Salome was Strauss's third opera. Its biblically based subject-matter and modernist musical style caused an immediate sensation and led to protests, official condemnation and even bans in several cities. Once the fuss died down, it emerged as a masterly piece of *fin-de-siècle* decadence, with its glittering orchestration, powerful characterization and grisly fascination with extreme psychological states. The text skilfully trims the text of Oscar Wilde's florid play, originally written in French in 1893.

ᙯ Plot

Salome is the daughter of Herodias by her first marriage. Now Herodias is married to Herod, Tetrarch of Judea, who has imprisoned John the Baptist, 'Jokanaan', in an underground cistern for preaching dangerous new doctrine and denouncing the decadence of Herod and his court.

Narraboth guards the cistern: he is obsessed with the beautiful teenage Salome, who has left Herod's banquet, disgusted by her stepfather's lustful looks and the dinner-table arguments of the Jews and Romans. Salome persuades Narraboth to open the cistern and fetch Jokanaan. Despite his fierce insults and refusal to look at her, she is erotically fascinated by Jokanaan's powerful presence. Jokanaan is sent back into the cistern, but Narraboth cannot bear to see Salome in love with another and kills himself.

Herod and Herodias appear: he is fearful of ill omens, she loathes Jokanaan, who shouts curses from the cistern. The Jews quarrel with the Nazarenes, and there is talk of another miracle-working prophet in the land – is he the Messiah, some ask. Herod lasciviously asks Salome to dance for him.

Despite her mother's disapproval, she agrees on the condition that when she has finished, he will give her whatever she asks. Her dance involves the seductive shedding of seven diaphanous veils. Herod is enthralled, but his superstitious nature recoils in horror when Salome asks for her reward – the head of Jokanaan on a silver platter. He offers her untold riches instead, but she persists. Finally, Herod yields and Jokanaan's severed head is laid before Salome. Deliriously she picks it up and reflects on what could have been: 'If you had looked at me, you would have loved me.' Herodias is delighted to be rid of Jokanaan, but when Salome kisses Jokanaan's bleeding mouth, Herod can take no more: he orders his soldiers to kill Salome, and they crush her beneath their shields.

✆ What to listen for

Strauss once admitted that *Salome* might on first hearing sound like 'a symphony with accompanying vocal parts', and much of the piece's power and originality is concentrated in the brilliant manipulation of the colours of the instrumental palette (for example, the short stabbing strokes on the bridge of the double bass, indicative of Salome holding her breath while Jokanaan is being executed). Coldly analysed and unpicked, a lot of the melodies (such as the tunes which make up the Dance of the Seven Veils) are banal, and Strauss is too ready to turn up the volume and pile up the notes in order to make an effect – the opera uses an enormous orchestra. Yet *Salome* provides a totally enthralling experience in the theatre, grounded in a flawless dramatic structure which moves inexorably over its hundred-minute span without a second's waste or tedium.

The role of Salome is alluring but difficult, ranging from a high B to low G flat, and requiring sufficient reserves of power and breath to ride the orchestral tumult of the duet with Jokanaan and the long final monologue in which Salome makes love to the severed head. And how many sopranos have the right bodies to impersonate convincingly the role of a beautiful teenage temptress? Teresa Stratas, Julia Migenes and Maria Ewing are among those who could look and sound sweet sixteen, but didn't have the heft to ride the climaxes; the more Amazonian Anja Silja and Catherine Malfitano lacked the silky innocence of voice that the music ideally requires. Singers of ampler physique often avoid embarrassment by deputizing the business of the Seven Veils to a professional dancer. Both Herod and Herodias present great opportunities for older sopranos (or mezzo-sopranos) and character tenors to indulge in melodramatic histrionics – neither has much to sing.

There are three slightly different versions of the opera: the original score of 1905; a revision which Strauss made in 1930 with the aim of reducing some of the orchestration so that lighter-voiced sopranos could sing Salome; and a later revision made to accommodate Wilde's original French text. The second is the edition most commonly used in opera houses today.

ॐ In performance
A production flamboyantly designed by Salvador Dalí and directed by the young Peter Brook, with the voluptuous Ljuba Welitsch in the title-role, caused a great stir at Covent Garden in 1949, introducing London audiences to the modern concept of staging opera.

Among successful recent productions are those by Peter Hall (seen in Los Angeles and at Covent Garden and the Met), in which Maria Ewing strikingly finished the Dance of the Seven Veils stark naked; Luc Bondy (Salzburg and Covent Garden), who presented Herod's palace as a bombed-out den in a city ravaged by war; and André Engel (WNO and Scottish Opera), who evoked the Arab harem paintings of Delacroix. Others striving to avoid the obvious Hollywood biblical kitsch have taken the symbolist paintings of Odilon Redon or the Secessionist eroticism of Gustav Klimt as their inspiration.

ॐ Recordings
CD: Cheryl Studer (Salome); Giuseppe Sinopoli (cond.). DG 431 810 2

Video: Catherine Malfitano (Salome); Christoph von
Dohnanyi (cond.). Covent Garden production. Decca 074
105 3

Teresa Stratas (Salome); Karl Böhm (cond.). German television film. DG 072 109 3

Elektra

One act. First performed Dresden, 1909.
Libretto by Hugo von Hofmannsthal

In 1903 Strauss saw a production of Sophocles' *Elektra*,
rewritten (under the influence of a reading of Freud) by
Hugo von Hofmannsthal and staged by the revolutionary
director Max Reinhardt. Struck by its operatic potential, he
approached Hofmannsthal for permission to set the text to
music – and thus began one of the great composer–librettist
partnerships. Strauss nevertheless worried that *Elektra* might
seem too similar in scope (one act, lasting about 110 minutes)
and subject-matter (a neurotic woman driven to an extreme
act) to its predecessor, *Salome*. The result is that *Elektra* was
scored for an unprecedentedly large orchestra – including
eight clarinets, eight horns and four Wagner tubas – and
broke new boundaries of fortissimo.

ᖇ Plot

Banished outside the walls of the palace of Mycenae,
Elektra squats in rags, mourning her dead father King
Agamemnon, murdered by his wife, Elektra's mother,
Clytemnestra, and her lover Aegisthus. Elektra is obsessed
with desire for revenge. Her emollient sister Chrysothemis,
desperate for a normal existence, begs her to be more cir-
cumspect.

Clytemnestra is haunted by nightmares. She comes out of
the palace to ask her daughter Elektra – whom she believes to
have magical powers – for help. Elektra taunts her aggres-

sively. News comes that Elektra's exiled brother Orestes is dead. Clytemnestra is delighted, but Elektra despairs: she always hoped that he would return and be the agent of her revenge. Elektra fails to persuade the timorous Chrysothemis to join with her in a murderous plot, and sets to work alone, digging up a buried axe.

A stranger enters. He questions Elektra, and once he is sure of her identity and loyalty, reveals himself to be Orestes – news of his death was false. Elektra is blissfully reunited with her brother, who has returned to do his duty. In disguise, he enters the palace, where he soon kills Clytemnestra and Aegisthus. Elektra's joy at the long-awaited slaughter drives her demented. She dances deliriously and falls dead, as the distraught Chrysothemis hammers on the palace door.

∾ What to listen for

After the opening scene, in which five servants and their overseer discuss the situation, Elektra does not leave the stage (although Birgit Nilsson, one of the greatest Elektras, found an opportunity during the digging-up of the buried axe to creep into the wings and swallow a fortifying pint of beer). The role is the ultimate *tour de force* for a dramatic soprano, exhausting not only vocally but emotionally too. Elektra is a woman of high intelligence and wit teetering on the edge of insanity, and her music persistently rises to high-lying climaxes indicative of her hysteria. The soprano also has to master a long, complex and sophisticated text, flavoured with the Freudian theory of the unconscious, and sustain an intensity which can embrace both the tendresse of the reunion with Orestes and the final explosive mad dance of fury. Chrysothemis is in contrast a more conventionally lyrical soprano role, and Clytemnestra provides a gift to an older contralto with crisp enunciation and a touch of ham. The male roles, Orestes and Aegisthus, are comparatively small and uninteresting.

Compared to the overripe, lip-smacking sensuality of *Salome*, the idiom of *Elektra* is cold, hard, and brazen – qualities appropriate to the depiction of a society ruled by a primitive blood-feud. There are moments when its harmonic dissonance is extreme and minutes when it descends into plain bombast, but after all the sound and fury, the score comes defiantly home in the basic key of C major – one of the little jokes which pepper Strauss's scores.

❧ In performance

It's no longer enough to present an approximation of Ancient Mycenae – contemporary productions envisage *Elektra* as taking place in a bunker, a prison, a mental hospital, or any location evocative of the brutality and psychosis of twentieth-century totalitarianism. How to keep the acting style clear of melodrama and do any sort of justice to the subtleties of Hofmannsthal's fascinating text is more of a problem.

❧ Recordings

CD: Birgit Nilsson (Elektra); Georg Solti (cond.). Decca 417 345 2
Video: Leonie Rysanek (Elektra); Karl Böhm (cond.). Decca 071 400 3

Der Rosenkavalier
(*The Knight of the Rose*)

Three acts. First performed Dresden, 1911.
Libretto by Hugo von Hofmannsthal

After *Salome* and *Elektra*, Strauss was desperate to write a comedy. Hofmannsthal obliged with the delicious confection of *Der Rosenkavalier*, a pastiche of rococo intrigue, combining ingredients drawn from Beaumarchais, Molière, Hogarth, Verdi's *Falstaff* and the *commedia dell'arte*, as well as the authentic social history of Maria Theresa's Vienna in the 1740s. With its sophisticated balance of farce, romance and world-weary wisdom, the result has been consistently admired and beloved since its first performance.

∾ Plot

While her husband, the Feldmarschall (Field-Marshal) is away, the aristocratic Marschallin Marie Therese is conducting a passionate affair with a much younger man, Count Octavian. Their love-making is interrupted by the arrival of Marie Therese's boorish and lecherous country cousin Baron Ochs, who has come to Vienna to solve his financial problems by marrying Sophie, the pretty teenage daughter of the *nouveau-riche* Herr von Faninal. Octavian disguises himself as Mariandel, a maidservant, and Ochs takes a misguided fancy to 'her'.

Ochs solicits the Marschallin's help – he needs someone to present Sophie with the silver rose which customarily accompanies a marriage proposal. The Marschallin mischievously suggests her 'cousin' Octavian for the task.

After her levee, the Marschallin bids farewell to Octavian, conscious that she is getting old and that he will soon be looking for women elsewhere. Octavian is appalled at the suggestion, but the Marschallin knows better, reflecting that one must accept the passage of time without sinking into self-pity.

In Faninal's house, there is great excitement as the bearer of the silver rose approaches. When Octavian appears to make the presentation, he and Sophie fall instantly in love. But Sophie is disgusted by Ochs's coarseness and immediately determines to reject him. Ochs's spies, Valzacchi and Annina, inform Ochs what is going on between Sophie and Octavian, and Ochs and Octavian fight an inconsequential duel. Sophie is taken away by her father Faninal and Octavian is shown the door. But Octavian now buys up the services of Valzacchi and Annina, and hatches his own little plot. He tells Annina to deliver Ochs a note from 'Mariandel', proposing an assignation in a suburban inn. Ochs cannot resist.

When he arrives at the inn, Ochs is perturbed by both Mariandel's reluctance to be seduced and her startling resemblance to Octavian. Then Annina arrives and noisily accuses

Ochs of being the father of several of her children. Faninal is summoned and witnesses further farcical complications, all carefully stage-managed by Octavian, which culminate in Ochs's total humiliation. Only the Marschallin's sudden and surprising arrival quells the hubbub. She firmly dismisses the disgraced Ochs, and shows a gracious and generous understanding of Octavian's new passion for Sophie. The two young lovers are left happily alone together.

ᠭᠣ What to listen for

An opera dominated by female voices and containing three of the repertory's most beautiful and gratifying roles for full lyric soprano (the Marschallin), a lighter high lyric soprano (Sophie) and high mezzo-soprano or low soprano (Octavian). Ochs is a great favourite of bass-baritones, too, though finding the balance in the characterization between the country gentleman and the lecherous boor is not easy: however coarse he may be, Ochs is still some sort of aristocrat.

Note the graphic description of sexual climax in the prelude (whooping horns depicting orgasm); the elaborately detailed scene-painting of the Marschallin's levee, full of typically Straussian little jokes; the almost Puccinian sweetness of the aria sung by the Italian tenor who serenades the Marschallin as she receives her guests; the suppleness and warmth of the conversations between Octavian and the Marschallin, and the subtle colouring of word and shaping of phrase with which a good singer will mark the Marschallin's melancholy monologue.

Act II centres on the dazzling scene of the Presentation of the Rose, a scene for Sophie and Octavian which serves as the classic example of Strauss's obsession with the shimmering silvery glamour of the soprano voice. Like the Italian tenor's aria, the waltzes at the end of Act II are an anachronism, but one that seems to fit the pastiche so perfectly that it is impossible to object. The over-egged farce of the first half of Act III melts into the rapturous trio ('Hab mir's gelobt') and the almost childlike innocence of the ensuing rocking duet for

Sophie and Octavian (modelled, it is believed, on the duet in *Hänsel und Gretel*, one of Strauss's favourite operas).

For all these marvels, *Der Rosenkavalier* remains an opera for those with a sweet tooth. It is a long work (three and a half hours of music) with a lot of text and a bewildering confusion of secondary characters, requiring superlatively disciplined conducting and magnificent singing if it is not to drag in the middle.

✎ In performance

An opera so intricately and meticulously written that it does not take kindly to being messed about with, though attempts have been made to lift it gently out of the 1740s Viennese setting and eliminate some of its whipped-cream and sugared-icing ingredients by updating the scenario to the turn-of-the-century era of its composition.

The list of great female singers who have given memorable interpretations of the Marschallin, Octavian and Sophie is endless. Many have graduated from Octavian to the Marschallin (Christa Ludwig), and several from Sophie to the Marschallin (Lucia Popp), but only three have also played Sophie – Lotte Lehmann, Lisa della Casa and Elisabeth Söderström. Outstanding recent interpreters of these roles include Felicity Lott and Renée Fleming (Marschallin), Ann Murray, Susan Graham and Anne-Sofie von Otter (Octavian) and Barbara Bonney and Kathleen Battle (Sophie). Strauss's score specifies that Octavian should be sung by a soprano, but in the interests of contrasting vocal weight and colour with the Sophie and Marschallin, the role is usually taken today by a high mezzo-soprano.

✎ Recordings

CD: Régine Crespin (Marschallin); Georg Solti (cond.). Decca 417 493 2

  Kiri Te Kanawa (Marschallin); Bernard Haitink (cond.). EMI 754 259 2

DVD: Felicity Lott (Marschallin); Carlos Kleiber (cond.). Vienna State Opera production. DG 073 008 9

Ariadne auf Naxos

**Prologue and one act. First performed Vienna, 1916.
Libretto by Hugo von Hofmannsthal**

Strauss and Hofmannsthal originally planned to append a
small-scale half-hour opera on the theme of the mythological
Ariadne to a version of Molière's play *Le bourgeois gentilhomme*,
for which Strauss would provide incidental music. In the event,
Molière was compressed and Ariadne expanded, and in 1912
the diptych was performed in Stuttgart. But it made for an
awkwardly long and ill-balanced evening, and the additional
expense and difficulty of hiring troupes of both singers and
actors meant that the work was never likely to establish itself.

In 1916, a shorter and more coherent revision was performed, and it is this version which, despite several substantial musical losses, has remained standard. In place of *Le bourgeois gentilhomme*, it substituted a prologue with themes and
setting loosely drawn from Molière, but newly focused on the
figure of the Composer, and the dilemmas of the creative
artist in a society which wants cheerful entertainment rather
than profound art.

❧ Plot

In the house of a rich Viennese gentleman, preparations are
under way for a theatrical entertainment. There is consternation when it is announced that, to save time and money, the
brilliant young Composer's serious opera on the tragic situation of the deserted Ariadne is to be performed with elements
of a farcical *opera buffa* intermixed. Zerbinetta, the vivacious
leading lady of the comic troupe, flirts with the Composer in
an attempt to unravel the plot of his opera. Idealistic though
he is on matters of both music and love, the Composer cannot help but be charmed by her gaily cynical attitude to the
tragic Ariadne. Then a bell rings: the performance is due to
begin, and it is too late for the Composer to prevent the
botch of his tragic masterpiece.

The opera-within-an-opera opens to reveal the incon-solable Ariadne lying outside a cave on the island of Naxos. She has just been abandoned there by her lover Theseus and, for all the efforts of the *opera-buffa* troupe to cheer her up, she longs to die. Zerbinetta preaches a more down-to-earth atti-tude – one man can soon be replaced with another. When Bacchus arrives, Ariadne at first mistakes him for Theseus, then the Herald of Death. But to Zerbinetta's satisfaction, Ariadne and Bacchus fall in love, celebrating their union in a long and rapturous duet.

ᖇ What to listen for

Most of *Ariadne auf Naxos* was composed in conscious reac-tion to the Wagnerian scale and effects of *Elektra* and *Der Rosenkavalier*. The orchestration is modest and contains several discrete arias – the tone is Mozartian. Yet Strauss could never altogether resist firing the big guns. *Ariadne* contains three female roles similar to those in *Rosenkavalier* – the Composer (high mezzo-soprano, although, as for Octavian in *Der Rosenkavalier*, the score specifies a soprano), Ariadne (full lyric soprano, requiring stronger and deeper low notes than the Marschallin or Arabella) and Zerbinetta (a lyric soprano with facility for coloratura and high notes) – as well as a cruelly testing and ungrateful role for the tenor Bacchus.

It is also a score which contains several magnificent out-bursts. The Composer makes an impassioned defence of the 'Holy Art of Music' at the end of the Prologue; Ariadne paints a moving vision of the kingdom of death in 'Es gibt ein Reich'; and in 'Grossmächtige Prinzessin', Zerbinetta shows Ariadne the error of her views. The latter is one of the great coloratura showpieces: its interminable 1912 version hits a stratospheric F; rewritten and mercifully shortened in 1916, it rises only to a more modest E (a semitone lower than the Queen of the Night's top F). Even so, few singers manage the trill on the top D and E which Strauss cruelly specifies at one point. The great blot on the score, by common consent, is the coarse, noisy and over-extended duet for Bacchus and Ariadne which ends an otherwise enchanting piece.

Note also the lovely music for the Rhinemaiden-like trio of nymphs who surround Ariadne, and the gently simple song, 'Lieben, hassen', crooned by the *opera-buffa* figure of Harlequin in an attempt to comfort Ariadne. It's a marvellous opportunity for a young lyric baritone hoping to make his mark.

ও In performance

Like *Der Rosenkavalier*, this opera offers three marvellous roles to female singers, but confronts directors with the difficulty of presenting an elegant farce through which Hofmannsthal's more serious themes – the meaning of sexual fidelity, for example – can also shine. Again, Hofmannsthal's libretto is so beautifully crafted and specifically detailed that there is not much that can be done in the way of updating or conceptualizing. Audiences always regret the way that the sympathetic figure of the Composer vanishes from the action after the Prologue: some productions compensate by having him silently watch the action of the opera-within-an-opera from a chair at the side of the stage.

ও Recordings

CD: Leontyne Price (Ariadne); Georg Solti (cond.). Decca 460 230 2
Video: Jessye Norman (Ariadne), Kathleen Battle (Zerbinetta); James Levine (cond.). Metropolitan Opera production. DG 072 411 3

Die Frau ohne Schatten
(*The Woman without a Shadow*)

Three acts. First performed Vienna, 1919.
Libretto by Hugo von Hofmannsthal

A twentieth-century rewriting of *Die Zauberflöte*, with the glory of human fertility as its theme. Although its orchestration is the most grandiose Strauss ever used and its physical landscape is cosmic, the opera is closely focused on individual dilemmas and marital relationships.

⌘ Plot

The daughter of Keikobad, ruler of the spirit world, has married a human Emperor. As she is neither mortal nor immortal, she cannot bear children – a sterility symbolized by her lack of a shadow. If she cannot find one within three days, Keikobad will turn the Emperor to stone. The scheming Nurse leads her to the mortal world and the house of a good man, Barak the Dyer, whose nagging and dissatisfied wife is also childless, much to Barak's disappointment. The Nurse bribes the Dyer's Wife with riches to sell the Empress her shadow. But the Empress is filled with remorse when she understands what misery this will cause Barak, and tells her father Keikobad that she cannot go through with the bargain. She pleads to save her husband, offering herself as a sacrifice. Finally, her resolution prevails. The Dyer's Wife learns to love Barak, and eventually both she and the Empress are allowed their shadows and the promise of children.

⌘ What to listen for

Strauss's most aurally glittering and spectacular score, rich in heavily underlined themes and virtuoso orchestral interludes, but lacking the obvious vocal 'highlights' of his previous operas and perhaps too rich in narrative complexity and symbolism for its own good. It marks a peak in Strauss's aspirations – his subsequent operas are either more modest in scale or formulaically repetitive of the successful elements of *Der Rosenkavalier*. The sort of Straussian soprano who wallows in *Der Rosenkavalier* tends to find the role of the Empress exhausting – she rises to a testing top D in the course of her long (and admittedly very beautiful) solo scene in Act III.

The Dyer's Wife is written for a heavy dramatic soprano with enough personality on stage to suggest that she is more than just a venal and loud-mouthed shrew. The Nurse is one of Strauss's few roles for contralto, but its rewards are entirely dramatic. The Emperor's music provides further evidence for the view that Strauss had something against tenors – and it is the baritone singing the sympathetic character of Barak who gets the opera's best tune, 'Mir anvertraut', sung at the beginning of Act III, in assertion of love for his wife.

⌘ In performance

A nightmare to stage – hugely expensive and complicated, and so overloaded with scenic transformations and special effects (including the *Peter Pan* problem of lighting the Empress so that she does not cast a shadow) that a director has little hope of communicating the human implications of the fable. Many productions end up in consequence resembling a cross between Santa's Christmas Grotto and an episode of *Star Trek*. Rather more tasteful is John Cox's staging, designed by David Hockney, and seen in Los Angeles and at Covent Garden. In Vienna, Robert Carsen presented the opera as a sort of Freudian nightmare, set at the time of the opera's composition on a stage dominated by a series of beds; at the Met (where star sopranos such as Leonie Rysanek and Deborah Voigt in the role of the Empress have made the opera very popular), Herbert Wernicke had surprising success with a glacially minimalist but highly evocative approach.

⌘ Recordings

CD: Julia Varady (Empress); Georg Solti (cond.). Decca 436 243 2
Video: Cheryl Studer (Empress); Georg Solti (cond.). Salzburg production. Decca 071 425 3

Arabella

Three acts. First performed Dresden, 1933.
Libretto by Hugo von Hofmannsthal

'A second *Rosenkavalier*, without its mistakes and longueurs' was what Strauss suggested to his librettist Hofmannsthal in 1923. Hofmannsthal obliged with an adaptation of one of his short stories, but tragically died in 1929 before he and Strauss had completed the fine-tuning of his draft libretto. In tribute to his memory, Strauss set Hofmannsthal's every word as he left it, which explains a certain wordy slackness in Acts II and III. A second *Rosenkavalier*, or a pale imitation of it? Or a subtle romantic comedy in its own right, with a rather more acid edge than its precursor?

ᐧᐁ Plot

Vienna, 1860. The impoverished Count Waldner is reduced to taking rooms in a hotel with his wife and two daughters, Arabella and Zdenka. All hope of a revival of the family fortunes depends on a wealthy husband for the charming and beautiful Arabella; Zdenka has been brought up as a boy, in order to save money.

Arabella rejects her playboy suitors, but falls for the mysterious Mandryka, nephew of an old army comrade of her father and the heir to some distant rural estates. At the Coachman's Ball (an actual annual event in mid-nineteenth-century Vienna), Arabella falls in love with Mandryka, but the happy ending is delayed by an intrigue and misunderstanding. Zdenka is in love with Matteo, one of Arabella's suitors. Zdenka gives Matteo a key, telling him that it belongs to Arabella's room. This is merely a ploy to get Matteo into bed with Zdenka, who impersonates her sister when Matteo makes use of the key. But Mandryka overhears Zdenka talking to Matteo, and believes that Arabella is betraying him. He resolves to return home without her.

Zdenka reveals her trickery just in time and Matteo transfers his affections to her. The opera ends as Mandryka rapturously watches Arabella radiantly descending the hotel staircase carrying a glass of water, symbolic of her chastity, in accordance with a country custom that Mandryka explained to her at the ball.

∾ What to listen for

The score is predominantly wistfully sweet and gentle in character, with the orchestration kept under firm rein. Arabella is a role with a high-lying lyric line that will 'fit' any singer of the Marschallin (in *Der Rosenkavalier*) like a glove. Highlights include the Act I duet for Arabella and Zdenka, 'Aber der Richtige', based on a Balkan folk-song; Arabella's monologue 'Mein Elemer' as she reflects on what life would be like if she is reduced to marrying her suitor Elemer; a daft coloratura number for the cabaret artiste Fiakermilli, who presides over the Coachman's Ball; and the lush Straussian orchestral apotheosis as Arabella descends the staircase with her glass of water.

∾ In performance

With its glamorous heroine, dashing hero (Mandryka is a sympathetic role for a handsome baritone) and splendid ball scene, *Arabella* is a romantic fairy-tale for grown-ups. Productions almost always limit themselves to a meticulous re-creation of the Vienna of the 1860s – including some gorgeous frocks for Arabella. Every generation has brought its great interpreters of this peach of a role – Lisa della Casa in the 1950s, Kiri Te Kanawa and Felicity Lott in the 1980s and more recently, Renée Fleming.

∾ Recordings

CD: Kiri Te Kanawa (Arabella); Jeffrey Tate (cond.). Decca 417 623 2
DVD: Kiri te Kanawa (Arabella); Christian Thielemann (cond.). Metropolitan Opera production. DG 073 005 9

Capriccio

One act (but often played with an interval). First performed Munich, 1942.
Libretto by the composer and Clemens Krauss

Inspired by a little comic opera by Mozart's rival Salieri entitled *Prima la Musica e poi le Parole* (*First the music, then the words*) and originally conceived as a curtain-raiser to Strauss's one-act mythological opera *Daphne* (1938), *Capriccio* grew into a nostalgic valediction to a civilization being destroyed by the brutality of the Second World War, as well as to the elderly Strauss's own fifty-year career as a conductor and composer of opera.

✍ Plot

An aristocratic salon in Paris, 1777, in the era when Gluck's music was controversial (see p. 5). Flamand the composer and Olivier the poet are rivals for the love of Countess Madeleine. They are contributing to a birthday entertainment in her private theatre. Along with the help of the worldly impresario La Roche and the Countess's brother, who is in love with the actress Clairon, they debate the aesthetics of opera, notably the question whether words or music should dominate. Various amorous intrigues run as undercurrent to the discussion, and the Countess promises to choose between her two suitors by eleven the next morning. La Roche finally asserts the glory of theatre, its ability to speak to hearts and minds and reflect all human preoccupations. The Countess is impressed and commissions Flamand and Olivier to write an opera to mark her birthday. The Count adds that it should be based on all that has passed within the Countess's salon and that the Countess must decide how the plot will end when Flamand visits her at eleven the next morning.

Night falls, and the Countess is left alone. In a long monologue, she questions her own heart but is unable to decide how she will bring the opera to an end – whether to choose Flamand or Olivier, music or words.

❧ What to listen for

A fluent, elegant, knowing diversion which wilfully averts its eyes from the ideology of the Third Reich and the horrors of the Second World War. Warm, serene and a touch smug in its conservatism and arch references to previous Strauss operas, *Capriccio* is structured round a series of conversations, broken by several declamatory speeches, the intrusion of a comic Italian soprano and tenor (with a dancer in tow), several amusing ensembles, all crowned by Strauss's self-conscious farewell to the operatic composition in the shape of an exquisite orchestral 'moonlight' interlude and the Countess's final monologue – a long meditation on art and love which evokes the shimmering soprano music written for the Marschallin, Ariadne and Arabella.

As befits an opera which debates the relative values of words and music, the text is set so that every syllable should be readily audible, and the opera is best performed in a smaller auditorium where none of the singers have to strain to project.

❧ In performance

Although the libretto firmly sets the action in pre-Revolutionary Paris, *Capriccio* works equally well when updated to the 1920s, a transformation effected with notable panache by John Cox's production at Glyndebourne. At the Berlin Staatsoper, Jonathan Miller eerily framed the opera with the sound of bombs and Nazi broadcasts – the background to the opera's first performances in war-torn Germany.

❧ Recordings

CD: Elisabeth Schwarzkopf (Countess); Wolfgang Sawallisch (cond.). EMI 567 394 2

Video: Kiri Te Kanawa (Countess); Donald Runnicles (cond.). San Francisco Opera production. Decca 071 426 3

Arnold Schoenberg (1874–1951)
Moses und Aron

Three acts (of which only two are normally performed).
First performed 1957. Libretto by the composer

In essence, a meditation on profound questions of the Jewish
religion. Schoenberg composed the first two acts between
1930 and 1932, shortly before he was forced to leave Nazi
Germany. In exile in California, he never found the inspiration to set his text for Act III to music, though he sanctioned
the solution of reciting it as an epilogue.

ᴥ Plot

Following the story in Exodus, the opera opens as Moses is
instructed by God, speaking through the Burning Bush, to lead
the Israelites from Egypt to the Promised Land. Moses doubts
his abilities, but is assured that his brother Aaron will act as his
mouthpiece. The Israelites are led out into the desert.

With Moses absent on Mount Sinai, the Israelites lose
heart and at Aaron's instigation, an orgy ensues around the
statue of the Golden Calf. On his return with the tablets of
the Ten Commandments, Moses is horrified by the depravity.
He and Aaron quarrel: Moses cannot see how the mystery of
God can be physically represented, but Aaron insists that
idols and miracles win the people's loyalty, and that even the
tablets are material symbols of the invisible. Aaron leads the
Israelites onwards, following a Pillar of Fire. Moses is left to
mourn his failure.

The unperformed, uncomposed Act III consists mostly of
the trial of Aaron before Moses, at the end of which Aaron
falls dead.

ᴥ What to listen for

The obvious highlight of this austere but mesmerizing opera,
largely written in the twelve-note or serial mode, is the

extended orgy scene in Act II, a vast musical tapestry which vividly depicts processions and dances of increasing wildness, culminating in violent rape and pillage before concluding in utter exhaustion.

The opera is predominantly choral, and some of this music is rhythmically spoken rather than sung. To dramatize the extreme contrast between their philosophical outlooks, Moses is composed for a bass speaking voice, Aaron for a singing tenor. The score is also notable for its use of small ensembles, such as the four naked virgins sacrificed during the orgy and the six voices representing God.

ᴥ In performance

The opera pivots on the contrast between Moses, whose religion is purely internal and spiritual, and Aaron, the man of action and rationality – a contrast which raises a parallel question: can Schoenberg's own vision be realized in theatrical terms, or is this opera better performed as an oratorio, its drama left in the mind's eye? Two important recent productions took different approaches: in Amsterdam, Peter Stein interpreted the elaborate stage directions quite literally, using floodlight to suggest the power and presence of God; in Frankfurt and Paris, Herbert Wernicke avoided any pretence of naturalism. At the Met, Graham Vick presented Moses as a tired corporate businessman, Aaron as his sleek spin-doctor, but such modern references seem both glib and tendentious.

ᴥ Recording

CD: Chris Merritt (Aron); Pierre Boulez (cond.). DG 449 174 2

Alban Berg (1885–1935)
Wozzeck

**Three acts (usually performed without an interval).
First performed Berlin, 1925. Libretto adapted by the
composer from the play by Georg Büchner**

When Georg Büchner died at the age of twenty-three in
1837, he left his play *Woyzeck* in a fragmentary and confused
manuscript (the spelling 'Wozzeck' is a misreading of almost
illegible handwriting). Attracted by its short scenes and emotional directness, Berg began to set the text to music during
the First World War, but did not finish it until 1922, by which
time he had himself experienced something of Wozzeck's situation as a miserable conscript in the Austrian army.

  Early performances caused a great stir, with the more conservative critics branding the music insane and obscene –
along with all Berg's 'decadent' *œuvre*, the opera was subsequently forbidden by the Nazis. Over the last half-century,
however, *Wozzeck* has been increasingly recognized as the
crucial masterpiece of operatic modernism, and its gritty
subject-matter, complex musical and dramatic structure have
proved profoundly influential on composers such as
Shostakovich, Stravinsky and Britten.

❧ Plot

In a small garrison town, the poor soldier Wozzeck is haunted
by hallucinatory visions and bullied by a sadistic Captain and
a Doctor, who uses him as a guinea-pig for his experiments.
Wozzeck's girlfriend Marie, mother of his son, is seduced by
a dashing Drum Major.

  After taunting hints are dropped by the Captain, Wozzeck
becomes suspicious of Marie, who feels terrible guilt at her
lapse. Wozzeck is involved in a fight with the Drum Major,
and then takes Marie out on a walk in the forest, where he
stabs and kills her.

Back in the town, Wozzeck visits a tavern where he is seen to have blood on his hands. In a state of terrible mental torment, he rushes back into the forest to retrieve the murder weapon and drowns in a pond, imagining himself to be covered in blood. Back in the town, Wozzeck's and Marie's son plays in the street as news breaks of the discovery of Marie's corpse.

⌘ What to listen for

The opera lasts barely a hundred minutes. Each of its fifteen scenes is tightly organized around one musical form (sonata, fugue, rondo, passacaglia), device or invention, all but two separated by orchestral interludes. The parallels and echoes between them are remarkably intricate and complex, but the effect of the music is anything but cerebral – the force of the drama is immediately and graphically striking. The opera bears the mark of Berg's teacher Schoenberg in its atonal elements, but it also contains folk-songs, dance-hall tunes and passages of searing orchestral lyricism. The vocal line is marked by '*Sprechgesang*', a style of singing which requires the voice to adapt a tone close to speech, while following musical rhythm and pitch.

⌘ In performance

The opera has often been staged as an exercise in the style of German expressionism, with visual references to the caricatures of George Grosz and a Brechtian theatrical flavour – the danger being that such an approach can end up making this most compassionate and involving of operas seem cold and cynical, with Wozzeck depicted simply as a moron-turned-psychopath and Marie as nothing more than a whore. More sensitive recent productions by Deborah Warner (at Opera North) and Patrice Chéreau (for the Châtelet in Paris and the Berlin Staatsoper) have rediscovered the opera's human heart, presenting Wozzeck and Marie as essentially decent people battered and manipulated by a brutal and exploitative social order.

∾ Recordings

CD: Anja Silja (Marie); Christoph von Dohnanyi (cond.).
Decca 417 348 2
Video: Waltraud Meier (Marie); Daniel Barenboim (cond.).
Berlin Staatsoper production. Warner 0630 16338 3

Lulu

**Three acts. First performed Zurich, 1937 (two acts);
Paris, 1979 (three act-version).
Libretto by the composer from two plays by Frank
Wedekind**

Berg worked on this opera, based on two scandalous plays written at the turn of the century, from 1928 until his death in 1935.
He left Act III slightly incomplete, and his widow refused to
sanction any posthumous completion. After her death,
Friedrich Cerha was able to complete the gaps in Act III, and
his edition, first performed in 1979, has now become standard.

∾ Plot

The Animal Trainer presents his menagerie, with the sexually devastating Lulu as the snake.

Lulu's lover, Dr Schön, and his son, the composer, Alwa
watch Lulu being painted. After they leave to attend a rehearsal of Alwa's new ballet, the Painter seduces Lulu. When Lulu's
husband bursts in, he is so shocked that he drops dead.

Lulu marries the Painter. She is visited by the sinister
Schigolch: it is not clear whether he is Lulu's former lover or
her father, but he expresses satisfaction at seeing Lulu in
comfortable circumstances. Schön wishes to be respectably
married and attempts to break off the affair he has covertly
been having with Lulu, but first he tells the Painter about her
sordid past. The Painter kills himself. Lulu presses Schön to
break off his engagement and marry her instead.

But even when she is established as Frau Schön. Lulu continues to attract admirers – including a desperate schoolboy, the lesbian Countess Geschwitz and Schön's son Alwa. When Schön hears the latter confessing love to Lulu, he is enraged and hands Lulu a revolver, suggesting that she kill herself. But Lulu kills Schön instead. A silent film interlude shows how Lulu is then arrested, imprisoned and contracts cholera. With the self-sacrificial help of the Countess Geschwitz, Lulu escapes from jail and takes up with Alwa.

They escape to Paris, where Lulu is blackmailed by a white-slave-trafficking Marquis, and then to London. To eke out her miserable existence – with Alwa, Schigolch and the Countess Geschwitz still in tow – Lulu takes to prostitution and is murdered by Jack the Ripper.

∾ What to listen for

Like *Wozzeck*, *Lulu* is a score of incredible formal intricacy, organized round classical forms and the twelve-note 'serial' system pioneered by Berg's teacher, Arnold Schoenberg. The musical material is tightly interwoven and thematically coherent, but the effect is of great agitation and volatility. Underpinning the nervosity is a sense of overwhelming sadness, which finally gushes out in Countess Geschwitz's lament over Lulu's dead body. The role of Lulu lies very high. The score specifies several top E flats and Fs, but sopranos like Teresa Stratas often take the lower options which Berg mercifully allows them.

∾ In performance

The fascination of this opera lies in the character of Lulu herself – is she prey or predator? A symbolic embodiment of the obsessive and amoral nature of male sexual desire or a selfish but suffering human being with the potential for something better? The opera can seem simply a bitter satire of a decadent bourgeoisie, populated with two-dimensional caricatures, but a good production such as Patrice Chéreau's in Paris (the first staging of Cerha's three-act version) will reflect the emotional complexity of the music and at least pay tribute to the sincerity of the love which Countess Geschwitz doggedly lavishes on Lulu.

❧ Recording

CD: Teresa Stratas (Lulu); Pierre Boulez (cond.). Paris Opéra production. DG 415 489 2

Kurt Weill (1900–50)
Die Dreigroschenoper
(*The Threpenny Opera*)

**Prologue and three acts. First performed Berlin, 1928.
Libretto by Bertolt Brecht**

An updated version of John Gay's *The Beggar's Opera*, banned
by the Nazis in 1933, but hugely popular on account of its
black humour and irresistibly slinky score. The band for the
first performance consisted of seven jazz musicians; later
Weill revised it for a more conventional band of twenty-
three. Brecht also made several different versions of the text.

∾ Plot
In London's sleazy Soho, the disreputable Mr and Mrs
Peachum are appalled to hear that their daughter Polly has
married the gangster Mack the Knife. Mrs Peachum bribes the
prostitute Jenny to betray Mack to the police, but he is helped
to escape from prison by Lucy, daughter of the corrupt police
chief Tiger Brown. Peachum threatens to disrupt the coronation if Mack is not dealt with, so Mack is arrested again and led
to the gallows. At the last minute, Mack is pardoned.

∾ What to listen for
Composed in reaction to the pomposity of post-Wagnerian
opera, *Die Dreigroschenoper* was aptly described by Hans Keller
as 'the weightiest possible lowbrow opera for highbrows and
the most full-blooded highbrow musical for lowbrows'. Like
The Beggar's Opera (with which it otherwise shares only one
tune), it consists of a number of discrete, short musical numbers, interspersed with dialogue, including the famous 'Ballad
of Mack the Knife' which opens the show.

∾ In performance
Conceived as 'a play with music', this piece requires a rough,

sharp ironic edge to make its full effect, and cabaret singers are often imported to create the right vocal atmosphere. Brecht didn't want the performance to be polished or genteel, and the characters are not meant to be sympathetic or attractive; this is socialist satire, not grand opera. But Weill did not want the music approximately rasped, in the inimitable style of his wife Lotte Lenya – he always hoped that opera singers would take it seriously and sing his notes precisely.

✎ Recording

CD: Ute Lemper (Polly); John Mauceri (cond.).
Decca 430 075 2

Aufstieg und Fall der Stadt Mahagonny
(Rise and Fall of the City of Mahagonny)

Three acts. First performed Leipzig, 1930.
Libretto by Bertolt Brecht

In 1927, Brecht and Weill collaborated on a twenty-five-minute 'anti-opera' entitled *Mahagonny Songspiel*. It consists of a series of musical numbers (sung by six soloists) linked to the theme of Mahagonny, the city dedicated to pleasure and vice. Orchestral interludes separate the songs and ensembles; there is no connecting dialogue or plot. Such was its success, however, that Brecht and Weill decided to expand this cantata into a full-length opera. It caused a riot at its first performance on account of its debunking cynicism and obscenity.

✎ Plot

Fatty, Widow Begbick and Trinity Moses, white-slave traders on the run, arrive in the city of Mahagonny in the American desert. Its values are based on dollars, whisky and sex: crime and prostitution are rampant. A lumberjack called Jim Mahoney buys the mulatto girl Jenny for thirty dollars and hopes for a lifetime of total selfish freedom and 'every man for himself'. A hurricane threatens to destroy Mahagonny, but it passes the city by.

All the vices flourish, until Jim loses all his money and even Jenny refuses to help him out with a loan. Jim is thrown into prison. In Mahagonny, not having money is the worst of crimes and Jim is sentenced to death and executed. God descends on Mahagonny. The city burns and Jim's relics are paraded before the audience.

✎ What to listen for

The score is rich in wit and ingenuity, with brilliant parodies of the clichés of dance-hall band tunes, honky-tonk, ragtime and operetta, as well as Weill's unique adaptation of the Bach chorale. Among the more celebrated numbers are the 'Alabama Song', with its amusing pidgin-English lyrics, and Jim's 'Denn wie man sich bettet, so liegt man' – you made your bed, now lie on it.

✎ In performance

Unlike *Die Dreigroschenoper*, *Mahagonny* is a true 'through-composed' opera rather than a superior form of musical comedy, although its rambling yet inert plot and cartoon characters make it difficult to pace and pitch in the opera house. Weill's bitter-sweet lyricism sometimes sits uneasily with Brecht's iconoclastic cynicism and his feeling that music primarily exists as a medium in which to communicate his political message.

Yet too many productions today end up neutering the satire, mistaking *Mahagonny* for the innocent farce of *The Best Little Whorehouse in Texas*.

✎ Recording

CD: Lotte Lenya (Jenny); Wilhelm Brückner-Rüggerberg (cond.). CBS 77341

Hans Werner Henze (1926–)
Elegy for Young Lovers

Five acts. First performed 1961.
Libretto by W. H. Auden and Chester Kallman

Over the last half-century, Henze has proved himself the most prolific and versatile of contemporary opera composers. His major works include the one-act *Boulevard Solitude* (1952), a modern take on the Manon Lescaut story; *Der Prinz von Homburg* (1960), an adaptation of Kleist's play exploring military values; the black comedy *Der Junge Lord* (1965); and *The Bassarids* (1966), a powerful version of Euripides' *The Bacchae*.

Elegy for Young Lovers has a sophisticated libretto, dealing with the question of how far an artist is morally entitled to exploit real life in order to create a work of art.

✍ Plot

The year is 1910. Accompanied by his mistress Elisabeth, his patron Carolina and his physician Dr Reischmann, the celebrated poet Mittenhofer visits a hotel in the Alps to seek inspiration from the hallucinations of Hilda Mack, a widow who has lived there since her husband was killed in a climbing accident during their honeymoon forty years previously. When a guide announces that he has found the frozen corpse of her husband, Frau Mack is distraught – she had always believed that her husband was still alive. Her hallucinations cease.

Reischmann's son Toni falls in love with Mittenhofer's mistress Elisabeth. When Mittenhofer finds out, he is both mortified and enraged, but he needs a new source of inspiration. He tells Toni and Elisabeth that he is planning a new poem about young love, and needs an edelweiss collected from the nearby mountain in order to complete it. Toni and Elisabeth volunteer for the expedition and are killed in a blizzard, as Mittenhofer intended.

The final scene shows a fashionable salon in Vienna where Mittenhofer is reading his new poem, 'Elegy for Young Lovers'.

∾ What to listen for

A chamber opera, full of what the composer called 'tender, beautiful noises' in which the orchestral texture is light and clean, with particular instruments associated with particular characters – brass for Mittenhofer, flute for Frau Mack, violin and viola for Toni and Elisabeth. Although there are several formal arias, duets and ensembles, the texture is so cunningly interwoven that the opera seems conversational and intimate. In emulation of Berg's Lulu, Frau Mack is required to sing some fearsomely high coloratura.

∾ In performance

With three acts divided into thirty-four short scenes, this is an opera which requires a small theatre and understated performance to make its proper mark. The role of Mittenhofer, composed for Dietrich Fischer-Dieskau, is a *tour de force* for a baritone who can act as well as he can sing.

∾ Recording

CD: Dietrich Fischer-Dieskau (Mittenhofer); Hans Werner Henze (cond.). DG 449 874 2

PART THREE

Italian Opera

Gioachino Rossini's operas swept through the gloom of post-Napoleonic Europe and brightened the spirit of the age. Rossini ranks among the laziest of great composers, constantly recycling his best tunes and shamelessly resorting to clichés when inspiration failed; he broke the rules of *opera seria* and *opera buffa* unsystematically, and an older generation thought his music coarse and needlessly loud.

But the young adored his fantasy, wit and energy, and even his more routine efforts have their passages of breathtaking beauty and originality. Gaetano Donizetti and Vincenzo Bellini followed in his wake. Donizetti was an indefatigable worker and a skilled craftsman rather than a genius: his best operas are probably his comedies, but his tragedies, several of them drawn from the historical novels of Walter Scott, are also highly effective and stageworthy. Vincenzo Bellini died before he had fully matured: his powers of orchestration were minimal and his forms often conventional. But he had a wonderful gift for intense elegiac melody as well as a fiery patriotic fervour, and his operas can rise to heights of emotional grandeur.

Both composers wrote keenly for the great singers of the day and their work is now often associated with the term *bel canto* ('beautiful singing'), used to indicate a vocal technique which emphasizes both smoothness of line and the capacity to execute fast passages with accuracy and precision. The profession of singing was changing. Napoleonic law banned the practices which led to the castrati, and by the 1820s they had become virtually extinct in the opera house. Public adulation now transferred to sopranos like Giuditta Pasta, Maria Malibran and Giulia Grisi, as celebrated for their acting as for their vocal abilities, and the male leads were increasingly taken by tenors like Gianbattista Rubini and Gilbert Duprez, notable for the ease and power of the top of their voices.

From the 1840s to the end of the century, the dominant figure in Italian opera was Giuseppe Verdi. He came from a peasant background and his early operas, like Rossini's, are more notable for sheer vigour than polish or subtlety. But he doggedly acquired mastery of his art, and the fifty years which separate *Nabucco* from *Falstaff* constitute one of the great journeys of the history of music. Verdi was more than a composer: his operas embody a passionate nationalistic idealism, and they played a significant propaganda role in the fight to reunify Italy as a democratic nation.

By the 1870s, however, a new generation of composers sought to move away from the high-minded, self-sacrificing characters and antiquated dramatic subject-matter that shaped Verdi's work. Operas of this period, like Amilcare Ponchielli's *La Gioconda* and Alfredo Catalani's *La Wally*, are devoid of political content, focusing more on the extreme emotional crises of tormented individuals; and at the end of the century, Pietro Mascagni's *Cavalleria Rusticana* set a fashion for dealing with sensational low-life crimes of passion, in harsh, febrile and often overheated music.

Of all those composers involved in this 'verismo' ('realism') movement (as it was labelled), the most sophisticated, original and successful was Giacomo Puccini. He drew on French music (in particular, the heart-throb sentimentality of Jules Massenet) and the 'through-composed' techniques of Richard Wagner, but he was also innately gifted as a vocal melodist and orchestral colourist. It is not surprising that his best operas, with their matchless ability to hit an audience's most tender emotional spots, remain the most popular in the world.

Under Mussolini and the Fascists, opera remained a beacon of national pride, but with Puccini's death in 1926, the tradition had reached some sort of climax. After the war, Luigi Dallapiccola made earnest attempts to raise the tone with operas that had absorbed the transalpine influence of Schoenberg and Berg, and in more recent years Luciano Berio has made some interesting experiments with the subversion of conventional narrative and musical structures. But Italian opera now lives on its past: it is not, and probably never again can be, what it was in the mid-nineteenth century.

Gioachino Rossini (1792–1868)
L'Italiana in Algeri
(*The Italian Girl in Algiers*)

Two acts. First performed Venice, 1813.
Libretto by Angelo Anelli

Rossini was still only twenty-one when he wrote this, his
eleventh opera and first major success in the field of comedy.
Written in less than a month, to an existing libretto, it has an
irresistible farcical energy and youthful sparkle which the
more mature composer never quite recaptured.

✿ Plot

Mustafa, the boorish Bey of Algiers, discards his wife Elvira
and orders her to marry his recently captured Italian slave,
Lindoro. Mustafa is then captivated by an Italian lady, Isabella,
who has come to Algiers in search of her lover Lindoro,
accompanied by her irritating elderly admirer, Taddeo. Isabella
uses her wiles to outwit both Mustafa and Taddeo, and after
various intrigues – involving Isabella's invention of an order of
husbands called the 'Pappatacci' who do nothing except eat,
sleep and leave their wives in peace – she and Lindoro escape
to Italy. Mustafa asks Elvira's forgiveness.

✿ What to listen for

The confrontation of east and west, Christian and Muslim, is
an old operatic theme (Mozart's *Die Entführung* is the most
obvious example), but in musical terms Rossini seems unin-
terested in suggesting oriental colours. The score is thoroughly Italian in spirit, and the role of Isabella is rich in vocal
opportunities for a mezzo-soprano like Marilyn Horne or the
pre-war Spanish singer Conchita Supervia, who combined
dazzling personality with a firm coloratura technique and
sense of slyly flirtatious fun. Her arias range from the lyrical
'Per lui che adoro' to the rousing 'Pensa alla patria', but it is

in the vividly comic duets and ensembles that her personality is most forcibly expressed. The dotty first-act finale, in which all the characters express their differing states of confusion in imitation of the orchestra, can send an audience rocking with laughter.

❧ In performance

One of the most successful modern productions, seen in Vienna and at Covent Garden and the Met, was directed by Jean-Pierre Ponnelle – a staging full of choreographed comic business which managed to be witty rather than irritating. Later attempts to suggest a feminist tinge to Isabella's strategy and more sinister imperialist undertones in the plot have foundered: *L'Italiana* is essentially farce, complete with racist and sexist stereotypes, and it is lightness of touch rather than depth of interpretation that counts in presenting them.

❧ Recording

CD: Agnes Baltsa (Isabella); Claudio Abbado (cond.).
DG 427 331 2

Il Barbiere di Siviglia
(The Barber of Seville)

Two acts. First performed Rome, 1816.
Libretto by Cesare Sterbini

Beaumarchais's original play, a companion piece to *The Marriage of Figaro*, had been adapted into operatic form ten times before Rossini attacked it. His version was composed at tremendous speed – nine days, according to one story – and although its première was a fiasco, it quickly became the most popular of all comic operas, hugely admired by Beethoven, Verdi and Wagner.

ॐ Plot

Seville, in the mid-eighteenth century. Young Count Almaviva is in love with the vivacious Rosina and has been serenading her under the name of Lindoro. She is duly impressed, but the affair can progress no further because she is kept under lock and key by her guardian, the elderly Doctor Bartolo, who wants to marry her himself. The quick-witted but mercenary barber Figaro comes to Almaviva's aid and together they hatch a plan: Almaviva will disguise himself as a drunken soldier and knock on Bartolo's door with a demand for billeting. The ruse works insofar as Almaviva gains admission to the house and reveals himself to Rosina as 'Lindoro', but suspicions are aroused and mayhem ensues.

Almaviva returns to Bartolo's house, this time disguised as a stand-in for Rosina's music teacher Don Basilio. A lesson of sorts ensues. Figaro arrives to shave Doctor Bartolo and steals the key which will allow Rosina to escape. However, Bartolo gets wind of the elopement plan, and decides to marry Rosina at once. But after further confusions and mis-understandings, the ever resourceful Figaro is still one step ahead, and he persuades the Notary to marry Rosina to Almaviva while Bartolo is out fetching the constabulary. Bartolo is eventually consoled by Rosina's dowry.

ॐ What to listen for

One reason that this opera is so frequently performed is that is relatively easy to cast. Rosina was originally written for a mezzo-soprano, but it can easily be sung by a soprano; Figaro is a gift for a high baritone (although few can articulate the light, crisp semiquavers in the duet with Rosina, 'Dunque io son'), Bartolo is great fun for a bass with a comic touch. It is in the duets, trios and ensembles that most of the opera's comedy effervesces: the Act I finale, 'Fredda ed immobile', is one of Rossini's most riotous inventions and the quintet 'Buona sera, mio signore' in Act II one of his wittiest. The characterization in the opera is sharp, even though several of the melodies are lifted from other works of very different plot and mood (including Rosina's 'Una voce poco fà', originally composed for a tragic opera about Elizabeth I). The opera also illustrates Rossini's genius for making something brilliant and beautiful from material that on paper looks simple and even mechanical.

✃ In performance

An opera which needs extensive rehearsal if the ensembles and repartee are to cohere and flow at the right spanking pace – if there is any drag or slump in the performance, the clichés (such as his trademark long crescendo) which underpin Rossini's inspiration begin to show through. Most productions opt for some degree of period realism, but occasionally something more surreal is attempted. Ruth Berghaus, for instance, in a controversial production staged in Munich, set the opera on a huge naked female torso, its bosom serving as Rosina's balcony; other directors have looked to the masters of cinematic farce – Chaplin, Keystone Cops, Fellini – for their inspiration.

✃ Recordings

CD: Thomas Allen (Figaro); Agnes Baltsa (Rosina); Neville Marriner (cond.). Philips 446 448 2
DVD: Cecilia Bartoli (Rosina); Gabriele Ferro (cond.). Arthaus 090

La Cenerentola (Cinderella)

Two acts. First performed Rome, 1817.
Libretto by Jacopo Ferretti

Loosely based on the Cinderella fairy-tale, but with all supernatural elements removed from the plot. An opera which has become increasingly popular since it was revived for the Spanish mezzo-soprano Conchita Supervia in the 1930s. Like

La Gazza Ladra (*The Thieving Magpie*), composed later the same year, it has a subtle and bitter-sweet flavour which distinguishes it from earlier farces such as *Il Barbiere di Siviglia*.

∾ Plot

In Don Magnifico's shabby mansion, his downtrodden daughter Cenerentola is busy with housework while her step-sisters Clorinda and Tisbe quarrel. Disguised as a beggar, Prince Ramiro's tutor Alidoro enters, sent by Ramiro to assess the girls' eligibility for his hand in marriage. Clorinda and Tisbe scorn the beggar; Cenerentola takes pity. Following Alidoro's reports of this virtuous and beautiful creature, Ramiro himself now appears, disguised as his valet Dandini, to look at Cenerentola. He and Cenerentola fall instantly in love.

Magnifico and his daughters are invited to Ramiro's ball, but the snobbish Magnifico refuses to allow Cenerentola to attend. Fortunately, Alidoro steps in and Cenerentola eventually arrives at the ball splendidly attired and veiled. Magnifico, Clorinda and Tisbe do not recognize her.

The real Dandini, disguised as Ramiro, is in love with Cenerentola too, but she rejects him in favour of the false Dandini, Ramiro, who offers to marry her. She gives him one of a matching pair of bracelets, telling him to find her again and learn her true identity. The real Dandini reveals that he is only a valet – and Magnifico is furious to realize that he has been fooled by a servant.

Back at Magnifico's mansion, Cenerentola resumes her housework and dreams of 'Dandini'. Meanwhile, Ramiro's coach is overturned in a storm outside the mansion, and he and the real Dandini come in for shelter. Ramiro recognizes the bracelet on Cenerentola's arm and announces that she is his bride. Magnifico, Clorinda and Tisbe are appalled, but the tutor Alidoro is delighted at the wisdom of Ramiro's choice. Cenerentola rejoices in the change of her fortunes and generously forgives all those who have done her wrong.

ᴥ What to listen for

The opera's most celebrated number – a rewriting of a tenor aria from *Il Barbiere di Siviglia*, usually cut today – comes at the very end. Cenerentola's exhilarating rondo 'Non più mesta' is a chance for the mezzo-soprano to show off her coloratura technique – especially if she is capable of rising into soprano regions for the climax. Note also Cenerentola's hauntingly melancholy 'once upon a time' folk-song that opens Act I and recurs later in the opera, and the sextet in the second scene of Act II, a number which illustrates Rossini's virtuosity at conveying a state of comic confusion. (Incidentally, Rossini did not intend all the words in the fast patter ensembles to be heard, *à la* Gilbert and Sullivan; he treats the voices as though they were orchestral instruments, and the text is mere nonsense.) Elsewhere, the score illustrates Rossini's habit of repeating material: this can be either tedious or exhilarating, depending on the conductor's skill at keeping the tempi buoyant without simply rushing through the faster passages headlong.

ᴥ In performance

La Cenerentola is more a sly moral tale than a little girl's fantasy of rags-to-riches. Directors tend to muddle the two, however, and even attempt to reinsert the glamorous magic-wand element that Rossini deliberately eschewed. The better productions heed the view of Rossini scholar Richard Osborne that the opera inhabits 'a harder, brittler world than that of, say, Mozart's *Le Nozze di Figaro*, and in some ways a more painful one'.

The title role has recently benefited from the talents of Cecilia Bartoli, a mezzo-soprano whose style and technique is probably very close to that of the singers of Rossini's day. The opera's first production at the Met was specially mounted for her in 1997. Singers such as Bartoli, more alert to issues of historical authenticity than their predecessors, follow traditional performing practice and provide extensive improvised ornamentation when the melodies are repeated within arias.

❧ Recording

CD and video: Cecilia Bartoli (Cenerentola); Riccardo
Chailly (cond.). Decca 436 902 2(CD); 071 444 3 (video)

Semiramide

Two acts. First performed Venice, 1823.
Text by Gaetano Rossi

Rossini's first great success, composed in 1813, was *Tancredi*,
a heroic opera based on a tragedy by Voltaire. Ten years later,
he returned to Voltaire for *Semiramide*, another work which
demonstrates his aspirations to forge a grand classical style.
The story had previously been the subject of some forty
operatic settings.

❧ Plot

Queen Semiramide ascended the throne of Babylon with the
help of Prince Assur, who murdered her husband King Nino
with her complicity. Now Semiramide is in love with the
army commander Arsace, unaware that he is her son, whom
she also attempted to kill. The ghost of Nino publicly
announces that Arsace will succeed to the throne and privately reveals to him the true circumstances of his assassination.

Arsace is appalled to discover that a woman as wicked as
Semiramide is his mother, but when he confronts her, he is so
moved by her remorse that they are reconciled. Assur attempts
to kill Arsace, but Semiramide interposes herself between them
and dies on her son's sword. Arsace is declared king.

❧ What to listen for

The title role, originally written for Rossini's first wife,
Isabella Colbran, is a showpiece for a dramatic coloratura
technique, with a fine aria in Act I, 'Bel raggio', in which
Semiramide celebrates her infatuation with Arsace; and two

imposing duets with Arsace, 'Serbami ognor' and 'Giorno d'orrore' (the latter a scene of confrontation and reconciliation often compared to that between Gertrude and Hamlet). Rossini excelled in duets for female voices – other fine examples can be heard in *Tancredi* and *La Gazza Ladra* – and they provide tests of breath control and synchronicity. It is vital to use two voices that 'blend' smoothly.

Semiramide is not a high soprano role, and it is sometimes sung by a high-lying mezzo-soprano. The 'trouser' role of Arsace, however, lies low for a mezzo-soprano. Its most successful exponents, like the American Marilyn Horne, exploit powerful chest notes to make the character sound convincingly masculine.

Note the grandeur of the finale to Act I, in which the ghost of Nino appears, and Assur's mad scene, in which his hallucinations, mental disturbance and return to sanity provide a great opportunity for a bass with vocal flexibility as well as a sense of the melodramatic.

∿ In performance
A long opera, difficult to cast or stage satisfactorily and usually performed with substantial cuts, but one which offers irresistible opportunities to first-rate virtuoso singers. For the director and designer, it is less gratifying: how does one depict Ancient Babylon without sinking into Hollywood biblical kitsch?

∿ Recording
CD: Joan Sutherland (Semiramide), Marilyn Horne (Arsace); Richard Bonynge (cond.). Decca 425 481 2

Guillaume Tell (*William Tell*)

Four acts. First performed Paris, 1829.
Libretto by Etienne de Jouy and Hippolyte Florent-Bis

In 1823, Rossini moved to Paris. There he revised two of his earlier tragic operas (*Maometto Secondo*, which became *Le Siège de Corinthe*; and *Mosè in Egitto*, which became *Moïse et Pharaon*) and wrote two original pieces, *Il Viaggio a Reims* and *Le Comte Ory*, in a lighter vein. His last opera, a version of Schiller's treatment of the story of the Swiss patriot William Tell, represents a remarkable new departure, tailored to the contemporary French taste for extensive choral and balletic episodes, spectacular processions and stage effects, all framed by subject-matter relating to the struggle for national self-determination.

Rossini later cut the opera to three acts, and various Italian abridgements were made during his lifetime, albeit without his authorization. Today, one is most likely to hear a (lightly cut) performance of the original French version.

⚭ Plot

In thirteenth-century Switzerland, the cantons are suffering from the repressions of Austrian domination. The freedom-fighter William Tell attempts to win Arnold, a young Swiss, to the cause of independence, but Arnold can only feign support because he is in service to Austria and in love with the Austrian Mathilde, sister to the evil governor Gessler. Tell helps a man who has killed an Austrian caught trying to rape his daughter – a gesture which provokes horrible reprisals.

Despite his love for Mathilde, Arnold is finally so outraged at the Austrians' murder of his father that he is converted to the cause of Swiss liberty. Gessler orders humiliating celebrations to mark the centenary of the Austrian occupation, but Tell refuses to participate and is arrested. Gessler sadistically commands Tell, on pain of death, to display his famous skill with the crossbow by shooting an apple placed on the head of his son Jemmy. Tell succeeds in this ordeal, but Gessler treacherously arrests him anyway. With Mathilde's support, Arnold takes over the leadership of the Swiss uprising and uncovers a cache of arms hidden by Tell.

Tell evades captivity and kills Gessler. The uprising succeeds and the Swiss hail the dawn of a new era of liberty.

∾ What to listen for

After the famous Overture with its prestissimo 'Lone Ranger' climax, the opera gets off to a slow start with the overlong Act I. But the drama soon builds momentum, and the subsequent acts contain some fine arias – for soprano, Mathilde's exquisitely lyrical 'Sombre forêt' in Act II; for tenor, Arnold's testing 'Asile héréditaire' in Act IV – and tautly developing ensembles, such as the trio in which Arnold learns of the murder of his father, or the scene in which Tell is obliged to shoot the apple from his son's head. Note also the charm of the folk-dances in Acts I and III, the austerely powerful chorus of oath-taking at the climax of Act II and the glowing hymn to liberty which brings the opera to a radiant ending.

Throughout the opera, there is a sense of a drama built on passionate declamation rather than pauses for vocal display interrupted by recitative – one of several respects in which *Guillaume Tell*, a work enormously admired by both Verdi and Wagner, points the way forward for nineteenth-century opera.

Throughout his career, Rossini wrote for a particular type of Italian tenor more noted for flexibility than power and using a light, sweet, heady tone in the falsetto-ish upper register. In Paris, however, a heavier, chestier, more masculine sound was in fashion, and at a performance of *Guillaume Tell* in 1837, Gilbert Duprez as Arnold became the first-ever singer to sing a full-throated chest-supported high C. Rossini hated the noise, and compared it to 'the squawk of a capon with its throat cut', but audiences went wild for it and have done so ever since, as the climax of 'Di quella pira' in *Il Trovatore* illustrates.

∾ In performance

Of all great operas, this is probably the least performed, and major houses like the Metropolitan and Opéra Bastille do not even have a production in their repertory. Why? Because *Tell* is a long piece without any obvious hit tunes outside the

Overture; because it requires large forces and a great conductor capable of keeping a firm grip on the piece's occasional longueurs; and because the role of Arnold in particular is so difficult to cast – few of today's tenors possess the power it requires in the higher register.

✎ Recording

CD: Cheryl Studer (Mathilde); Chris Merritt (Arnold); Riccardo Muti (cond.). Philips 422 391 2-4. In Italian

Gaetano Donizetti (1797–1848)
Anna Bolena (*Anne Boleyn*)

Two acts. First performed Milan, 1830.
Libretto by Felice Romani

Anna Bolena was Donizetti's thirtieth opera and first major
international success. It is one of three operas he drew from
Tudor history, an era made popular by the novels of Walter
Scott; the other two are *Maria Stuarda* (1835), based on
Schiller's play about the confrontation between Mary, Queen
of Scots and Elizabeth I, and *Roberto Devereux* (1837), about
Elizabeth's affair with the Earl of Essex. None of their plots
bear close relation to historical reality, but they are none the
less gripping and effective.

❧ Plot

In Windsor Castle, the courtiers discuss Enrico's (Henry
VIII's) neglect of his second wife, Anna (Anne Boleyn), and
his flirtation with her lady-in-waiting, Giovanna (Jane
Seymour). Enrico plans to entrap Anna by recalling her former lover Percy from exile. When Anna nobly resists Percy's
protestations, he draws his sword and threatens to kill himself. Enrico appears and decides to interpret the scene before
him as a conspiracy. Anna and Percy are arrested.

Giovanna visits Anna is prison and admits that Enrico has
asked her to succeed Anna as his wife and queen. Giovanna
persuades her that if she pleads guilty to adultery, Enrico
will be only too glad to grant her clemency. At the trial,
Anna's infatuated page Smeaton claims to be her lover, but
the ruse fails: Percy and Anna's brother Rochefort are pardoned, but Anna is sentenced to death and they choose to
die with her.

In her cell, the mentally unhinged Anna recalls former
happy days with Percy. She is restored to her senses by the
sound of the cannon announcing Enrico's marriage to

Giovanna, and as the hour of her execution draws near, she begs heaven to have mercy on them.

ও What to listen for

An opera of confrontations rather than arias – the quintet of conspiracy in the second scene, the enthralling first-act finale in which Enrico (bass) bursts in on Anna (soprano) and Percy (tenor); the duet between Anna and Giovanna (mezzo-soprano) which travels through a remarkable range of emotions; the trio 'Ambo morrete' in which Enrico expresses his desire for revenge as Anna despairs and Percy asserts his love for her – all these show Donizetti as a great musical dramatist only surpassed in nineteenth-century Italian opera by the mature Verdi.

The role of Anna is very difficult to cast. It lies generally low for most sopranos, with sudden flights high into the top register – a passage that most singers find difficult to negotiate – and culminates in a taxing twenty-minute final scene containing three short arias (the second of them based on 'Home, sweet Home') linked by some highly dramatic recitative. The final cabaletta is thick with trills and runs descriptive of Anna's defiance in the face of her unjust execution.

The roles of Enrico and Giovanna are also unusually challenging and rewarding: oddly, Enrico has no solo aria, but in all his utterances in ensemble and recitative, he is every inch the king.

ও In performance

Anna Bolena may be historically inaccurate, but it is strongly characterized and theatrical. The title role is a great vehicle for a soprano with the histrionic abilities to match its tricky vocal requirements. Donizetti tailored the role for one of the greatest of all sopranos, Giuditta Pasta, and in 1957–8 Maria Callas gave electrifying performances of the role at La Scala, Milan. Recordings show that even she had to make some cuts in order to conserve her strength for the demands of the final scene.

∾ Recording

CD: Maria Callas (Anna); Gianandrea Gavazzeni (cond.).
EMI 66471

L'Elisir d'Amore (The Elixir of Love)

Two acts. First performed Milan, 1832.
Libretto by Felice Romani

Composed in only six weeks, this is one of the most charming and shapely of comic operas, sharply characterized and holding a delicate balance between farce and sentiment.

∾ Plot

In an Italian village, the simple and timid peasant Nemorino pines with love for the rich and beautiful landowner Adina. But she is more taken with the dashing Sergeant Belcore, who has been billeted nearby, so Nemorino buys a 'love potion' from a visiting quack, Dulcamara. It is nothing more than a bottle of claret, and when Nemorino gulps it down, he suddenly becomes much less inhibited and, in his cups, appears to forget about Adina altogether. The secretly piqued Adina agrees to marry Belcore before his regiment transfers.

The wedding is celebrated, but Adina puts off signing the contract. Nemorino sobers up, then feels the need for more of the surprisingly intoxicating potion. As he is penniless, the only way to some cash is to enlist in Belcore's regiment.

Then news comes that Nemorino's rich uncle has died, leaving him a lot of money. Suddenly Nemorino finds himself the focus of widespread amorous attentions – a phenomenon he ascribes to the miraculous effect of the potion. Dulcamara tells Adina about the potion, and she is deeply touched by this evidence of Nemorino's devotion. She buys back his enlistment document and after both of them play a little hard to get, they fall into each other's arms. Belcore stands down, and there is a run on Dulcamara's potion.

∾ What to listen for

Unlike so many of Rossini's comic operas, *L'Elisir* is free of dud or flat passages. Good tunes abound from the beginning, and recitative and coloratura are sparingly used. The opera's most famous aria, memorably sung by great Italian tenors from Caruso to Pavarotti, is 'Una furtiva lagrima', sung towards the end of Act II as Nemorino notices for the first time that Adina is softening towards him. Nemorino is a relatively easy role in most respects, but this aria is deceptively difficult to sing – much of it lies just at the point at which the voice has to modulate from a sound produced in the chest to one produced in the head, and vice versa. The art lies in making the transition sound impeccably smooth, rather than a scrunching gear-change.

The opera is also full of delightful duets, notably Adina and Dulcamara's catchy barcarolle, 'Io son ricco, tu sei bella' and Adina and Nemorino's melting 'Prendi, per me sei libero'.

This opera was a great favourite of the Victorians, and the early Gilbert and Sullivan operetta *The Sorcerer* is broadly based on it.

∾ In performance

A piece which requires the lightest of touches from conductor, director and singers. It has responded happily to a variety of updatings and relocations – from the dustbowl of the American Depression to a backwater Italian seaside resort in the 1950s – but is always the better for a dry, tart flavour. For all its essential good nature, *L'Elisir* has a sharp edge: Nemorino is a fool, Adina a minx, and both the baritones, Belcore and Dulcamara, are cynical rogues exploiting peasant gullibility.

∾ Recordings

CD: Placido Domingo (Nemorino); John Pritchard (cond.). Sony 34585

Roberto Alagna (Nemorino); Marcello Viotti (cond.). Erato 998 483 2

Video: Luciano Pavarotti (Nemorino); James Levine (cond.). DG 072 423 3

Lucia di Lammermoor

Three acts. First performed Naples, 1835.
Libretto by Salvatore Cammarano

The best known of Donizetti's tragic operas, distantly based on Sir Walter Scott's now little-read novel *The Bride of Lammermoor*, skilfully trimmed of its sub-plots.

❧ Plot

On the wild borders of sixteenth-century Scotland, the Protestant Lord Enrico Ashton is determined to revive the family fortunes by marrying his over-sensitive sister Lucia to Arturo. Lucia, however, loves Edgardo, the Laird of Ravenswood, a Catholic house against whom the Ashtons have long been feuding. Edgardo wants to resolve their enmity and ask for Lucia's hand in marriage, but Lucia knows that her brother is implacable. Lucia and Edgardo exchange rings and vows as Edgardo leaves to fight for the Stuart cause in France.

Enrico has been spying on the affair between Lucia and Edgardo. He forges a letter from Edgardo announcing that he has fallen in love with another woman. Lucia is devastated when she reads this, and Enrico forces her to proceed with the marriage to Arturo. Lucia considers herself spiritually married to Edgardo, but even the chaplain Raimondo refuses to support her.

At the wedding of Lucia and Arturo, Edgardo unexpectedly bursts in. Misunderstanding the situation, he sees Lucia's name on the marriage contract, curses her apparent treachery and storms out. Enrico challenges him to a duel. In the bridal chamber, Lucia goes mad and kills Arturo. In her deranged state, she returns to the wedding party in a bloodstained dress and hallucinates marriage to Edgardo before collapsing.

As Edgardo waits outside the castle for his duel with Enrico, he hears a funeral knell. Raimondo tells him that it signals Lucia's death. Grief-stricken, Edgardo kills himself.

∿ What to listen for

Lucia is a strongly characterized role, and a good interpreter will make the girl's mental instability quite clear from the aria in the second scene. Some accomplished prima donnas have themselves performed the harp obbligato on stage. Her personality develops through superb duets with Edgardo and Enrico – the first expressing rapturously hopeful love, the second defiance melting into despairing resignation. At the centre of the opera is the superb sextet which builds within itself from the first tenor–baritone duet and then moves into a grandly scaled finale which brings Act II to a close. Act III opens with a sometimes omitted encounter between Edgardo and Enrico. It continues with Lucia's celebrated mad scene and concludes with an almost equally impressive aria for the mourning Edgardo.

There has been much debate in the last forty years over the type of soprano which should sing Lucia. Its two most famous recent exponents, Maria Callas and Joan Sutherland, both had large voices with extraordinary flexibility and fullness in the upper range, capable of sustaining heavy dramatic assignments such as Turandot, but the role was originally written for Fanny Persiani, who by all accounts had a thin, light, piercing soprano: Beverly Sills may therefore be considered a more 'authentic' Lucia than Callas or Sutherland. Similarly, the role of Edgardo seems to have been intended for a lighter- and brighter-voiced tenor than is commonly cast today: certainly few of today's exponents could reach anywhere near the top E flat dictated by Donizetti at the end of the duet with Lucia.

As notated in Donizetti's manuscript score, the mad scene does not contain the famous extravagantly florid cadenza sung with flute obbligato – this evolved through the applause-seeking tendencies of several nineteenth-century prima donnas eager to show off their high notes and agility.

❧ In performance

The characterization of Lucia – the overimaginative girl, mourning her mother's death and prey to visions – sometimes leads producers such as Robert Carsen in Geneva or Francesca Zambello at the Met into the realms of expressionist fantasy. Efforts to stay within the Scots setting usually end up reminiscent of the tartan shortbread biscuit box, and this is not an easy opera to stage well, unless the cast is led by singers whose acting falls the right side of ham.

❧ Recording

CD: Maria Callas (Lucia); Herbert von Karajan (cond.). EMI 63631 2

Don Pasquale

Three acts. First performed Rome, 1843.
Libretto by Giovanni Ruffini and the composer

The last of the great comic operas in the witty, quicksilver Rossinian style.

❧ Plot

In nineteenth-century Rome, the fussy old bachelor Don Pasquale is determined to marry in order to disinherit his nephew Ernesto, who has fallen in love with the spirited young widow Norina. Pasquale asks his friend Dr Malatesta to help him. Malatesta agress, although he is secretly in league with Ernesto and Norina, and the lady he introduces to Pasquale as his convent-educated sister Sofronia is none other than Norina in disguise.

Pasquale is smitten by this apparently demure creature whose only hobby is sewing. But the moment he has signed the marriage contract, bequeathing 'Sofronia' half his fortune, she turns nasty, nagging him mercilessly, making extravagant demands and turning his household upside-down.

When Pasquale catches 'Sofronia' in assignation with another man (in fact Ernesto), various complications and confusions ensue, all of them craftily engineered by Malatesta. Eventually, Sofronia's true identity is revealed and Pasquale ends up happy to divest himself of a troublesome wife by annulling the marriage and blessing the union of Norina and Ernesto.

∾ What to listen for

The score was written in a couple of weeks, absorbing several pieces lifted from obscure areas of the composer's *œuvre*. One would never know it: the music radiates an effortless unity of style, every bar is full of wit and charm, and there isn't a dull moment. The most memorable numbers include Malatesta's baritone aria 'Bella siccome un angelo', Norina's characterful soprano aria in the second scene and Ernesto's serenade followed by his duet with Norina in the final scene. All the roles are gratifying to sing, though Ernesto lies high for most modern tenors, and the cabaletta of his aria is frequently transposed down. So many baritones with a comic touch want to sing the essentially bass role of Pasquale that they often cheat by leaving out some of the low notes!

Perhaps the very first comic opera to use strings, rather than the traditional harpsichord or fortepiano, as accompaniment for the recitative.

∾ In performance

The scenario updates nicely: Patrick Mason's production at ENO shows Norina running a souvenir kiosk and Malatesta riding a Vespa scooter, but such gags should be balanced by characterization which suggests the poignancy of Pasquale's situation and a compassionate element in Norina's personality.

∾ Recording

CD: Mirella Freni (Norina); Riccardo Muti (cond.).
EMI 47068 2

Vincenzo Bellini (1801–35)
I Capuleti e i Montecchi
(*Capulets and Montagues*)

Two acts. First performed Venice, 1830.
Libretto by Felice Romani

Only indirectly drawn on Shakespeare's *Romeo and Juliet*. Although it contains its trite and formulaic passages, this opera offers music of grave and noble beauty to the singers of the two central roles. Very rarely performed last century, until a revival conducted by Claudio Abbado in 1966 precipitated its return to the repertory.

✒ Plot

In Renaissance Verona, Capellio, head of the Capuleto family, refuses to allow Giulietta to marry Romeo, a member of the rival Montecchio family. Instead he orders her to marry Tebaldo, who has taken a vow to revenge himself on Romeo for the (accidental) killing of Capellio's son. Romeo cannot persuade Giulietta to elope, so he and his supporters storm the Capuleto palace as she is about to marry Tebaldo. There is general outrage and the wedding is called off. Romeo escapes.

After the fracas, the sympathetic doctor Lorenzo gives Giulietta a sleeping potion that will counterfeit death and save her from marriage with Tebaldo. Lorenzo goes to find Romeo to explain his plan to reunite him with Giulietta and bring peace between their families. But he is too late – Romeo has an angry confrontation with Tebaldo and hears the news that Giulietta has been found dead. Distraught, Romeo breaks into the Capuleto family vault and, seeing Giulietta laid out like a corpse, takes poison. As his strength fades, Giulietta revives. They are briefly reunited, but when Romeo dies, Giulietta collapses lifeless over his body.

ᔓ What to listen for

Wagner admired much of Bellini's music, on the grounds that 'it is strongly felt and intimately bound up with the text'. Despite the thinness of the orchestration (often nothing more than repeated string arpeggios) and the aggressive but dull scoring for the feuding males, the music for the lovers is quite sublime.

Juliet is written for a lyric soprano, Romeo for a mezzo-soprano, although the music has occasionally been transposed to suit a tenor. Romeo confronts the singer with tremendous challenges: the role is long and high-lying (with several exposed high Bs in Act I) and many long and highly expressive phrases, both in the duet with Juliet in Act I, and the opera's final scene. Juliet's very first line, 'Eccomi in lieta vesta', is extraordinarily difficult to sing: the very first note, set to a vowel, requires a perfectly steady and controlled 'swelling' and diminishing (known as a '*messa di voce*') – if the singer can get that right, the omens for the rest of the performance are good. Although it does not involve any startling flights of coloratura, much of this role is marked to be sung *piano* – a dynamic much trickier to sustain than *forte*.

ᔓ In performance

The success of a performance will depend on finding a pair of singers whose voices blend and contrast elegantly, and who understand that in singing Bellini, emotional expressiveness must be balanced by respect for the melodic integrity of the vocal line.

A small-scale production by Dominic Cooke at Grange Park Opera made a brave attempt to relocate the story to the world of forties *film noir*, with the Capulets and Montagues presented as feuding mafiosi.

ᔓ Recording

CD: Agnes Baltsa (Romeo); Edita Gruberova (Giulietta); Riccardo Muti (cond.). EMI 64846 2

Norma

Two acts. First performed Milan, 1831.
Libretto by Felice Romani

Undoubtedly the masterpiece of early nineteenth-century Italian tragic opera. Bellini and his librettist adapted the plot from a French neo-classical play in Racinian style, cutting a mad scene for Norma and emphasizing the character's gentler side rather than her Medea-like desire for vengeance.

✎ Plot

Gaul simmers with rebellion against the occupying forces of the Romans. Against the wishes of her bellicose father Oroveso, Norma, High Priestess of the Druids, urges peace for the time being. She has secretly borne two sons to Pollione, Proconsul of the Roman army, and although she has lost his affection, she is still torn by her love for him. What she does not know is that he has become involved with the young Druid priestess Adalgisa, who agrees to return to Rome with him.

Adalgisa confides in Norma, who turns on Pollione in fury and threatens to kill their children in revenge. But Norma cannot bring herself to commit the deed; she tells Adalgisa her own secret, and Adalgisa is so moved that she decides to renounce Pollione and urge him to return to Norma.

Pollione is adamant, however, and Norma strikes the sacred gong of the Druids, heralding war against the Romans. Pollione is captured attempting to abduct Adalgisa. He is led as a prisoner to Norma's presence, and she privately threatens to kill him, their children and Adalgisa. Then she summons her father Oroveso and the Druids, announcing that she knows the name of a guilty priestess who must be immolated on the sacrificial pyre. Challenged to reveal the culprit's identity, she admits that it is none other but herself. Imploring her father to look after her sons, Norma ascends the sacrificial pyre. Moved by her nobility of spirit, Pollione follows her.

❧ What to listen for

Norma stands or falls by the soprano who takes the title role. In the operatic annals, it is indelibly associated with its creator Giuditta Pasta and, in our own time, Maria Callas – both of them magnificently domineering actresses with dark, strong, flexible voices and stage personalities capable of switching between the imperious high priestess, the scorned lover and the affectionate mother with equal conviction. Since Callas, all sopranos (even the supreme vocal acrobat Joan Sutherland, in a technically immaculate partnership with Marilyn Horne's Adalgisa) have tended to realize one aspect of the role much more effectively than the others – and a singer who is mistress of the seamless melody of 'Casta Diva' is unlikely to manage the fire and brimstone of the Act I finale or the Gluckian grandeur of the final scene with equal conviction.

Adalgisa is an odd role. She has no aria, only a long declamatory recitative, and vanishes unsatisfactorily from the drama in the last act. Today, it is customary to cast a mezzo-soprano in the role, but this necessitates some downward transposition, and the contrast with Norma – and the blend of their duets – works far better if Bellini's original intention is observed by casting a light, bright lyric soprano of virginal timbre. Pollione is a dramatically unsympathetic and vocally ungrateful role which no self-respecting tenor ever relishes.

❧ In performance

Charging the personal drama of *Norma* is the political dimension of the Gauls' fight against the occupying Romans – subject-matter with an obvious resonance in the Austrian-occupied regions of northern Italy in the 1830s. Directors today, anxious to avoid evoking the cartoon-strip imagery of Asterix, often like to emphasize this aspect of the opera by suggesting visual parallels with modern nationalist struggles.

∾ Recording

CD: Maria Callas (Norma); Tullio Serafin (cond.).
EMI 47304 8

I Puritani (*The Puritans*)

Three parts. First performed Paris, 1835.
Libretto by Carlo Pepoli

Bellini's last opera, written months before his premature death. Although the librettist was inexperienced and the plot is unintentionally ludicrous, *I Puritani* shows formal innovations and harmonic and instrumental sophistication which can only leave one wondering how Bellini's genius would have developed had he lived.

∾ Plot

During the time of the English Civil War, Elvira, daughter to the governor of the Puritan-held fortress at Plymouth, loves Arturo, a Royalist (or cavalier). She, however, is loved by another Puritan, Riccardo, to whom she was promised by her father.

Arturo and Elvira are allowed to marry, but at the wedding celebrations Arturo is forced to help the disguised Enrichetta, the widow of Charles I, to escape from captivity. Elvira misinterprets Arturo's interest in this mysterious lady and goes mad. Arturo is condemned to death, and Riccardo and Elvira's uncle Giorgio ride out to find him.

Three months later, Arturo returns from hiding and explains to Elvira the reasons for his peremptory departure from the wedding. She recovers her sanity, only to lose it again when Riccardo and Giorgio arrive to arrest Arturo. Elvira resolves to die with Arturo, but the situation is resolved when a messenger announces that the Royalists have been defeated and an amnesty is declared. Elvira recovers her sanity again, and is finally united with Arturo.

‹◊ What to listen for

The absence of an overture, the blurring of boundaries between aria and duet and several instances of remarkable rhythmic experimentation are features of this opera.

Elvira is a fine vehicle for a lyric coloratura soprano. It contains two showpieces, the vivacious polonaise 'Son vergin vezzosa', with its chromatic scales, arpeggios and staccatos; and the long Mad Scene, memorably sung by Maria Callas, in which the slow aria, 'Qui la voce sua soave' provides a wonderful example of the achingly lyrical melancholy which so impressed Chopin. Unusually, the opera also features a rousing martial duet for baritone (Riccardo) and bass (Giorgio), 'Suoni la tromba', which in the right throats can bring the house down at the end of Part Two.

The role of Arturo lies impossibly high for most modern tenors, requiring a voice which can rise to top Ds and even an F – notes which can only be sung in a light, almost falsetto head voice that only bel-canto specialists can produce. Other tenors tend to find tactful substitutes. Note also the way Arturo's lovely 'A te, o cara' in the third scene of Part One is turned into a quartet, with choral accompaniment.

‹◊ In performance

An opera tailored to the talents of a celebrated quartet of great singers who often performed together: soprano Giulia Grisi, tenor Gianbattista Rubini, baritone Antonio Tamburini, and bass Luigi Lablache. Grisi (Elvira) was a great beauty and an accomplished actress, famous for her mad scenes (both on- and off-stage), Rubini (Arturo) had a light, high-lying, bright-toned voice of great flexibility, Tamburini (Riccardo) was prized for his immaculate legato and breath control, while Lablache (Giorgio) was a giant figure with a voice and personality to match. Today, *Puritani* is often regarded as a vehicle for a star coloratura soprano (such as Joan Sutherland or Edita Gruberova), but properly performed, it emerges as a subtly calibrated ensemble piece.

For directors, the big problem is how to deal with Elvira's psychologically implausible alternations between sanity and insanity.

❧ Recording

CD: Joan Sutherland (Elvira); Luciano Pavarotti (Arturo); Richard Bonynge (cond.). Decca 417 588 2

Giuseppe Verdi (1813–1901)
Nabucco

Four parts. First performed Milan, 1842.
Libretto by Temistocle Solera

Verdi's third opera, *Nabucco*, caught the rising tide of nationalistic feeling in Italy and went on to establish the composer's
fame all over Europe. More than any other of his operas,
wrote the Verdi scholar Julian Budden, it 'resembles a series
of vast tableaux, rather than a drama relentlessly moving
towards its denouement'. The character of Nabucco, or
Nebuchadnezzar, bears a distant relation to an episode in the
Old Testament book of Daniel, but the plot is more closely
drawn from a popular ballet of the time.

❧ Plot

Inside the temple of Solomon, the Hebrews pray for protec-
tion from the invading Babylonians, led by their king
Nabucco. The Hebrew high priest Zaccaria holds Nabucco's
daughter Fenena as hostage: she is in love with the Hebrew
prince Ismaele, who vows to set her free.

Nabucco's other daughter, Abigaille, also loves Ismaele and
offers to help save the Hebrews if he will love her in return.
Ismaele rejects her. The Hebrews are defeated, but Zaccaria
threatens to kill Fenena if Nabucco enters the temple sacrile-
giously. For love of Fenena, Ismaele disarms Zaccaria. The
temple is destroyed and the Hebrews driven into exile.

In Babylon, Abigaille discovers to her fury that she is the
daughter of a slave, not of Nabucco. She vows revenge on
him and Fenena, who has converted to Judaism. When
Nabucco returns, claiming to be the one true god, he is struck
by a thunderbolt and goes mad. Abigaille seizes his throne
and tricks Nabucco into signing a warrant for the execution
of the Hebrews.

Nabucco is full of remorse and prays to the Hebrew God

for forgiveness. He is restored to sanity, rescues the condemned Fenena and the Hebrews and proclaims his conver-
sion to Judaism with a promise to rebuild their temple. The
Babylonian idol Baal shatters. The remorseful Abigaille takes
poison, and dies begging the Hebrew God for forgiveness.
Zaccaria returns the crown to Nabucco amid rejoicing.

∾ What to listen for

In the words of Julian Budden, this opera is 'the supreme
instance of the triumph of the whole over the parts' – by
which he means that despite several coarse and crude passages, an overall energy carries the score forward irresistibly.
The chorus dominates and gets the best tunes – notably the
heart-rending 'Va, pensiero', which has come to mean to
Italians much what 'Land of Hope and Glory' means to the
English. Although it is marked to be sung *sotto voce*, with
respect to the underlying melancholy, the tempo should not
drag – this is music which should lilt on a wing and a prayer.

Nabucco is a fine role for a strong, rich-toned baritone,
and the character's descent into madness and then repen-
tance offers great histrionic opportunities. Zaccaria is the
first of several dignified priestly basses to appear in Verdi's
œuvre, and he is graced with two magnificent and taxing arias
which extend over a wide range. This is not easy to cast well.
Even more problematic, however, is the killer role of
Abigaille. Aside from the young Maria Callas (who only sang
three performances), it is hard to think of any soprano who
hasn't resorted to shrieking, shirking or skirting in order to
negotiate the fearsome demands of range, agility and stamina that Verdi makes of her in the big aria of evil intent and
the leaps and thrusts of her duet with Nabucco. Ismaele is a
tenor role of scant interest, but Fenena has a beautiful prayer
to sing in the final scene, and the role is noticeably more lyrical than Verdi's subsequent dealings with the mezzo-soprano
range.

∾ In performance

A grand spectacle of an opera, whose subject-matter regularly tempts producers (such as David Pountney for ENO, Tim Albery for WNO and the Royal Opera and Robert Carsen at the Opéra Bastille) to evoke visual parallels with the persecution of present-day Jews and the crisis in the Arab world.

∾ Recording

CD: Piero Cappuccilli (Nabucco); Giuseppe Sinopoli (cond.). DG 410 512 2

Ernani

Four parts. First performed Venice, 1844.
Libretto by Francesco Piave

Based on Victor Hugo's play *Hernani*, this is one of the most cogent and vigorous of Verdi's early operas. Hugo himself disliked the adaptation.

∾ Plot

The dashing outlaw-nobleman Ernani loves the courtly lady Elvira, who is being forced to marry her aged guardian, Silva. Carlo, the power-hungry new King of Spain, also loves Elvira.

On the day of Silva's wedding to Elvira, Carlo takes Elvira hostage. Ernani is captured by Silva. Ernani, who wants revenge on Carlo for the killing of his father, strikes a deal with Silva: he will join in Silva's plot against Carlo – and as guarantee of his honour in the matter, Ernani promises on his father's memory that he will kill himself if he should ever hear Silva blow a certain horn-call.

Carlo is elected Holy Roman Emperor and Ernani and Silva's conspiracy is uncovered. Moved by Elvira's pleas,

Carlo forgives them both, and magnanimously allows Elvira to marry Ernani.

But Silva still wants revenge, and blows his fatal horn. Ernani feels obliged to honour his bargain and to Elvira's horror, he kills himself.

⌘ What to listen for

Like *Nabucco*, *Ernani* is an opera notable for providing particularly strong roles for baritone (Carlo) and bass (Silva). It is written very much in the style of Donizetti, with an uninhibited energy and swagger that is a trademark of Verdi's early work; bad performances tend to use these qualities as an excuse for a lot of shouting – and some heavy cuts. But neither Ernani (tenor) nor Elvira (soprano) are easy roles – Elvira's opening aria 'Ernani, involami', for example, requires a range of over two octaves and has a fiendish cabaletta that is beyond the range of all but a few.

⌘ In performance

Because of its lack of ambiguity, there isn't much that a director can do with this gloves-off tale of love, honour and revenge: productions usually evoke the paintings of Velázquez.

⌘ Recording

CD: Leontyne Price (Elvira), Carlo Bergonzi (Ernani); Thomas Schippers (cond.). RCA GD86503

Macbeth

Four acts. First performed Florence, 1847.
Libretto by Francesco Piave and Andrea Maffei

Verdi's tenth opera, and his first drawn from a Shakespearean source. Interestingly, the original play had not been performed in Italy at the time of the opera's composition and, like *Nabucco*, was best known as a ballet. Verdi substantially revised the score in 1865 for a French production; both the first and second versions, or a mixture of the two, are regularly performed today.

ᴑᴥ Plot
Broadly the same as Shakespeare's play.

ᴑᴥ What to listen for
An opera which represents a great leap forward in Verdi's development, notably in the hushed extended duet – more like a dramatic dialogue – between Macbeth and Lady Macbeth before Duncan's murder.

Macbeth is a magnificent role for the mature Verdi baritone who can also sing Iago and Rigoletto, although his only major aria comes at the very end of the opera: 'Pietà, rispetto, amore' is a lament for his decline into evil, comparable to Shakespeare's 'Tomorrow, and tomorrow, and tomorrow'.

Lady Macbeth is notoriously difficult to cast. Verdi specified a soprano voice that was deliberately dark and even ugly, and the notes also specify a voice capable of enormous range and flexibility – the end of the sleepwalking scene demands a high pianissimo D flat that many singers simply can't muster, and there are tricky coloratura passages in the nervous Brindisi in the banqueting scene. Both sopranos and mezzo-sopranos may be heard in the opera house; Maria Callas proved one of the rare singers who has filled the bill consummately.

Note also the arias for Banquo and Macduff, both fine examples of Verdi's style at this period of his compositional life. The apparent jollity of the witches' choruses has been much mocked, but a great Verdi conductor like Riccardo Muti can bring out their latent daemonic quality, and the scene in which the apparitions are raised is splendidly spooky.

Verdi revised the score for a Paris production in 1865, and it is this version which is generally favoured today, although the original version (lacking among other things the haunting chorus 'Patria oppressa' which opens Act IV and Lady Macbeth's aria 'La luce langue') has occasionally been revived.

∾ In performance

At La Scala, Milan, Graham Vick's production revolved around a giant rotating cube, which symbolized both the fortress of Macbeth's power and the prison in which his evil deeds imprison his conscience.

Whether the Macbeths are presented in homespun medieval robes or in the guise of twentieth-century dictators, the problem for a director is the presentation of the witches. In Hamburg, Steven Pimlott went the whole hog and showed them disappearing on broomsticks. For Luc Bondy's fine production for Scottish Opera, they were not so much toothless old hags as a coven of bored suburban housewives, who treat some of their jauntier music as an excuse for a knees-up. This worked surprisingly well.

∾ Recording

CD: Shirley Verrett (Lady); Piero Cappuccilli (Macbeth); Claudio Abbado (cond.). DG 449 9732 2

Luisa Miller

Three acts. First performed Naples, 1849.
Libretto by Salvatore Cammarano

Based on Schiller's play *Kabale und Liebe* (*Conspiracy and Love*), although censorship forced Verdi to tone down some of its more scandalous aspects.

∾ Plot

In an eighteenth-century Tyrolean village, Luisa Miller, daughter of an old soldier, is in love with a young peasant lad who courts her. The vicious Wurm, himself lusting after

Luisa, informs her father that the young man is in fact Rodolfo, son of the local landowner, Count Walter, Wurm's employer.

The duchess Federica is expected to make a dynastic marriage to Rodolfo, but he tells her that he loves Luisa, to whom he now reveals his true identity. Count Walter is enraged by Rodolfo's behaviour and takes reprisals against Luisa's father. To save his life, Luisa is forced to write a letter renouncing Rodolfo and offering to marry Wurm. Rodolfo finds the letter and is so shocked by its contents that he resolves to kill both himself and Luisa. Having made her confirm that she did write the letter, he produces some deadly poison which they both drink. As she is dying, Luisa reveals the truth to Rodolfo, who manages to muster enough strength to kill the nefarious Wurm.

❧ What to listen for

Like many of Verdi's earlier works, the musical quality of *Luisa Miller* rises as the opera progresses, picking up from a slow start to reach a conclusion of great intensity. Much of the vocal writing harks back to Donizetti, but there is also evidence of a more poetic, inward quality which Verdi's previous operas lacked. The role of Luisa is problematic, requiring a soprano who can handle high-lying coloratura (as in her first aria, with its staccati) but who also commands more weight than the traditional ingénue.

The opera is also unusual in containing two strong baritone roles in Walter and Miller, whose arias succeed each other. Tenors relish Rodolfo and the plangently lovely aria 'Quando le sere al placido'. Other highlights include the unaccompanied quartet in Act II, Luisa's 'Tu puniscimi, o signore' and her duet with Miller 'La tomba è un letto'.

❧ In performance

Because the setting of this opera is more intimate and domestic than Verdi's other early operas, several attempts have been made to put the scenario into a modern suburban context –

not easy to make convincing, given the conventional melo-drama of the plot.

ᖇ Recording

CD: Placido Domingo (Rodolfo): Lorin Maazel (cond.).
DG 459 481 2

Rigoletto

**Three acts. First performed Venice, 1851.
Libretto by Francesco Piave**

Verdi thought Victor Hugo's play *Le Roi s'amuse* to be 'perhaps the greatest drama of modern times', and despite problems with the censors, he and Piave managed to transform it into one of the strongest and most coherent of Italian opera libretti.

ᖇ Plot

In the decadent Renaissance court of the libertine Duke of Mantua, the vicious hunchback jester Rigoletto is terrified when he is cursed by Monterone, whose daughter has been seduced by the Duke and who has now been arrested for denouncing him. Some cynical courtiers decide that they will abduct a beautiful young woman whom the widower Rigoletto is said to keep locked away in his house. This is in fact Rigoletto's beloved daughter Gilda. Unbeknownst to her father, Gilda has fallen in love with a handsome young student – the Duke in disguise – whom she has met in church and who secretly visits her at home. The courtiers trick Rigoletto into helping them abduct Gilda.

The Duke is delighted by this prank and uses the opportunity to seduce Gilda. When Rigoletto discovers what has happened, he vows revenge on the Duke, despite the pleading of Gilda, torn between loyal filial devotion to her father and love for the Duke. In a sleazy inn, on a stormy night,

Rigoletto pays the professional assassin Sparafucile to murder the Duke and deliver his corpse in a sack. The Duke is enticed to the inn by Sparafucile's exotic sister Maddalena, who is so charmed by him that she persuades Sparafucile to trick Rigoletto and substitute an innocent passer-by. Hiding outside the inn, Gilda overhears all this, but because nothing can quench her love for the Duke, she decides to sacrifice herself in order to save him: she enters the inn and is duly murdered. Sparafucile hands the sack over to Rigoletto, who opens it to find the body of his daughter, as the voice of the Duke is heard gaily singing in an upstairs room. Monterone's curse has been fulfilled.

∾ What to listen for

One of Verdi's most strongly characterized operas – the Duke, Rigoletto and Gilda are all masterly psychological studies, and Gilda, in particular, torn between love for her father and the Duke, makes one of the most touching of operatic heroines.

Each of the three principal roles also offers great vocal challenges. Rigoletto is written for a high-lying baritone. All aspects of his complex character are embodied in the scene at the end of the second act, when he confronts the courtiers and is then reunited with Gilda. The singer must in turn convey the playful hunchback jester, the tragic father, the crazed avenger. He must shout his anger with roof-raising force, sing his grief with a firm legato, convey his fatherly love with a gentle warmth and take care that he doesn't drown Gilda out in their concluding duet.

The Duke is a fine role for a lyric tenor, although many find the rum-ti-tum cabaletta to the Act II aria so difficult that they cut at least its second verse. Conductors like Riccardo Muti who are strict about performing only the notes that Verdi wrote (rather than those that show-off tenors have traditionally interpolated) also insist that the tenor performs 'La donna è mobile' without a cadenza and concluding high B (a note which Verdi cleverly saves for the recurrence of the tune, when Rigoletto realizes that the Duke has not been murdered). Gilda's virginal purity misleads some opera houses to cast a very light or soubrettish soprano. This is not wise: even though more mature voices sometimes have difficulties with the high-lying 'Caro nome' and its staccati and trills, most of the role requires a stronger lyric timbre.

Rigoletto also ranks as one of Verdi's most innovative scores, avoiding both conventional aria structures and large-scale ensembles, as well as using long duets to advance the drama. Note also the recurrent use of the 'Maledizione' theme, the all-male chorus, and the absence of an overture. The last act – with the moans of an off-stage chorus representing the looming storm, the wonderful quartet for the flirting Duke and Maddalena, the love-lorn Gilda and the wretched Rigoletto (in which each voice is brilliantly contrasted and distinguished), the airy bravado of the Duke's 'La donna è mobile', the fury of the breaking storm and Rigoletto's discovery of the dying Gilda combine to make an exemplary piece of operatic story-telling.

ᰡ In performance

A taut and exciting drama, written, as Verdi put it, 'without arias or finales' – certainly not of the obvious kind. The most celebrated modern production is undoubtedly that of Jonathan Miller for ENO, who relocated the action to the territory of *The Godfather*: New York's Little Italy with the Duke as a young gang-leader, and Rigoletto as his henchman-cum-barman. 'La donna è mobile' emerges as a tune from a juke-box, to which the Duke sings along. Miller's concept has been much imitated.

Other productions have concentrated on the idea, resonant in our own era, of the Duke's court as a place of extreme decadence – a moral line which provides a splendid excuse for plenty of titillatingly orgiastic goings-on in the opening scene.

∾ Recordings

CD: Placido Domingo (Duke); Piero Cappuccilli
(Rigoletto); Carlo Maria Giulini (cond.). DG 457 753 2
DVD and video: Luciano Pavarotti (Duke); Riccardo
Chailly (cond.). Decca 071 401 9 (DVD); 071 401 3 (video)

Il Trovatore

Four parts. First performed Rome, 1853.
Libretto by Salvatore Cammarano

Verdi intended to follow *Rigoletto* with another opera on a
father-daughter theme, based on Shakespeare's *King Lear* (a
project he considered and rejected several times in the course
of his career). Instead, he returned to the Spanish ambience
of *Ernani* and adapted a play by a fiery young imitator of
Victor Hugo, Garcia Gutiérrez. *Il Trovatore* was a huge
instant success. A few critics cavilled about the gloomy
atmosphere (almost every scene takes place at night) and the
morbidity of the plot. 'But is not life all death anyway?' the
composer retorted with a shrug.

∾ Plot

In war-torn fifteenth-century Spain, Ferrando, a commander
in the army of the Count di Luna, tells a strange story. Years
ago, the Count had a baby brother who died after being given
the evil eye by an old gypsy. The Count's father had this
gypsy burned at the stake. In revenge, the gypsy's daughter
Azucena stole the baby, and a few days later, some charred
baby bones were found at the foot of the stake. But because of
doubts as to whether these were the bones of his brother, the
young di Luna has continued to search for him.

As the opera opens, the young di Luna is in love with the
noble lady Leonora. But Leonora is smitten with Manrico, a
mysterious wandering troubadour who serenades her. He and

di Luna fight a duel over Leonora; Manrico wins, but 'a voice from heaven' stays his hand and he lets di Luna go free.

In a gypsy encampment, Azucena tells her son Manrico what happened all those years ago – in a frenzy, Azucena mistakenly flung her own baby son into the flames. Manrico wonders about his parentage. Azucena quickly reassures him that he is her son.

Believing Manrico to be dead, Leonora decides to enter a convent. As di Luna attempts to abduct her, Manrico comes to her rescue. Di Luna's forces invade the gypsy encampment in search of Manrico and arrest and torture Azucena.

Manrico hears this news as he and Leonora are about to be married. He rushes off to save his mother, but is himself captured by di Luna and condemned to death. Leonora offers herself to di Luna if he will spare Manrico's life. Di Luna agrees, but Leonora takes poison rather than submit, dying in Manrico's arms. Manrico is dragged off to execution, and Azucena reveals to di Luna the terrible truth that Manrico is not her son, but his long-lost brother, the kidnapped baby. Di Luna is appalled, but Azucena is triumphant – at last her mother is avenged.

✵ What to listen for

A notoriously difficult opera to cast – you will often hear it said that it requires 'the four greatest singers in the world'. This may not literally be the case, but it is certainly hard to assemble four voices of equal or balancing excellence. Leonora used to be taken by the type of big, dark soprano who could also sing Aida – Leontyne Price, for example; today, it has become fashionable to cast a lighter voice, on the basis that in Verdi's day those who sang the virginal Gilda in *Rigoletto* were also often cast as Leonora. The role requires one of the widest ranges of any in Verdi's *œuvre*, from a low A flat to a top D flat: both her arias are sumptuous in their broadly arched phrases and rich melodies. Manrico is a splendid role for a strong lyric tenor, making no potentially embarrassing demands for coloratura flexibility: the infamous top C which traditionally crowns 'Di quella pira' – thrillingly macho when the singer nails it, disastrously comic when it wobbles or misses the pitch – is an interpolation which does not appear in the score, though Verdi is known to have sanctioned it. In defence of authenticity, purist conductors like Riccardo Muti insist on excluding it. The jewel for the baritone singing the unsympathetic character of di Luna is the graceful serenade 'Il balen'. It lies high, however, and some heavier voices find this a strain.

But the most interesting and complex role is that of Azucena (invariably sung by a mezzo-soprano, though in fact the range is scarcely different from that of Leonora), one of the few mother-figures in Verdi's *œuvre* and a character whose fierce passions and desire for revenge offer great histrionic opportunities.

For all its energy, brilliance and conventional orchestration, this is not a coarse or noisy opera, and it is up to a conductor to communicate its Mozartian qualities – intimacy, melancholy, clarity.

ᴄᴡ In performance

For the director, perhaps the most unrewarding of all Italian operas, not least because so much crucial action takes place off-stage and shrouded in the darkness of night. Each scene is in effect a tableau – this, as the Verdi scholar Julian Budden put it, is 'an opera of the expanded moment', in which the characters are powerful archetypes rather than the credible personalities of *Rigoletto* or *La Traviata*. Yet whatever the complexities and absurdities of the plot, *Il Trovatore* has a classical symmetry – each of the four principal characters has two arias and they finally come together in the immaculately constructed last scene.

Some attempts (including one by Andrei Serban, seen at Opera North and elsewhere) have been made to use the period of the Spanish Civil War to make the clash of Manrico and di Luna plausible, but producers nowadays tend to opt for a gloomy abstraction which creates atmosphere but doesn't elucidate the plot.

❧ Recording

CD: Placido Domingo (Manrico); Carlo Maria Giulini (cond.). DG 423 858 2

La Traviata

Three Acts (four scenes); First performed Venice, 1853. Libretto by Francesco Piave

Based on Alexandre Dumas's play *La Dame aux Camélias*, dramatized from Dumas's own novel in 1848 and originally drawn from his romantic involvement with the enchanting courtesan Marie Duplessis, who had died in 1846 at the age of twenty-three.

Verdi had a personal identification with the subject – he himself had been living since 1848 in Paris with Giuseppina Strepponi, a retired soprano with illegitimate children, who in 1859 was to become his second wife. So he knew at first hand something of the prejudice that women in Violetta's position faced: 'a subject for our age' is how he described the opera.

❧ Plot

The glamorous courtesan Violetta Valéry (soprano) is dying from tuberculosis. At a party, she falls in love with Alfredo Germont (tenor), who has long admired her from a distance. The two of them live happily together in the country, until Violetta is secretly visited by Alfredo's father, Germont (baritone). He demands that Violetta leave his son, since the scandal of her past threatens to destroy his daughter's chance of a good marriage. Fearful that Alfredo's love would in any case fade, she sadly agrees. Germont is moved by her nobility of spirit; she asks him not to tell Alfredo the truth until she is dead. Violetta returns to Paris and an old lover; Alfredo pursues her to a party, where he publicly denounces her.

Deserted by her fashionable friends, Violetta sinks into poverty and becomes mortally ill. Germont tells Alfredo the truth about her selfless sacrifice, and he hastens to her bedside. Joyously reunited, they talk of leaving Paris and a fresh start, but it is too late – Violetta dies in Alfredo's arms.

ᖇ What to listen for

Violetta is a role often said to require three different voices. Her long aria at the end of Act I moves from a gently expressive musing ('Ah! fors'è lui') to a brilliant florid climax ('Sempre libera', which some brave sopranos crown with a high E flat, not in fact written into the score). A fuller, richer sound is required for the complex feelings which animate her interview with Germont, as well as considerable resources of breath for the expansive phrases with which she bids Alfredo farewell ('Amami, Alfredo'). For the final death scene, the singer must both darken her tonal colour and suggest Violetta's ebbing strength. A strong lyric voice, properly trained in coloratura, like that of Angela Gheorghiu, is probably the type best suited to all aspects of the role.

The roles of Alfredo (for lyric tenor) or Germont (a mature baritone) are less problematic. In the past, it was the custom to cut the uninteresting cabalettas to both their arias in Act II, but these are usually included in performances today. The preludes to both Acts I and III, both requiring refined string playing, display a reflective melancholy beauty and freedom of line that is new to Verdi's orchestral music. Also remarkable is the use of Violetta's spoken voice, over a plangent violin solo, for her reading of Germont's letter in the last scene.

ᖇ In performance

La Traviata was unsuccessful at its première – mainly because the audience at La Fenice in Venice was incredulous of a grossly fat soprano who scarcely suggested a fragile consumptive. Verdi forbade any further performances until he found a singer more physically appropriate. In 1854, the opera was slightly revised and then relaunched with the slim and pretty Maria Spezia as Violetta. From then on, it made emotional sense, and has stood ever since as one of the most popular pieces in the repertory.

Verdi had originally planned to stage *La Tráviata* in contemporary costume, but the management of La Fenice in Venice, which had commissioned the piece, found this unacceptable, and the libretto ended up specifying that the action takes place in 1700. Producers and designers have invariably ignored this date, and the great majority of stagings present the drama in Dumas's Paris of the 1840s. However, in a quest for a more visually splendid setting, Luchino Visconti transplanted it to the 1870s (at La Scala, Milan, with Maria Callas) and to the 1890s (at Covent Garden).

More recently, several productions have also attempted to draw parallels between Violetta's tuberculosis and the AIDS epidemic, while Jonathan Miller, a qualified doctor as well as a director, made a great point (in productions for ENO and Opéra Bastille) of presenting the pathological details of her illness accurately. But *La Traviata* is a direct and simple drama, which does not lend itself to radical reinterpretation.

In 1981, a lavish film version, soupily directed by Franco Zeffirelli and starring the immensely vulnerable and appealing Teresa Stratas, proved very successful and brought the opera to new audiences.

Many sopranos have been attracted to the role of Violetta and its vocal and dramatic possibilities, but few can be said to have truly mastered its complex demands. In the last half-century, Maria Callas remains outstanding: sadly, she never made a proper studio recording of the opera. Among her successors, the Romanian Ileana Cotrubas ranks for many as the most touching and musical interpreter; and in 1994, her compatriot Angela Gheorghiu's sensational Covent Garden début in the role led BBC television to clear an entire evening to broadcast the performance.

ᙅ Recordings

CD: Ileana Cotrubas (Violetta): Carlos Kleiber (cond.).
DG 459 089 2
   Angela Gheorghiu (Violetta); Georg Solti (cond.). Decca
448 194 2
Video: Teresa Stratas (Violetta); James Levine (cond.).
DG 0 73 120 3.

Simon Boccanegra

**Prologue and three acts. First performed Venice, 1857.
Libretto by Francesco Piave**

Based on another play by the author of *Il Trovatore*, García
Gutiérrez. Criticized at its first performance both for its tangled plot and for a score whose dark tone and severity was
unrelieved by *Trovatore*'s immediate melodic vitality, *Simon
Boccanegra* was substantially revised in 1881 with the help of
the librettist Arrigo Boito. It is this later version, most
notable for the creation of the magnificent Council Chamber
scene (substituting for two more narratively muddling and
musically conventional scenes) which is normally performed
today and which is described below.

ᙅ Plot

In fourteenth-century Genoa, the plebeian Simon
Boccanegra is elected Doge. He hopes to marry the noble-
woman Maria, who has already born him a daughter. But
Maria dies, the baby vanishes and Boccanegra is cursed by
Maria's father, Fiesco.

   Twenty-five years later, Boccanegra is still in power. He
rediscovers his daughter, who has been brought up by his
political enemies, the Grimaldis. Her name is Amelia, and the
loathsome Paolo, one of Boccanegra's henchmen, lusts after
her. Paolo schemes to abduct Amelia, but the plot is foiled

when Amelia's favoured admirer Gabriele Adorno murders the abductor.

This provokes the people of Genoa to break angrily into the chamber where Boccanegra presides over the city's council. Gabriele knows nothing of Amelia's true parentage and denounces Boccanegra under the misapprehension that he was behind the attempted abduction. Amelia enters dramatically and restrains Gabriele from murdering Boccanegra, but the rioting is only stopped when Boccanegra points menacingly at Paolo and commands him to find the traitor.

Paolo continues to plot against Boccanegra and attempts to win both Gabriele and Fiesco to the cause of armed rebellion. But when Gabriele finds out that Amelia is Boccanegra's long-lost daughter, he agrees to fight on his behalf. Paolo's forces are defeated and after his arrest he confesses all. But it is too late – Boccanegra has already swallowed a slow-acting poison administered by Paolo. As it takes effect, Boccanegra is reconciled to his old enemy Fiesco and tells him that Amelia is his granddaughter. In his last moments of life, Boccanegra names Gabriele as his successor.

✃ What to listen for

Because of its lack of obvious tunes or brilliance, as well as its over-complicated plot, *Simon Boccanegra* has never been popular, though in terms of intensity and nobility it ranks as one of the most elevated and moving of Verdi's operas. It contains some fine arias – notably Fiesco's brooding 'Il lacerato spirito' and Amelia's first aria 'Come in quest'ora bruna', with its evocation of the shimmering Mediterranean – but as the opera progresses, it is the highly charged duets and trios which impel the drama towards the heart-rending final scene of confrontation. The scene in the council chamber is extraordinary both for Boccanegra's peroration 'Plebe! Patrizi! Popolo!', which the musicologist Julian Budden called 'Verdi's noblest monument to the baritone voice', and for the way it builds the dramatic tension, pitching soloists against chorus and building towards a climax which descends to a massive whisper before exploding in an equally massive shout.

Note also the persistent idea of the lilting sea, its ebb and flow rippling through the orchestra, and the sombre dignity of the opera's ending.

∾ In performance

Surely few opera productions have provided such a perfect visual embodiment of the music as Giorgio Strehler's *Simon Boccanegra*, first seen at La Scala in 1971 and subsequently much travelled: the brooding atmosphere of a medieval city riven by political faction and the romantic landscape of the sea were magically conveyed by Ezio Frigerio's gauzy russet sets, and Strehler brilliantly dramatized both the grand public and intimate personal struggles which drive the plot.

A very different interpretation was presented by David Alden at ENO in 1986 – a mixture of medieval and modern, with an abstract setting featuring a giant iron hand, symbolizing both fate and power, which loomed above the Council Chamber, descending when the plebeians invaded.

∾ Recordings

CD: Piero Cappuccilli (Boccanegra); Claudio Abbado (cond.). DG 449 752 2
Video: Kiri Te Kanawa (Amelia); Georg Solti (cond.). Covent Garden production. Decca 071 423 3

Un Ballo in Maschera
(*A Masked Ball*)

Three acts. First performed Rome, 1859.
Libretto by Antonio Somma

Based on Scribe's play about the assassination of Gustavus III of Sweden in 1792, the plot was considered inflammatory by the Bourbon censors in Naples – an Italian terrorist had recently made an attempt on the life of the French Emperor Louis Napoleon – and for the first performance the location was re-sited in a purely fictitious seventeenth-century Boston under British rule. Today, the Swedish setting is generally preferred.

ᰛ Plot

Gustavus III (Riccardo in the 'Boston' version) is planning a masked ball when he is warned by his friend and minister Anckarstroem (Renato) of a plot on his life. A petition urges the banishment of the fortune-teller Mademoiselle Arvidson (Ulrica) whose utterances command widespread respect. Along with his page Oscar, Gustavus decides to assume a disguise and visit her for himself.

Gustavus and Anckarstroem's wife Amelia are secretly in love. Amelia comes to ask Mademoiselle Arvidson how to put a stop to such adulterous feelings. Mademoiselle Arvidson tells her to gather a magic herb from beneath the gallows at midnight. Gustavus overhears and makes plans to follow her there.

Still disguised, Gustavus consults Mademoiselle Arvidson who tells him to beware the next man who shakes his hand. This turns out to be Anckarstroem, so Gustavus gaily laughs the prediction off.

At the gallows at midnight, Gustavus finds Amelia and they express their turbulent emotions. When Anckarstroem appears to warn Gustavus of the danger of lurking conspirators, Amelia draws a veil over her face. Gustavus escapes and Anckarstroem offers to escort the veiled lady to safety. But they are waylaid by the conspirators Ribbing and Horn (Sam and Tom), and in the ensuing confusion Amelia's identity is revealed to Anckarstroem, who is so appalled that he decides to side with the conspirators.

Anckarstroem plans to kill his wife, but decides that it is Gustavus who has led her astray and who must die. He orders Amelia to draw lots for the task of killing Gustavus. She picks Anckarstroem's name. When Oscar arrives with an invitation to Gustavus's masked ball, Anckarstroem realizes that such an event will provide an ideal time to strike.

Gustavus resolves to send Anckarstroem, with Amelia, to England as his envoy. At the ball, as Gustavus bids Amelia farewell, Anckarstroem shoots him in the back. Before he dies, Gustavus affirms that Amelia is innocent and nobly pardons Anckarstroem.

∾ What to listen for

One of Verdi's most polished and elegant scores, even if it only touches the heart in its final moments. By this stage of his career, Verdi had abandoned the aria model which uses a slow cavatina connected by recitative to a fast cabaletta, in favour of shorter, more flexibly paced and shaped arias. *Ballo* is also notable for the interplay of melodramatic political conspiracy with the airy gaiety associated with the elegant, insouciant and generous-hearted Gustavus (a favourite tenor role, which demands graceful style as much strong high notes or flexibility) and his spritely page Oscar, sung by a boyish-looking coloratura soprano. Led by them, the ensemble at the end of the first scene sounds like something out of an Offenbach operetta, and the quintet 'E scherzo o dè follia' is early evidence of a sophisticated jokey strain (albeit one underpinned here by a certain nervous unease) which Verdi would again indulge in *Falstaff*.

But the mood of the opera darkens: the love duet between Gustavus and Amelia is in the grand romantic mould, as is the ensuing scene in which Anckarstroem confronts Amelia, a conventional soprano tragic heroine, torn between personal inclination and moral duty. Her hesitant first aria, as she approaches the gallows at midnight, concludes with one of those magically soaring imprecations which are a special feature of Verdi's genius, even though only the most luscious of voices (Leontyne Price or Montserrat Caballé in their prime) can realize their full sumptuous glory. Anckarstroem's big moment comes in Act III – 'Eri tu' is one of Verdi's most virile baritone showpieces.

∾ In performance

A production in Stockholm in the late 1950s by Goeran Gentele was the first to follow historical actuality and present Gustavus as an effete homosexual, clearly more sexually interested in Oscar than Amelia. A more extreme line was taken by David Alden at ENO in 1989. Gustavus was presented as a dithering Hamlet figure, and the sets were dominated by images of time, fate and black magic – in the final ballroom scene, a statue of the horseman of the apocalypse, one of its hoofs resting on a clock-face, loomed above the stage. Other productions have explored ideas of the mask, of play-acting, of illusion and reality and the genuine and feigned emotions of Gustavus and Amelia.

∾ Recording

CD: Placido Domingo (Gustavus); Riccardo Muti (cond.). EMI 5 66510-2

La Forza del Destino
(*The Force of Destiny*)

Four acts. First performed St Petersburg, 1862.
Libretto by Francesco Piave

Like *Il Trovatore*, this is based on a sprawling, action-packed Spanish romantic drama. Interestingly, it is the only Verdi opera with an abstract title, although it has often been pointed out that the idea of 'coincidence' more aptly describes the plot than 'destiny'. First performed in St Petersburg (where it greatly impressed Mussorgsky and influenced the composition of his *Boris Godunov*), it was not particularly successful. Verdi revised the opera for a production at La Scala, Milan in 1869, substituting the now familiar overture for a shorter prelude and changing the original ending (Alvaro committing suicide by jumping off a cliff) into something less melodramatic. It is this latter version which is normally performed today.

∾ Plot

Seville, during the eighteenth century. As the noblewoman Leonora is about to elope with Alvaro, a figure of Byronic mystery and Inca descent, her father bursts in to thwart them. When Alvaro surrenders by throwing down his pistol, it accidentally fires and kills the old man. Leonora and Alvaro flee separately, each believing the other to be dead. Leonora's brother Carlo pursues them both, seeking revenge for the disgrace they have brought upon the family. After narrowly missing an encounter with Carlo, Leonora asks the Padre Guardiano, head of a monastery, to provide her with shelter and he agrees to house her in a lonely hermitage.

Both Alvaro and Carlo assume different names and join a Spanish contingent fighting in Italy in the War of Austrian Succession. Alvaro saves Carlo from being murdered by ruffians. Unaware of the other's true identity, the two men swear friendship. Then Alvaro is badly wounded in battle. He entrusts Carlo with a small casket of personal effects, asking that it should be opened after his death. Carlo's suspicions of Alvaro's true identity are confirmed when he treacherously looks inside the casket and finds a portrait of his sister Leonora. Once Alvaro has recovered, Carlo insults him and provokes an inconclusive duel. Alvaro returns to Spain and coincidentally enters the same monastery that gave Leonora her hermitage.

Several years later, Carlo tracks Alvaro down and challenges him to another duel outside the hermitage. Alvaro mortally wounds Carlo, and knocks at the hermitage in search of a holy person to give him the last rites. Leonora emerges and is startled to be reunited with Alvaro, but the still vengeful Carlo summons his ebbing strength and manages to stab her to death. The Padre Guardiano attempts to bring religious consolation to the despairing Alvaro.

∾ What to listen for

A failure on the grand scale – an opera whose extreme contrasts never gel into one convincing narrative line; least successful is probably the Italian battlefield episode of Act III, despite Alvaro's big aria 'O tu che in seno' and his stirring duet with Carlo. Among the finest sequences are Leonora's arrival at the monastery where she is granted shelter – her urgent aria 'Madre, pietòsa Vergine' is followed by a long and varied duet with the Padre Guardiano and concludes with the serene hymn 'La Vergine degli Angeli' – and the brief but electrifying final scene in which Leonora's famous aria 'Pace, Pace, mio Dio' is (in the later version of 1869) swiftly followed by an impassioned trio.

Leonora is not one of Verdi's more difficult soprano roles in terms of range or flexibility, and the singer assuming it has about two hours to recuperate in her dressing-room between 'La Vergine degli Angeli' and 'Pace, Pace, mio Dio'. But Verdi does demand from her a rare ability to spin soft high notes in contrast to a hard, thrilling forte. Alvaro is a monster role, and is gratifying only to the sort of dramatic tenor who can master Otello or Andrea Chénier. For light relief, Verdi presents Trabuco the pedlar, Preziosilla the camp-following gypsy and the grumbling monk Fra Melitone. None of these figures adds much to the central drama, though Preziosilla's roulades and 'Rataplan' lend proceedings a welcome *élan*. The opera's arresting overture, which opens with the 'destiny' theme which recurs throughout the action, is often played separately as a concert piece.

∾ In performance

It is a brave opera house which undertakes *La Forza del Destino*. Aside from the problems it presents in terms of casting, the sprawling range of action, character locale, and mood also make it almost impossible to stage coherently. In Toulouse, Nicolas Joel transferred the action to the 1940s, and the evoked atmosphere of world war certainly made some of the more outlandish coincidences in the plot more plausible. The Kirov Opera mounted the original St Petersburg version, with sets copied from the original designs, but the result was no more convincing than more radical efforts.

∾ Recordings

CD: Leontyne Price (Leonora); Placido Domingo (Alvaro); James Levine (cond.). RCA RD8 1864

Galina Gorchakova (Leonora); Valery Gergiev (cond.). Philips 446 951 2. Original St Petersburg version

Don Carlos

Five acts. First performed Paris, 1867.
Libretto by Joseph Méry and Camille du Locle

With its exploration of the clashes between Church and state, Catholic and Protestant, national liberty and imperial repression, political expedience and private passion, Schiller's play *Don Carlos* inspired Verdi to one of his very greatest operas. It was originally composed to a French text for the Paris Opéra, where certain conventions – such as a ballet and a spectacular procession scene – had to be rigidly observed. This necessitated many alterations in rehearsal and increased the length of the work beyond Verdi's ideal measure. When he revised the opera in 1882 for an Italian production, Verdi made substantial cuts and changes (among them the elimination of the first scene in the forest at Fontainebleau, when Carlos first meets Elisabeth) in an attempt to make the opera more concise. Modern taste has now reverted in favour of the French version, although the various recensions are so complex that there can never be a definitive version of the score.

❧ Plot

1568: Elisabeth, daughter of the King of France, has fallen in love with Carlos, the Infante of Spain, but political considerations require her to marry his father, the widowed King Philip II. Carlos seeks solace in the monastery of San Yuste, where his noble grandfather Charles V is thought to be still living in anonymous seclusion and meditation. There Carlos encounters his great friend Rodrigo, Marquis of Posa, to whom he confesses his passion for Elisabeth. Posa is sympathetic, but attempts to persuade Carlos to forget his personal troubles and join him in taking up the cause of Protestant Flanders, a province of the Spanish empire currently suffering from Catholic repression. Carlos and Posa swear eternal friendship.

Princess Eboli, a lady of the court and secret mistress to Philip II, is in love with Carlos and misinterprets his agitation as a sign that he returns her feelings. Elisabeth grants Carlos an interview, ostensibly to hear his suit on behalf of the Protestants of Flanders. But when they are alone, Carlos breaks down in passion, forcing the tormented Elisabeth to remind him that she is now his stepmother. The jealous and suspicious King Philip is furious to discover that the queen has been left unattended.

Posa pleads with Philip on behalf of Flanders. Philip admires Posa's idealism and confides in him his fears about Carlos and Elisabeth, but claims that he himself is restrained by the unbendingly reactionary attitudes of the ancient Grand Inquisitor.

In the gardens of the palace during a masked ball, Carlos waits for a lady who has summoned him with an anonymous note. He believes that its author is Elisabeth, and shows consternation when Eboli appears. She is enraged by his indifference to her advances, and threatens to expose him to the king.

At an *auto-da-fé*, the ceremony marking the burning of heretics, six deputies from Flanders appear to plead their cause before Philip. Carlos publicly speaks out on their behalf and draws his sword in a symbolic gesture of defiance. Posa, who deplores such hot-headed tactics and believes he can win Philip over by more rational means, gently disarms Carlos and hands the sword to Philip. As the pyre is lit around the heretics, a voice from heaven is heard promising redemption.

Alone in his study, Philip laments that Elisabeth does not love him. The Grand Inquisitor appears, suggesting that the greatest threat to stability is Posa's liberalism. Elisabeth is distraught at the theft of her casket. She sees it on Philip's table – when he opens it, he finds her miniature portrait of Carlos and accuses her of adultery. Eboli reveals to Elisabeth that she stole the casket out of jealousy and admits that she has been Philip's mistress. Elisabeth banishes her, either to exile or a convent.

Carlos has been arrested for his treasonable behaviour and Posa visits him in prison. Posa tells Carlos that he has implicated himself as the leader of the Flemish deputies, nobly hoping that this will gain Carlos his freedom. Posa is shot by the king's assassins – as he dies, he tells Carlos that Elisabeth has agreed to one last meeting with him outside the convent of San Yuste. A rebellious mob attempts to set Carlos free, but the Grand Inquisitor quells it with threats against those who lift their hand against God's anointed rulers.

Elisabeth and Carlos meet outside the convent. As they take a sad leave of each other, Philip emerges from the shadows and demands that the Grand Inquisitor arrest him as a heretic. At that point, a mysterious cowled monk – who may or may not be Carlos's saintly grandfather, Charles V – emerges and leads Carlos into the safety of the monastery.

◑ What to listen for

Every role in this opera is wonderful both to sing and to act: Elisabeth requires no extreme high notes or coloratura, and the only drawbacks are the problem of spinning high-lying pianissimi in her first brief aria, 'O ma chère compagne', sung to her banished lady-in-waiting, and the long wait for her big moment: the magnificent 'Toi qui sus le néant' does not come until Act V. Eboli is a classic example of a role which contains arias of such different character and style – the sly, flirtatious 'Veil' song in Act II, and the boldly emotional 'O don fatal' in Act IV – that almost all singers excel in one at the expense of the other. But the character is superbly drawn, and 'O don fatal' can bring the house down.

Carlos and Posa are not as demandingly hefty as the leading tenor and baritone roles in *Forza*, *Aida* or *Otello*, and both are well suited to good-looking younger singers who can make much of their thwarted idealism. Philip is a dream role for any bass: not just a regal cipher, he is a man tortured by the conflicts between his personal morality and political considerations, as well as his unhappy marriage – all embodied in the first scene of Act IV, where his monologue, 'Elle ne m'aime pas' is succeeded by his epic confrontation with the Grand Inquisitor.

The orchestration is notable for masterly use of the lower strings, and only in some pompous and inappropriate jauntiness in the scene of the burning of the heretics does Verdi's inspiration falter.

✎ In performance

Two magnificent interpretations have dominated the staging of this great opera. Luchino Visconti's 1958 production of the Italian version at Covent Garden was an exercise in old-fashioned historical realism, and although its painted flats came to look unsophisticated over the years, the sense of courtly grandeur and dignity encasing the characters' turbulent emotions remained enormously impressive.

Luc Bondy's staging of the French version, first seen at the Châtelet in 1996, was more austerely stylized, although still suggestive of the sixteenth-century historical period. More focused on the intense personal conflicts than on the broader political drama, it brought a dreamlike quality to the scene in Philip's study and an intense poignancy to the thwarted love between Carlos and Elisabeth.

❧ Recordings

CD: Montserrat Caballé (Elisabetta); Placido Domingo (Carlo); Carlo Maria Giulini (cond.). EMI 567 401 2. Italian version

CD, video and DVD: Karita Mattila (Elisabeth); Thomas Hampson (Posa); Antonio Pappano (cond.). Directed by Luc Bondy. French version. EMI 4243 5 56152 2 (CD); EMI 0630 163 183 (video); and BBC NVC Arts 0630 16318 2 (DVD)

Aida

Four acts. First performed Cairo, 1871.
Libretto by Antonio Ghislanzoni

In 1869, Verdi was asked by the Khedive of Egypt to inaugurate a new opera house being built in Cairo as part of the celebrations surrounding the completion of the Suez Canal in 1870. Verdi failed to finish the score by the deadline and the Franco-Prussian war prevented the scenery being transported out of Paris, so the Cairo Opera House opened with *Rigoletto*. *Aida* eventually received its première there on Christmas Eve 1871.

Verdi took meticulous care to furnish correct archaeological detail for the libretto, and this may be one reason why it seems rather stiff and conservative – this is a piece with roots in the outdated conventions of French grand opera and eighteenth-century *opera seria*. From a musical point of view, however, the score ranks as a technical marvel – remarkably original in its orchestration, well-nigh perfect in terms of balance, proportion and clarity – as well as a treasure-trove of melody and dramatic master-strokes.

❧ Plot

Ancient Memphis. The warrior Radames secretly loves Aida, a beautiful Ethiopian captive who has been made slave to the

King of Egypt's daughter, Amneris. He does not know that Aida is the daughter of the King of Ethiopia or that Amneris herself is in love with him. War is declared against the resurgent Ethiopians and Radames is named commander of the Egyptian army. As he is sent off to fight her compatriots, Aida is torn between loyalty to her homeland and love for Radames.

Amneris goads Aida into confessing the truth about her relationship with Radames and then reveals that she, too, loves him. Radames returns from the war in triumph and is acclaimed by the populace. Among the prisoners is Aida's father Amonasro, unrecognized as the King of Ethiopia. As a reward for his military success, Radames is given Amneris as his bride – an offer he cannot refuse.

Aida awaits a secret final meeting with Radames at night by the banks of the Nile. Amonasro has guessed her feelings for the Egyptian general. Outraged, he plays on her sense of patriotism and persuades her to wheedle some crucial military intelligence out of Radames. Reluctantly, Aida consents. Amonasro hides, as Radames arrives and protests that he still loves Aida alone. As they plan to flee to Ethiopia together, Radames unwittingly reveals the military information which Amonasro requires to ambush the army. But from another hiding place, Amneris and the High Priest Ramfis have also been listening. Aida and Amonasro escape, but Radames is arrested as a traitor.

Radames is tried by Ramfis and the priests. Outside the court, Amneris paces up and down, torn between thwarted love and the desire for revenge. Amonasro has been killed, but Radames refuses to denounce Aida and the court condemns him to be buried alive in the temple crypt. Aida finds her way into his tomb and they die together, as a repentant Amneris kneels in remorseful prayer above them.

✎ What to listen for

An opera which poses singers a variety of problems. For Aida herself, these are focused on the sustained high C, marked '*dolce*', at the climax of her aria which opens the Nile scene. Because there is so little support from the orchestra, and because of the ascent which precedes it, the note is horribly difficult to achieve, and many otherwise qualified sopranos avoid the role entirely because they are so frightened of flunking it. Like Leonora in *Forza*, Aida is a Verdi role which makes great play of the contrast between *piano* and *forte* singing, and those who simply belt it out can never do it justice.

Amneris is written for a high mezzo-soprano similar to Eboli in *Don Carlos*. Unusually, the role involves no set-piece aria, though the dramatic declamation in the scene in which she awaits the verdict of Radames's trial for treason is a tremendous *tour de force* for any singer with a stentorian chest voice and an Olympic level of stamina. Radames confronts his biggest hurdle in the first minutes of the opera, when his aria 'Celeste Aida' ends with a top B flat which is meant to die away pianissimo. Very few heroic tenors can even approximate this, and almost everybody simply hits the note fortissimo, destroying a beautiful musical effect.

Like several other Verdi operas (*Il Trovatore*, for instance), *Aida* has a reputation for being a rousing blockbuster. But it is also a score of remarkable refinement and delicacy – note the sinuous oriental colourings and the bright-toned pseudo-Ancient Egyptian idiom of the dance and processional music; the enthralling development of the duet between Aida and Amneris; the masterly construction of the Nile scene, with the simplicity of its exquisite orchestral evocation of the atmosphere; and the final duet for Aida and Radames, in which the shortness of the phrases brilliantly suggests their struggle for breath. The famous Triumph Scene contains a great deal of strong melody and martial splendour; it is much more convincing than the similar *auto-da-fé* scene in *Don Carlos*, and exemplifies Verdi's mastery of large-scale theatricality, building climax upon climax.

❧ In performance

Despite being celebrated as opera's equivalent of a Hollywood blockbuster and often presented on vast arena or open-air stages (notably in Verona and Luxor), *Aida*, like *Don Carlos*, is focused on human relationships at the mercy of public conflicts, even though neither the characterization nor the political perspective is anything like as subtle as it is in *Don Carlos*.

The Ancient Egyptian setting is impossible to represent without lapsing into kitsch, though audiences continue to want this opera to look like a fifties biblical epic starring Charlton Heston and Gina Lollobrigida (who did indeed play Aida in a dubbed film version). An elegant solution was provided by Philip Prowse for Opera North, when his handsome staging updated the action to the time of the opera's composition and a time of dubious colonial adventurism. More controversially, a production in Frankfurt directed by Hans Neuenfels had the dancers in the Triumph Scene making Nazi goose-steps and salutes, with the chorus of Egyptians presented as a bourgeois opera audience applauding from tiers of boxes. The idea that the Egyptians represent an aggressive Fascist power (redolent of Mussolini and his Abyssinian expedition) has become a commonplace.

❧ Recording

CD: Montserrat Caballé (Aida); Placido Domingo (Radames); Riccardo Muti (cond.). EMI 5676 13 2

Otello

Four acts. First performed Milan, 1887.
Libretto by Arrigo Boito

Verdi's trust in the highly intellectual and cultivated librettist and composer Arrigo Boito had consolidated when Boito helped him revise *Simon Boccanegra* in 1881. Their rapport inspired Verdi to return to Shakespeare for what would be his first new opera for over fifteen years and a work of masterful technical polish and theatrical grandeur.

∾ Plot

Broadly the same as Shakespeare's play, omitting its initial Venetian scenes, and opening with the citizens of Cyprus anxiously watching the sea as Otello fights off the invading Turkish navy.

∾ What to listen for

Verdi was thought to be very old-fashioned at the time of *Otello*'s composition, but the score showed his critics how wrong they were. Although there are grand-opera elements (such as the big ensemble finale to Act III), the score also displays the influence of Wagner in its use of motifs and the technique of 'through-composition', in which the drama proceeds without any obvious breaks or division into separate numbers.

The role of Otello is one of the summits of any tenor's aspirations, requiring enormous power, stamina and sensibility. Over the last thirty years, Jon Vickers, Placido Domingo and Vladimir Galuzin are probably the only three singers (none of them Italian-born) to have mastered its demands. The difficulties begin with the character's first entrance and the trumpet phrases of 'Esultate' which rise to a high B before the singer has had any chance to warm up. The love duet at the end of Act I is warmly lyrical, while the duet with Iago at the end of Act II is brazenly ferocious. The singer must convey both the noble warrior and the ardent husband, as well as suggesting a decline into paranoid insanity. Many tenors fudge the written high C in the Act III duet with Desdemona; and even fewer can bring to Otello's sombre final utterances the right mixture of dignity, remorse and tenderness.

Iago is another challenge, written for a powerful dark-hued baritone who can bring a light, wry touch to the Brindisi in

Act I and a sardonic snap to the monologue in Act II. Mere roarers need not apply. Desdemona is the last in the line of pure-hearted Verdi heroines – 'the type of resignation, goodness, self-sacrifice', as Verdi wrote. Softer-grained sopranos find the character's outbursts in Act III a strain, but come into their own in the soft, high-lying passages of the 'Willow' Song and Ave Maria in Act IV. Note also the magnificent scene-painting of a storm-tossed sea which opens the opera, the delicate madrigal in Act II, and the eerie quietness and economy with which Act IV is orchestrated.

Verdi revised the ensemble which concludes Act III: the original and longer version, in which it is undoubtedly difficult to hear all the different contrapuntal vocal strands, remains the more commonly performed; the shorter and simpler version, less frequently heard today, was written for a production in Paris in 1894.

‪ In performance

More radical producers want to see the racial question as the heart of the opera, but it was of little concern to Verdi or Boito (or Shakespeare, for that matter). Part of the success of Peter Stein's 1986 staging for WNO was that it reflected its roots in both Shakespearean tragedy and Victorian melodrama, presenting the opera in sets based on flat-perspective early Renaissance painting and using a language of theatrically heightened gesture. But this is not an opera which responds kindly to being messed about with, and more aggressive attempts to update it (as in David Freeman's production for ENO, set in a present-day military compound covered with barbed wire and barrels of explosives) end up seeming simply irrelevant.

‪ Recordings

CD: Placido Domingo (Otello); James Levine (cond.). RCA GD 82951 2
DVD: Placido Domingo (Otello); Georg Solti (cond.). Covent Garden production. Pioneer 452 736 089204

Falstaff

Three acts. First performed Milan, 1893.
Libretto by Arrigo Boito

When a newspaper article suggested that he was incapable of writing a comic opera, Verdi was stung – his one attempt at the genre, *Un Giorno di Regno* (*King for a Day*, 1840), had been completely forgotten. So at the age of seventy-five, he began work with Boito on an adaptation of Shakespeare's farce *The Merry Wives of Windsor*. To cover himself, he made out that the project was something he was undertaking 'to pass the time' rather than for performance. What eventually emerged surprised the first-night audience at La Scala – the octogenarian composer had produced something sparkling, sly and witty in a style entirely unlike that of his previous work. As Boito wrote to Verdi, 'After having sounded all the shrieks and groans of the human heart, to finish with a burst of laughter – that is to astonish the world.'

Among several earlier operatic adaptations of the play, the most notable is Otto Nicolai's *Die lustigen Weiber von Windsor* (1849), known to Verdi; later came Ralph Vaughan Williams's charming *Sir John in Love* (1935).

✥ Plot

Broadly the same as *The Merry Wives of Windsor*, in which Mistress Ford leads a comic female conspiracy designed to teach the lecherous Sir John Falstaff a lesson. A sub-plot involves Mistress Ford's jealous husband and his reluctance to let their daughter Nannetta marry young Fenton.

✥ What to listen for

Otello is the culmination of the Italian grand-opera tradition; *Falstaff*'s mercurial fluency and wit transforms and perfects Rossinian *opera buffa*. As the dazzling double ensemble at the end of the second scene and the vast, uproarious final fugue indicate, this is an opera designed for an immaculately rehearsed team with sharp ears, superb diction and quick musical responses rather than a line-up of star soloists, although both the title role (written for a *buffo* with a range which covers both bass and baritone) and Ford (written for the same sort of baritone as Rigoletto and Iago) are vocally tricky – as is Nannetta, a lovely role for a very young soprano with superb breath control and the ability to spin confident high pianissimi in her exchanges with Fenton (light tenor) in the second scene.

Rather than providing complete arias, Verdi scatters the score with memorable melodic phrases which seem to grow naturally out of the comedy – one thinks of the gorgeous soprano line unfurled in Alice Ford's half-mocking, half-seductive outburst in the second scene, of the snatched encounters and kisses of Nannetta and Fenton ('always disturbed and interrupted and always ready to begin again', as Boito put it), of the contralto Mistress Quickly's ludicrous curtsey, 'Reverenza', in the third scene. More substantial highlights of the score also include Falstaff's tiny but perfect aria 'Quand'ero paggio', sung as he describes his nimble youth to Mistress Ford, and lasting only a matter of seconds; Ford's monologue at the end of third scene, a parody of the conventions of operatic melodrama; and the fairy music in the last scene, its spooky daintiness creating an atmosphere quite new to Verdi's *œuvre*.

✵ In performance

In big opera houses like the Met or the Salzburg Festspielhaus, the fizzing comic vivacity of *Falstaff* tends to fall flat, and it is not an opera which responds happily to star singers elbowing forward to steal the show. It is always at its most enjoyable when a team has been intensively rehearsed in the sort of collegial conditions that Glyndebourne offers. In other respects, it is open to any number of approaches – pure carry-on farce (Graham Vick for Covent Garden) or ambivalent bitter-sweet comedy (Peter Stein for WNO, Matthew Warchus for Opera North), in Elizabethan (Jonathan Miller for the Berlin Staatsoper), late Victorian (Declan Donnellan for Salzburg) or modern dress (David Pountney for ENO).

✤ Recordings

CD: Giuseppe Valdengo (Falstaff); Arturo Toscanini (cond.).
RCA GD 60521

   Bryn Terfel (Falstaff); Thomas Hampson (Ford); Claudio
Abbado (cond.). DG 471 194 2

DVD: Bryn Terfel (Falstaff); Bernard Haitink (cond.).
Covent Garden production. BBC OA 08 12 D

Pietro Mascagni (1863–1945)
Cavalleria rusticana
(Rustic Chivalry)

One act. First performed Rome, 1890.
Libretto by Giovanni Tragioni-Tozzetti and Guido Menasci

Based on a play and novella by Giovanni Verga, this opera pioneered what became known as the 'verismo' style. This was a movement among young Italian opera composers, much influenced by Bizet's *Carmen* and the novels of Emile Zola, in which the focus was turned on violent and highly emotional episodes of modern life, usually drawn from proletarian or peasant characters – in marked contrast to the historical and 'noble' subject-matter favoured by Verdi. *Cavalleria Rusticana* is usually performed with *Pagliacci* (see p. 208) – a pairing known to opera lovers as '*Cav* 'n' *Pag*'.

∾ Plot

Easter morning in a Sicilian village. Most of the action occurs while the population is celebrating Mass in church. After being made pregnant by Turiddu, Santuzza has been excommunicated. Turiddu is now infatuated with a married woman, Lola, and refuses to honour his obligations to Santuzza. In revenge, Santuzza informs Lola's husband Alfio of the affair, and Alfio kills Turiddu in a duel.

∾ What to listen for

For all its crude orchestration and harmony, this is indisputably a strongly characterized and constructed opera, dominated melodically by a 'tragic destiny' motif which accompanies Santuzza's entrance and which is restated at its climax. At the centre of the opera is the long impassioned duet between Santuzza and Turiddu, but both these characters also have striking solo arias – Santuzza's narrative 'Voi lo sapete' and

Turiddu's drinking song. For the chorus, there is the 'Easter Hymn', led by Santuzza, and for the orchestra, the plangent Intermezzo, the melody of which is based on the Hymn. Much verismo is written as if to imitate the speaking voice and therefore only uses high notes to mark moments of great emotional stress and eschews coloratura. Santuzza can thus be sung by either a soprano (such as Maria Callas) or a mezzo-soprano (such as Tatyana Troyanos), though the mezzos often omit the top C at the end of the opera. Turiddu requires a tenor who can both out-belt the prima donna in the duet and muster some sweetness for the high-lying serenade at the beginning of the opera.

Bizet's *Carmen* was the great influence on this opera, as one can most obviously hear in Alfio's aria, which is strongly reminiscent of the toreador Escamillo's song.

∾ In performance

An opera whose effectiveness depends on singers willing to give their histrionic all, and one which can withstand a certain degree of coarse singing if the emotional commitment is sufficiently intense. Perhaps the most successful production of the piece has been that of Franco Zeffirelli, seen in different versions in various opera houses. It realistically evokes the life and look of a Sicilian hill town, and makes a great point of establishing characters for each member of the chorus. A production at the Berlin Staatsoper tried the experiment of performing *Cav* after *Pag*, presenting the former as a sort of ritualized Greek tragedy, ignoring the specified rural Sicilian setting.

∾ Recordings

CD: Renata Scotto (Santuzza); Placido Domingo (Turiddu); James Levine (cond.). RCA 7 4321 39 5002

Video: Placido Domingo (Turiddu); Georges Prêtre (cond.). Philips 070 104 3. Directed by Franco Zeffirelli. Coupled with *Pagliacci*

Ruggero Leoncavallo (1857–1919)
Pagliacci (*Strolling Players*)

Prologue and two acts (normally performed without an interval).
First performed Milan, 1892.
Libretto by the composer

Leoncavallo drew the plot from an incident remembered from his own childhood – his father was the magistrate who presided over the case.

❧ Plot

Tonio peeps through the curtains to introduce the audience to the drama which will ensue. The violent and jealous Canio leads a troupe of travelling players who pitch up in an Italian village. Canio's unhappy wife Nedda rejects the coarse advances of Tonio, a fellow actor. Tonio then spies on Nedda's meeting with her lover Silvio, with whom she plans to elope. In revenge, Tonio summons Canio. Silvio escapes, and Nedda refuses to reveal his identity, despite Canio's threats.

Before the assembled villagers, a performance of the evening's play begins. It is a comedy of marital intrigue, and for the disturbed Canio, fiction becomes confused with reality. He breaks out of character and again demands to know the name of Nedda's lover. When she continues to defy him, he stabs her. As she dies, Nedda cries out for Silvio. When he instinctively rushes out of the audience to help her, Canio stabs him to death too. Tonio ironically announces that 'La commedia è finita' – 'the comedy is over'.

❧ What to listen for

Written in conscious imitation of *Cavalleria rusticana*, although its score is more refined, varied and ambitious. Ever since the days of Caruso, the role of Canio has provided a *tour de force* for a dramatic tenor – Vickers, Domingo and

Pavarotti have been outstanding among recent interpreters – not least because the climax of its hit number, 'Vesti la giubba' doesn't demand a killing high C; Nedda, a gift for any attractive young soprano who can convey febrile sexuality, is more subtly composed, and the score even asks for trills in her aria, though few sopranos today are capable of providing them. Older, heavier Italian baritones relish Tonio's big prologue aria, usually sung in front of the curtain; younger, lighter ones cut their teeth on Silvio, a nice role offering several gracefully arching phrases.

ॐ In performance

The appearance of Tonio in front of the curtain to announce the drama to the audience may seem an odd break with the naturalism of what follows, but it is of a piece with the gap between reality and pretence which overtakes 'the drama within a drama' at the climax. For WNO, Elijah Moshinsky made a plausible transposition of the scenario to the world of post-war Italian neo-realist cinema; a production by Franco Zeffirelli in Los Angeles went further and set it on a modern tower-block estate, under the concrete piers of a highway. This had the effect of making the idea of a troupe of two-bit travelling players drawing an excited audience somewhat implausible. Several productions have intensified the twinning with *Cav* by using the same set.

ॐ Recordings

CD: José Cura (Canio); Riccardo Chailly (cond.). Decca 467 086 2

Video: Teresa Stratas (Nedda); Luciano Pavarotti (Canio); James Levine (cond.). Met production. DG 072 448 3
Coupled with Puccini's *Il Tabarro*.

Umberto Giordano (1867–1948)
Andrea Chénier

Four acts. First performed Milan, 1896.
Libretto by Luigi Illica

This costume drama emulates the torrid intensity of Puccini's
Manon Lescaut and verismo operas such as *Cavalleria
Rusticana* and *Pagliacci*. There was a real André Chénier, a fine
poet guillotined during the French Revolution, but the
opera's plot, based on a novelette, bears no other relation to
historical actualities.

∾ Plot

Just before the outbreak of the French Revolution, the aristocratic Maddalena de Coigny is smitten with the idealistic poet
Andrea Chénier, who speaks out on behalf of the poor and
oppressed in the hope of a better world. Gérard, a retainer in
the service of Maddalena's mother, nurses both amorous feelings for Maddalena and revolutionary sentiments.

Five years pass, and the revolution is in full swing. Chénier
is advised to flee the increasingly dangerous situation, but he
is held back by an arrangement to meet a woman who has
been sending him impassioned anonymous letters. It is
Maddalena, and the two of them are soon ardently in love.
Gérard, now one of Robespierre's cronies, continues to be
infatuated with Maddalena.

Chénier is arrested as 'an enemy of the people' and Gérard
is asked to sign the indictment. Conscience pricks him, but
his desire for Maddalena is overwhelming and he signs the
paper. Maddalena offers Gérard her body in exchange for
Chénier's freedom. When he hears how Maddalena has suffered from the horrors of the revolution, Gérard has a change
of heart: at the trial he supports Chénier's self-defence and
publicly admits that the indictment is fraudulent. But
Chénier is sentenced to death.

In the prison of Saint-Lazare, Chénier awaits execution. With Gérard's connivance, Maddalena gains admittance. The jailor agrees to let Maddalena substitute herself for another condemned female prisoner. Chénier and Maddalena are rapturously but briefly reunited before they are summoned to the guillotine.

Ꮼ What to listen for

Giordano's melodies seem to promise much more than they deliver, and he doesn't rate highly as a composer for the orchestra. The score nevertheless offers great vocal opportunities for the three principals, in arias which have narrative rather than lyrical shape: for Chénier (tenor), the idealistic 'Un dì, all'azzurro spazio', in which he contrasts the glory of nature with the selfishness of mankind; for Maddalena (soprano), 'La mamma morta' (made famous by its inclusion in the movie *Philadelphia*) in which she describes the horrible circumstances of her mother's death; for Gérard (baritone), 'Nemico della patria', in which he asks himself whether he can denounce Chénier. Best of all is the barnstorming duet in Act IV: it reaches a frenzied climax as Chénier and Maddalena mount the tumbril together sharing a triumphant high B – although heavier, more baritonal tenors often transpose this high-lying episode down a semitone.

Ꮼ In performance

Like *Pagliacci*, this is an opera which primarily offers a great vehicle for a dramatic tenor, preferably one with matinée-idol good looks – Franco Corelli, Placido Domingo and José Cura, for example. Although the score and libretto are both overheated melodramatic hokum and the modern school of producers find it quite uninteresting, the opera can still pack a punch.

Ꮼ Recording

CD: Placido Domingo (Chénier); James Levine (cond.) RCA GD82046

Giacomo Puccini (1858–1924)
Manon Lescaut

Four acts. First performed Turin, 1893.
Libretto by Domenico Oliva and Luigi Illica

Based on the novel of 1731 by Abbé Prévost. The composition of this, Puccini's third opera, was long and tortured, complicated by the recent success of Massenet's version of the same text (see p. 262–4).

∾ Plot

Mid-eighteenth-century France. Outside a coaching inn in Amiens, the susceptible young Chevalier des Grieux is captivated by the teenage beauty Manon Lescaut as she passes on her way to a convent. An old lecher, Geronte, plans to abduct her, but Manon and des Grieux thwart him by eloping in Geronte's own coach. Geronte's fury is assuaged when Manon's sinister and manipulative brother assures him that Manon will soon need a rich protector.

Sure enough, Manon is soon set up as Geronte's mistress. She confesses to her brother, however, that the pleasures of being a fine lady fail to satisfy her and she yearns for the romance and simple life that she shared with des Grieux. Lescaut agrees to fetch des Grieux, and the lovers are passionately reunited. When Geronte unexpectedly returns to find the pair in each other's arms, Manon taunts him and he leaves, outraged. To des Grieux's disappointment, Manon now proves reluctant to abandon her life of luxury. But then the police, summoned by the furious Geronte, arrive to arrest her as a prostitute.

At the harbour of Le Havre, Manon awaits deportation to Louisiana. Lescaut's plan to help her escape fails, and des Grieux begs the captain of the convict ship to allow him to make the crossing and follow Manon to America.

Once arrived in New Orleans, Manon and des Grieux manage to escape the authorities. They wander out into the desert and there, starving, delirious and despairing, Manon dies in des Grieux's arms.

What to listen for

A badly proportioned work – Acts I and II seem too long compared to Acts III and IV, and for all the outbursts of ardour, Puccini fails to convince us that Manon and des Grieux are ever happy with one another, thus reducing the pathos. There's too much doom and gloom, not enough sweetness and tenderness (an imbalance Puccini corrected in *La Bohème*). Manon is presented here not as the fragile and flirtatious teenager that she is in Massenet's opera, but as a passionate, worldly woman best interpreted by the sort of soprano who also sings Tosca – there are some big high Cs and heavy climaxes to negotiate. The attraction of the role is a pair of strongly expressive arias, 'In quelle trine morbide' and 'Sola, perduta, abbandonata', the latter in effect an electrifying death scene. The tenor doesn't have it easy either: many of Puccini's roles for this voice (Cavaradossi, Rodolfo and Pinkerton, for example) are relatively easy to sing, but des Grieux demands stamina and a wide range – his finest moment coming at the end of Act III as he pleads to be allowed to board the deportees' ship.

In performance

An awkward piece to direct, and one which does not happily move out of the rococo period; the best scene, theatrically speaking, is the brief but gripping Act III, in which the dockside parade of deported prostitutes provides an opportunity for members of the chorus to overact. Designers have a problem with Act IV, set in the Louisiana 'desert', and often present it as though the lovers remain in Paris as pariahs, the city's glamour turned bleakly hostile and imprisoning.

Recording

CD: Mirella Freni (Manon); Placido Domingo (Des Grieux); Giuseppe Sinopoli (cond.). DG 413 893 2

La Bohème

Four acts. First performed Turin, 1896.
Libretto by Luigi Illica and Giuseppe Giacosa

Loosely based on Henri Murger's novel and play *Scènes de la vie de Bohème*, and Puccini's recollections of his own student days. Leoncavallo's *La Bohème*, with a plot line that gives more prominence to Marcello and Musetta, was written simultaneously, amid much rivalry and dissension between the two composers. It had some initial success, but was soon thoroughly overshadowed by Puccini's version. Modern revivals, however, show that it has its own charms.

∾ Plot

Rodolfo the poet, Marcello the painter, Colline the philosopher and Schaunard the musician live a cheerful but hand-to-mouth existence in a Parisian garret, *circa* 1840. On Christmas Eve, they are about to consume an unexpected feast, only to be interrupted by the landlord demanding rent. The Bohemians humiliate him. When his friends go out on the tiles, Rodolfo stays in to write. There is a timid knock on the door – it is Mimi, an impoverished consumptive seamstress who lives in the apartment below and she has come in search of a light for her candle. After some innocently scheming flirtation, Rodolfo tells Mimi about himself and she responds with an account of her own life. Soon they are falling in love, and Rodolfo invites Mimi to join his friends at the Café Momus. There they witness a rumpus, as Marcello's former lover Musetta arrives with an elderly admirer, Alcindoro. Eventually, Musetta and Marcello are reunited and as the party leaves to follow the Christmas celebrations, Alcindoro is left with a huge bill.

A couple of months later, on a cold winter's morning, Mimi seeks out Marcello at the inn by the city gates where he is painting. She begs him for help with Rodolfo, whose jealousy is becoming intolerable. Mimi hides as Rodolfo appears and gives his side of the story, followed by a lament for Mimi's terrible physical condition. Mimi emerges, and as Marcello begins another quarrel with Musetta, she and Rodolfo agree to stay together until spring.

Some weeks later, both couples have split up. Rodolfo and Marcello try to work, but their thoughts turn to their lost loves. They are joined by Colline and Schaunard in some horseplay. Suddenly Musetta bursts in with the dying Mimi. Musetta sells her earrings and Colline pawns his coat in order to pay for some medicine, but it is too late. Mimi and Rodolfo briefly remember happier days, and then she quietly passes away, leaving Rodolfo desolate.

❧ What to listen for

Act I contains the opera's most famous music, in the shape of the charming sequence in which Mimi (soprano) and Rodolfo (tenor) become acquainted and fall precipitately in love: first comes Rodolfo's aria 'Che gelida manina' (often transposed down a semitone for the sake of tenors frightened of its top C), answered by Mimi's 'Sì, mi chiamano Mimì', and culminating in the ensuing duet 'O soave fanciulla'. Mimi's final floated top C is easy enough to reach, so long as Puccini's direction to sing it from off-stage is followed, allowing the soprano to attack it at an easier mezzo-forte which the audience should hear as an ethereal piano. The soprano Mary Garden remembered how radiant a celebrated early Mimi, Dame Nellie Melba, could make the note: 'it left Melba's body, it left everything and came over like a star . . . and went out into the infinite'.

Musetta used to be cast with squeaky soubrettes, but the fashion now is to mark the contrast with Mimi's lyric soprano by giving the role to a stronger voice with the heft to ride the din at the end of Act II. Marcello (baritone), Schaunard (baritone) and Colline (bass) are all enticing and uncomplicated roles for young singers, with Colline's haunting farewell to his old coat, 'Vecchia Zimarra', in Act IV winning him a moment of prominence late in the evening.

Nothing could demonstrate Puccini's genius as a musical dramatist better than Act III, the scene at the city gates. The music provides a seamlessly fluent twenty minutes which seems to move in a perfect curve, immaculately attuned to the wintry atmosphere and the emotions of the characters. The end of the opera is perhaps too heavy with musical reminiscence of what has gone before, but the final effect should never be merely sentimental – there's bitterness and anger in the stabbing chords which mark Mimi's death, and one should remember that, historically speaking, these Bohemians would soon be manning the barricades of revolution.

✍ In performance

An absolutely fail-safe piece, which can survive any mauling or incompetence but which works best when played by a good-looking young cast in a smallish house. Today, it is frequently updated – Jonathan Miller (at the Opéra Bastille) took it into the 1930s; both Baz Luhrmann (for Australian Opera) and Phyllida Lloyd (for Opera North) have successfully translated it to the Paris of 1950s; while David McVicar (for Glyndebourne) gave it a modern American flavour and even showed the Bohemians snorting cocaine. Several productions of the 1980s and 1990s suggested that Mimi was a victim of AIDS; others have presented Mimi as Murger did – a rather more tough, knowing and sexually assertive creature than Puccini shows. But modern settings can't easily convey the sense of young people resourcefully having a good time even though they are cold, hungry and penniless – and sometimes one can forget that *La Bohème* is basically a romantic comedy with a sudden tragic ending.

✍ Recordings

CD: Victoria de Los Angeles (Mimi); Jussi Björling (Rodolfo); Thomas Beecham (cond.). EMI CDS7 47235 8

Angela Gheorghiu (Mimi); Roberto Alagna (Rodolfo): Riccardo Chailly (cond.) Decca 466 070 2

Video: Cheryl Barker (Mimi); Julian Smith (cond.). Directed by Baz Luhrmann. Decca 071 176 3

Tosca

Three acts. First performed Rome, 1900.
Libretto by Luigi Illica and Giuseppe Giacosa

Victorien Sardou's melodrama *La Tosca* was a hugely popular
vehicle for the great French actress Sarah Bernhardt.
Puccini's adaptation strips away much of the play's extraneous
detail, and focuses on strong characterization and dramatic
impetus. Sophisticated opera-goers have little time for *Tosca*:
Joseph Kerman notoriously described it as 'a shabby little
shocker', and Benjamin Britten was appalled by 'its cheapness
and emptiness', but this remains an opera which has held its
huge popularity with the broader public for over a century –
and however glib and nasty it looks on the page, it seldom
fails to work in the theatre.

❧ Plot

Rome, 1800, in the repressive era during which the Bourbon
regime opposed the Napoleonic onslaught. Angelotti, an
escaped prisoner, takes refuge in a chapel of the church of
Sant' Andrea della Valle. Angelotti's friend and fellow freedom-
fighter, the painter Cavaradossi, is working on a painting of
Mary Magdalene – inspired by both Angelotti's sister, the
Marchesa Attavanti, and Cavaradossi's lover, the glamorous
but temperamental prima donna, Floria Tosca. Angelotti
asks Cavaradossi for help, but their plans are interrupted by
the sound of Tosca calling from outside the church.
Irrationally jealous of Cavaradossi's interest in the Marchesa,
she is furious when she detects the latter's presence in his
painting. Cavaradossi reassures her and, after she leaves,
accompanies Angelotti to his villa outside Rome. The Chief
of Police, Baron Scarpia, enters the church, looking for
Angelotti. Tosca returns to find Cavaradossi and is distraught to spot a fan belonging to her rival, the Marchesa,
by his easel. The lecherous Scarpia plays on Tosca's vulner-
abilities, hoping both to snare Angelotti and win Tosca for

himself. False news has come that Napoleon has been defeated at Marengo, and there is fervent singing of a victory *Te
Deum*, led by Scarpia.

Cavaradossi is arrested and brought for interrogation in
Scarpia's rooms in the Palazzo Farnese. Denying all knowledge of Angelotti's hiding-place, he is taken off to be tortured. Tosca appears after singing at a concert. Horrified by
Cavaradossi's screams of agony, she reveals Angelotti's whereabouts to Scarpia. Scarpia summons Cavaradossi back to
humiliate him with Tosca's betrayal, when news is brought
that Napoleon has triumphed after all. Cavaradossi exults at
Scarpia's discomfiture and is then dragged back to prison.
Alone together, Scarpia plays with Tosca, promising that in
return for her sexual favours, Cavaradossi will go free after a
mock-execution at dawn. As he writes out a safe-conduct for
her and Cavaradossi, Tosca spots a table knife. She uses it to
stab him to death.

Cavaradossi awaits execution on the ramparts of the
fortress of Castel Sant' Angelo. Tosca appears and explains
what has happened, assuring him that the firing squad's car-
tridges will be blank. But Scarpia has tricked her: when
Cavaradossi is shot, he falls dead. As Scarpia's body is discovered and soldiers rush to arrest her, Tosca proclaims that she
will meet Scarpia before God and flings herself from the ramparts to her death.

∾ What to listen for

Tosca is a role that falls awkwardly between the domains of
the lyric and dramatic soprano: Act I and 'Vissi d'arte' in Act
II are written for a warm, lyric voice, whereas the scenes with
Scarpia in Act II call for dramatic declamation and some loud,
exposed high Cs above a heavy orchestra. 'Vissi d'arte' falls in
the middle of the latter, and singers often find themselves too
tired to do justice to its calmer, long-breathed legato.
Cavaradossi is in contrast a gratifyingly easy role for a tenor,
with lyric arias at the beginning of Acts I and III, and only Act
II's audience-rousing cries of 'Vittoria! Vittoria!' (sung as he

hears of Napoleon's victory at Marengo) in between. Scarpia is also a gift to a bass-baritone with the right baleful presence. The trouble often comes from conductors who let the orchestra rip, pushing the singers to bellow and take unmusical extra breaths in order to increase volume.

∾ In performance

The classic *Tosca* production is that directed by Franco Zeffirelli, originally produced for Maria Callas and Tito Gobbi in 1964 at Covent Garden – a splendid spectacle, with 'realistic' representations of the interior of Sant' Andrea della Valle, the Palazzo Farnese and the Castel Sant' Angelo, as well as plenty of dramatic exits and entrances. Jonathan Miller's updating of the opera to Fascist Italy of the early 1940s (a production first seen in Florence) didn't work as well as one might have anticipated. Elsewhere, directors such as Nikolaus Lehnhoff (in Amsterdam) have striven for a more expressionistic approach to the piece, emphasizing its brutal and sadistic sexuality. On the latter note, it is important that Scarpia emerges as more magnetic and domineering than the clean-cut romantic Cavaradossi – Act II becomes much more exciting if there is a sense that Tosca is unconsciously fighting against her attraction to him. And Tosca should convey that the woman is not only a prima donna, in all senses of the term, but also a resourceful peasant who knows how to make a bargain and when to break a vow.

There is no more popular operatic myth than the one about the fat prima donna playing Tosca who leaps from the parapet and then bounces back into the audience's view from the waiting trampoline or mattress below. Making this climax convincing is certainly a problem for the singer and director, but no firm evidence of any Tosca reapppearing in this manner has ever been cited.

∾ Recordings

CD: Maria Callas (Tosca); Tito Gobbi (Scarpia); Victor de Sabata (cond.). EMI 47 175 8

Angela Gheorghiu (Tosca); Ruggero Raimondi (Scarpia); Antonio Pappano (cond.). EMI 557 173 2

Madama Butterfly

Two (or three) acts. First performed Milan, 1904.
Libretto by Luigi Illica and Giuseppe Giacosa

Based on a play by David Belasco, in turn dramatized from a short story based on an actual incident involving a Scottish whisky importer named Glover, whose geisha bride committed hara-kiri when he abandoned her. Puccini first saw Belasco's play performed in English in London, and without understanding a word of it, instantly saw its operatic potential. The first performance was a disaster, however, and Puccini withdrew the score to make substantial alterations. The revised version – with Pinkerton's character softened and less space given to the comedy of Butterfly's relations in Act I – was instantly a huge success and the opera went on to be one of the most admired and influential of the early twentieth century. Puccini continued to tinker with the score, and the resulting variants account for small differences that those familiar with the opera may note between various productions.

∾ Plot

Nagasaki, in the mid-nineteenth century. Goro the marriage broker arranges for the visiting American naval lieutenant Pinkerton to marry the beautiful fifteen-year-old geisha Cio-Cio-San, nobly born but now orphaned and impoverished, known as Madama Butterfly. The American consul Sharpless counsels caution: he is worried that Butterfly has renounced her religion in preparation for life as an American wife, whereas Pinkerton is clearly an easy-going fellow who will not take the marriage seriously. The wedding goes ahead, interrupted by Butterfly's uncle who curses Butterfly for betraying her religion and her roots. The couple are finally left alone: Butterfly is shy and doubting, until Pinkerton reassures her with expressions of his ardour and loyalty.

Three years later, and Pinkerton is long gone, leaving Butterfly with a little son known as Trouble. Butterfly still clings to a belief that Pinkerton will honour a promise to come back to her and refuses an offer of marriage from the wealthy and eligible Prince Yamadori. Her servant Suzuki is appalled, not least as money is fast running out. Sharpless has heard that Pinkerton is about to return – with his new American wife. He starts to tell Butterfly, who is so overjoyed by the first part of the news that Sharpless cannot bear to continue and let her know the whole truth. A cannon in the harbour announces the docking of Pinkerton's ship. Butterfly and Suzuki decorate the house with flowers in his honour and sit up all night waiting for his arrival.

Next morning, as a disappointed and exhausted Butterfly sleeps, Pinkerton appears with his wife Kate and Sharpless. Pinkerton tells Suzuki that he has come to take his son back to America. He is, however, stricken with remorse, and cannot face confronting Butterfly in person. When the situation is explained to her, Butterfly reacts with dignity, wishes the new Mrs Pinkerton well and asks the visitors to leave her alone for half an hour; Pinkerton may then have his son. Butterfly then commits hara-kiri, expiring just as Pinkerton returns.

∾ What to listen for

Butterfly is one of the most coveted roles in the Italian soprano's repertoire, not least as she is seldom off-stage and the tenor has such a thoroughly subsidiary part to play! There are difficulties, however. Although the role requires enormous stamina and a note of steely determination, it also needs fragility, pathos and charm – a combination which among recent prima donnas, only Renata Scotto has filled to perfection. Another problem is that Butterfly's entrance is an enormous hurdle – before the singer has had a chance to warm up, Puccini prescribes high-lying phrases, mostly marked piano, with an optional high D flat which few are brave enough to dare. The famous aria 'Un bel dì' in Act II is in fact one of the easier passages, demonstrating Puccini's ability to extract maximum emotional impact from minimal vocal effort; much trickier is the gentle lullaby at the beginning of the second scene of Act II – long phrases and a floated high B being required at a point at which energies are usually flagging.

Pinkerton is not a nice fellow and tenors don't much enjoy playing him: to soften his character, Puccini gave him an aria of remorse in the second scene of Act II, 'Addio, fiorito asil', when he revised the opera. Some critics feel that it does not ring true, and weakens the drama. Sharpless (baritone) and Suzuki (one of Puccini's few roles for mezzo-soprano) are much more sympathetic, but neither of them is given an aria. Other highlights include the rapturous Act I love duet (Puccini's longest); the overwhelming orchestral outburst as Butterfly reveals the existence of her son Trouble to Sharpless; and Butterfly's 'flower' duet with Suzuki, which gives way to the humming chorus and an impassioned orchestral intermezzo which allows the soprano a few minutes to recover herself.

Puccini uses some half-dozen authentic Japanese melodies in the score, accompanied by standard orchestral instruments in strange combinations (harp, piccolo, flute and bells, for instance) and some whole-tone harmonic scales to provide pseudo-oriental colour. In contrast, note the quotation of 'The Star-Spangled Banner' in Act I. This is a far more subtly coloured and harmonized score than either *Tosca* or *La Bohème*, and ranks as one of Puccini's masterpieces.

∾ In performance

Pity the poor Asian soprano forced to sing the title role over and over again, throughout her career, whatever her vocal capacities. Still, Cio-Cio-San is one of the great soprano roles in the Italian repertory, especially now we have grown out of conceiving of Butterfly as a twee, giggling and fan-fluttering ickle-girl and can appreciate a young woman's courage, dignity and strength of character. Good productions, such as those of Graham Vick at ENO and David McVicar for Scottish Opera will also convey a proper sense of the delicate politics of inter-racial marriage against a background of Yankee colonialism (for instance, Butterfly is often shown as dressing in western style following her marriage). Two matters open to interpretation are the degree to which Butterfly can be regarded as mentally dis-turbed in her obsessive determination and belief in Pinkerton's return, and the degree to which Pinkerton truly loves Butterfly when he marries her. Some stagings have introduced elements of classical Nōh and Kabuki vocabulary, but such stylization does not sit happily on either the naturalistic story-line or the overwhelming emotional impact of Puccini's music.

∾ Recording

CD: Renata Scotto (Butterfly); John Barbirolli (cond.).
EMI 769654 2

La Fanciulla del West
(The Girl of the Golden West)

Three acts. First performed New York, 1910.
Libretto by Guelfo Civinini and Carlo Zangarini

Having abandoned ideas of using Marie Antoinette or the Hunchback of Notre Dame as a subject, Puccini returned to David Belasco, whose play had inspired *Madama Butterfly*, for his next opera. *Fanciulla* was given its first performance at the Metropolitan Opera in New York. Despite its huge initial success and the superb score, its libretto has dated badly and today it is less frequently performed than it merits.

∾ Plot

California, during the Gold Rush of the 1850s. In the Polka Saloon, the formidable God-fearing Minnie presides over the

bar and teaches the miners to read and write. It's a struggle –
when the men are not complaining of homesickness, they are
gambling or brawling. News comes of the whereabouts of the
bandit known as Ramerrez. The Sheriff, Jack Rance, woos
Minnie and is jealous of her attentions to the mysterious
stranger Dick Johnson. A member of Ramerrez's gang is captured and offers to lead a posse to Ramerrez's hideout: this is
a ploy to empty the Polka Saloon and allow the bandits to
raid the gold that is kept there. Ramerrez is in fact Johnson,
but he is so smitten with Minnie that he refuses to collaborate
in the plan.

In her log-cabin, Minnie is visited by Johnson. They
declare their love for each other. A sudden blizzard means
that Johnson is obliged to stay the night. When a posse led by
Rance demands admittance, Johnson hides. Rance enters,
announcing that Johnson's cover has been blown and he has
now been identified as Ramerrez. After they leave, Minnie
berates Johnson for his deceit. Johnson explains that when his
bandit-father died six months ago, he was forced into ban-
ditry to feed his mother and brothers. Now, however, he has
fallen under Minnie's spell and vowed to change his wicked
ways. Johnson leaves and is shot at by the posse. Minnie
decides to believe his protestations. She conceals the wounded
man in her loft and denies all knowledge of his whereabouts
when Rance returns. He makes a pass at Minnie, which she
rejects – and he then accuses her of being in love with
Johnson.

Blood falls from the ceiling and Rance uncovers Johnson's
hiding place. Johnson collapses unconscious and Minnie
boldly challenges Rance to three hands of poker. If she wins,
Johnson's life is in her hands; if he wins, both Minnie and
Johnson are his. Rance can never resist a wager. Each wins
one hand, and then Minnie asks Rance to get her a drink.
While he is thus distracted, she removes some cards hidden
in her stocking and wins the third hand with three aces and a
pair. Rance leaves the cabin and Minnie laughs hysterically at
the success of her scheme.

Rance cheats on his bargain and Johnson is captured. A lynch-mob of miners prepare to hang him. With the noose around his neck, Johnson pleads that Minnie should be told he has gone free. At the last minute, Minnie appears on horseback. She appeals to the miners to spare Johnson's life: over hard times, she has given them so much, now she begs them to grant her this one wish. The miners agree, and Minnie and Johnson leave California for a new life together.

✎ What to listen for

Unlike other Puccini soprano roles which mostly lie in the middle of the voice, Minnie (like Turandot) is written for high and low extremes. No singer has ever found it easy, and given that the role also lacks a show-stopping aria (the nearest it gets to one, 'Laggiù nel Soledad', contains a killer high C that has embarrassingly floored several great names), it is not surprising that the part is so difficult to cast.

The tenor has a much easier time – the role of Dick Johnson was written for Enrico Caruso, and 'Ch'ella mi creda', his brief, intensely melodic outpouring in Act III, is an obvious hit tune (according to Lord Harewood, it was very popular with the troops during the First World War). Jack Rance is written for the same sort of singer as Scarpia in *Tosca*.

The score is rich and ambitious, with atmospheric and colourful orchestration. 'Ch'ella mi creda' aside, this is not an opera of extractable numbers (which may provide another reason why it has never won the popularity that is its due), but the scene of the card game between Rance and Minnie is one of Puccini's great theatrical *coups*, and the lavish, intoxicating duets for Minnie and Dick Johnson in Acts I and II show how vastly more subtle and varied a composer he had become since the crudity of *Tosca* a decade earlier. Note the superb curtains to each act – the opera's final moments provide the great original of the 'riding off into the sunset' cliché of so many western movies.

∾ In performance

The tragedy of this marvellous opera is that its gunslinger action and bible-bashing heroine make it almost unstageable without some degree of ludicrousness or parody – and given the additional problem of finding a dramatic soprano who can impersonate Minnie convincingly, it is not surprising that *Fanciulla* is not often heard today. Productions such as that by Robert Carsen in Antwerp actually incorporate elements of the cinematic western, using film clips and conventions in an artful manner. Far better to spend a lot of money building a 'real' log-cabin on stage – as Piero Faggioni did for his fine production at Covent Garden – and try to take the melodrama at its face value.

∾ Recording

CD: Placido Domingo (Dick Johnson); Zubin Mehta (cond.). DG 419 640 2

Il Trittico (*The Trilogy*)

Il Tabarro (*The Cloak*), one act, libretto by Giuseppe Adami; *Suor Angelica* (*Sister Angelica*), one act, libretto by Giovacchino Forzano; *Gianni Schicchi*, one act, libretto by Giovacchino Forzano.
First performed New York, 1918

After *La Fanciulla del West*, Puccini tried his hand at something in the Viennese style of *The Merry Widow*, with its blend of light comedy, gentle romance and sentimental melodies. But *La Rondine* (1912) was only moderately successful, and Puccini was drawn back to the school of violent and erotic French melodrama which had served him so well in *Tosca*: *Il Tabarro* is based on a stage hit of the time, Didier Gold's *L' Houppelande*.

Later, at the prompting of the librettist, he decided to

frame it with a gentler, sentimental tragedy and a sharp comedy – the result being a brilliant exercise in the matching and contrasting of operatic mood, colour and idiom. *Suor Angelica* is an original story; *Gianni Schicchi* is developed from a passing reference to a man who cheated on a will in Canto 30 of Dante's *Inferno*.

∾ Plot

Il Tabarro

A barge moored on the banks of the Seine in Paris. Giorgetta is the pretty young wife of Michele, its gruff, middle-aged owner. She is infatuated with a young stevedore, Luigi, with whom she makes a secret night-time assignation. Luigi will wait for her to give the signal of a lighted match before he approaches the barge.

Michele suspects what is going on, but fails to rekindle his wife's feelings for him. They quarrel and she goes off to bed. Michele sits on the deck and lights a pipe. Watching from the bank, Luigi takes this as the signal from Giorgetta and creeps aboard the barge, only to be seized by Michele, who forces him to confess the affair with Giorgetta and then strangles him to death. He wraps the corpse in Giorgetta's cloak, and triumphantly unfurls it when she comes up on deck.

Suor Angelica

Sister Angelica has been a nun for seven years, without ever hearing from her aristocratic family, who sent her to the convent after she gave birth to an illegitimate son. But now the Abbess tells Angelica that her aunt, an elderly Princess, has come to see her. Angelica is delighted, but the Princess is stern and unforgiving. She wants some documents signed and tells Angelica that her son died two years ago.

Angelica is distraught. She takes poison, then worries that the sin of suicide will damn her and that she will never be united with her son in heaven. Her prayers to the Virgin Mary are answered with a miracle – the Virgin appears, lead-

ing her son towards her. To the sound of heavenly choirs,
Angelica dies happily.

Gianni Schicchi

In a mansion in medieval Florence, Buoso Donati dies. His
relatives weep crocodile tears, thinking only about the money
they will inherit. They are appalled to discover that he has
left everything to a monastery. They decide to solicit the help
of the crafty Gianni Schicchi, whose daughter Lauretta wants
to marry Buoso's nephew Rinuccio. Schicchi agrees to impersonate the dying Buoso and dictate a new will which will
favour the relatives.

A notary is summoned. But the new will which Schicchi
then dictates leaves piffling amounts to the monastery and
the relatives, instead bequeathing the bulk of Buoso's estate
to Schicchi himself. The relatives are furious, but Lauretta
and Rinuccio can now be comfortably married.

❧ What to listen for

Il Tabarro is Puccini's one true exercise in verisimo style, not
only in terms of its lurid, proletarian subject-matter, but also
in its declamatory vocal writing for dramatic soprano
(Giorgetta), tenor (Luigi) and baritone (Michele). Like
Fanciulla, it offers no real set numbers, but colour comes
from the painting of the Parisian landscape and its canalside
characters. The whistle of a tug-boat, a foghorn, automobile
klaxon and an out-of-tune hurdy-gurdy can all be heard.

The entirely female *Suor Angelica* is in contrast more gentle and meandering, at least in the pastoral opening minutes,
with its pretty musical depiction of the nuns going about
their daily business. The opera really takes off dramatically
with the dialogue between the fearsome Princess (contralto)
and abject Angelica (lyric soprano), followed by Angelica's
delicately scored and deeply touching aria, 'Senza mamma', a
lament for her dead son which closes with a testing pianissimo high A. The final scene of the miraculous revelation
uses several off-stage instruments – including two pianos, an

organ, three trumpets and cymbals to enhance the sense of supernatural incursion. Like Butterfly, Angelica is a role which requires occasional bursts of vocal heft (including some screaming!) as well as pathos, fragility and charm – Teresa Stratas is widely considered to have been incomparable in this role. Among the minor roles, that of Suor Genovieffa stands out for some lovely phrases, especially those sung at her entrance.

Gianni Schicchi is full of sharply delineated character roles and is ideally performed in a tightly integrated ensemble of quicksilver responsiveness. Schicchi himself is composed for the sort of baritone who could also sing the title role in Verdi's *Falstaff* – an opera to which *Gianni Schicchi* is clearly indebted. Lauretta is for a young lyric soprano: she has the one famous aria, 'O mio babbino caro' (sung a plea to her father to help her courtship of Rinuccio) but in the dramatic context it should be sung with freshness, simplicity and sincerity rather than as a self-conscious diva's showpiece. It has often been remarked that this is an opera that makes little impact on the gramophone, but it comes delightfully alive in a good live performance.

✎ In performance

Although all three of these operas stand as individual masterpieces and the balance and contrast between them is brilliantly calculated, their total duration (four hours, including two intervals) makes the sum of *Il Trittico* just too long for the ordinary Puccini audience and too draining of an opera house's resources (it is, for instance, virtually impossible to present three such different operas on one unit set and only a limited amount of cross-casting is advisable). Consequently, both *Il Tabarro* and *Gianni Schicchi* often appear paired with one other one-act opera.

In Antwerp, Robert Carsen cleverly skirted these problems by combining the different worlds of the three operas and presenting them all as rehearsals in which the (uncostumed) singers appear to be improvising their roles.

❧ Recording

CD: Renata Scotto (Angelica), Tito Gobbi (Schicchi); Lorin
Maazel (cond.). Sony M3K 79312

Turandot

Three acts. First performed Milan, 1926.
Libretto by Giuseppe Adami and Renato Simoni

Puccini's magnificent last work, left unfinished at his death
from cancer. At the first performance in 1926, the conductor
Arturo Toscanini famously laid down his baton at the point at
which Puccini's score ceased – the funeral procession for Liù
– and announced to the audience, 'The opera ends here
because at this point the maestro died.' But since then
Turandot has customarily been heard in a version completed
from surviving sketches by Puccini's pupil, Franco Alfano.

❧ Plot

In ancient Peking, the cruel but beautiful Princess Turandot
lives only to revenge the rape of her ancestor Lou-Ling. She
will marry anyone who can answer her three riddles, but those
who fail will be executed. All comers have failed the challenge
and suffered the penalty, but when Calaf, son of Timur, the
deposed King of Tartary, arrives in Peking in disguise, accompanied by Timur and the adoring slave girl Liù, he resolves to
try his luck, despite the warnings of Turandot's ministers Ping,
Pang and Pong and the protestations of Timur and Liù.

Ping, Pang and Pong lament the unhappy despotism which
rules over China and long for their rural homes. Presided over
by the elderly Emperor, the ceremony of the three riddles takes
place in the palace before a great crowd. Turandot is dismayed
when Calaf, presenting himself as an anonymous stranger,
answers them all correctly. She claims that she would die of
shame if she had to marry, but the Emperor insists that the

terms of the test are unbreakable. Calaf now presents Turandot with another challenge – if she can discover his name before daybreak, he will release her from her obligation.

Turandot orders that nobody in Peking shall sleep until the stranger's name is uncovered. In the palace gardens, Ping, Pang and Pong attempt to bribe Calaf, but he is adamant. Meanwhile, Timur and Liù have been arrested. To save Timur, Liù steps forward and claims that she alone knows the stranger's name. Under torture, she then refuses to reveal it. Turandot asks her what gives her such magnanimity: love, replies Liù, who then kills herself.

Calaf is left alone with Turandot. He rails at her coldness and cruelty and then kisses her passionately. No man has ever done such a thing to her before, and under the spell of his ardour, her ferocity melts. She begs Calaf to leave with his secret intact, but he tells her his name and puts his life in her hands. In the presence of the Emperor, she announces at dawn she has discovered the stranger's name – it is Love.

∾ What to listen for

With its hints of Debussy, Ravel, Strauss and Schoenberg, the largely choral Act I is a kaleidoscope of early modernistic styles, effects and influences, with an ensemble finale which seems to encapsulate the whole tradition of nineteenth-century Italian opera. Puccini takes a great theatrical risk with Turandot herself – although she makes a brief, silent appearance in Act I, she only begins to sing half-way through Act II, by which point audience expectation is intense. The role is written for a dramatic soprano with an inexhaustible top register: her aria 'In questa reggia', in which she explains the reasons for the challenge of the riddles, is exceptionally difficult in that nothing precedes it, and the voice therefore has had no chance to warm up. Even trickier are the two long climactic phrases at the end of Act II in which she pleads with the Emperor, rising to top Cs which are expected to ride over the orchestra and chorus. It amounts to a gruelling twenty minutes for even the steeliest soprano throats.

Calaf is in comparison a relatively easy role – Puccini is kinder to tenors than he is to sopranos, and it seems unfair that 'Nessun dorma' (made even more famous by Luciano Pavarotti when it was adopted as the official theme-tune for the 1990 World Cup) should earn the singer so much applause for so little effort. It is Liù (lyric soprano), however, who has the most beautiful solo music in the opera: 'Signore, ascolta', the first of her two arias is very exposed, ending with the ascent to a high floated pianissimo B flat which sounds magical if – and it is a big if – it is executed correctly. The trio of Ping (baritone), Pang and Pong (tenors) can have great fun with the witty and elegant interlude that Puccini wrote for them at the beginning of Act II: Ping in particular has some fine lyric phrases.

The orchestration of the opera is dazzling in its exoticism and shimmer. The falling-off in quality when Alfano takes over is palpable – the completion is four-square, if not clumsy, mechanically recycling melodic material from earlier in the opera without imagination or sensitivity. How one regrets the loss of the crowning glory which Puccini would surely have provided for the final love duet! Some performances stop with Liù's funeral procession, but this is hardly satisfactory in the theatre, and several composers, including Luciano Berio, are now attempting to provide this extraordinary opera with a more fulfilling conclusion.

✎ In performance

An opera which can be used as an excuse for pantomime spectacle – as in the hideously overblown oriental kitsch produced by Franco Zeffirelli at the Met, or the much more subtle and elegant staging by Andrei Serban for Covent Garden – or as a piece in which the terror and repression of Turandot's Peking foreshadows the Fascistic authoritarianism which was to overwhelm Italy shortly after Puccini's death.

✎ Recording

CD: Joan Sutherland (Turandot); Luciano Pavarotti (Calaf); Zubin Mehta (cond.). Decca 414 274 2

PART FOUR

French Opera

Until this century, Paris was the undisputed operatic capital of the world, though its glamour and excitement have emanated as much from foreign influences as from native traditions. As early as 1752, the visit to Paris of an Italian *opera-buffa* troupe caused a great stir – its pace, fun and naturalness made the courtly baroque opera–ballets of Lully and Rameau seem slow and cumbersome. Some twenty years later, the operas of a German, Gluck, also caused heated controversy.

The Revolution of 1789 inevitably brought great changes to public taste, opening opera up to a wider audience and the principles of *Liberté*, *Egalité*, *Fraternité*. Composers like André Grétry and Etienne Méhul wrote in the style known as *opéra comique*, in which the static aria gave way to more dynamic musical interchanges. Spoken dialogue was used between numbers, and plots were no longer confined to the dilemmas of aristocratic or mythological personages. Instead, partly inspired by the philosophy of Rousseau, the action embraced exotic settings and supernatural effects, focusing on adventurous deeds of ordinary folk (heroic rescues were particularly popular – a concept borrowed by Beethoven for *Fidelio*).

Thus began the development of nineteenth-century 'Grand Opera'. Heavily subsidized by the state and almost invariably performed at the Paris Opéra (an institution first housed in the rue Le Pelletier and, since 1875, in the Palais Garnier, where it still functions today), this was a form which gradually lost its revolutionary edge to become a mere formula, top-heavy with empty spectacle and stage effects, cynically calculated to appeal to audiences more interested in show than in music. Using some episode in European history, usually connected to the fight against religious or political tyranny, a Parisian 'grand opera' proceeded through the fixed points of a long ballet interlude (often entirely unrelated to the drama); a procession; a duel or battle; a flood, fire or similar cataclysm; a big love duet and a long, loud ensemble for as many people as could be fitted on to the stage – all crammed into the central three of its five acts, so that the fashionable crowd who came late or left early wouldn't miss the highlights.

Although French composers like Daniel Auber made their contributions, many of Paris's grand operas were written by Italian composers: in the early years of the century, Luigi Cherubini and Gasparo Spontini; then Rossini and Donizetti and, finally, Verdi, whose *Don Carlos*, first performed in 1867, is one of the last – and perhaps the greatest – examples of the genre.

But undoubtedly the most successful of grand-opera composers was a German Jew, Giacomo Meyerbeer, who collaborated with the prolific French librettist Eugène Scribe on pieces such as *Les Huguenots* and *Le Prophète* – the mid-nineteenth century's nearest equivalent to the Hollywood epic. Meyerbeer's fame and fortune was bitterly resented by the anti-Semitic Richard Wagner, whose half-hearted attempt to modify his opera *Tannhäuser* for the Paris audience in 1861 was virtually booed off the stage because the ballet occurred too early in the evening.

At a distance from the grand-opera tradition stood one of the great non-conformists of musical history, Hector Berlioz. Like Wagner, he scorned the bombast and parade of Meyerbeer, and proposed a return to the dignity and purity of Gluck. But he was also a romantic dreamer with a lively sense of humour – and too much of an original to have been a success in his own day.

Grand opera primarily appealed to the wealthy and socially pretentious. Middle-class audiences generally preferred Paris's smaller, less daunting and expensive opera houses like the Théâtre-Lyrique and the Opéra-Comique (or Salle Favart), where they enjoyed the easy, tuneful sentimentality of Charles Gounod and the sparkling talent of Georges Bizet, who died young, unaware that in *Carmen* he had written what probably ranks as the world's most popular opera.

The allure of grand opera had declined by the 1870s, and in the final decades of the century, Wagner became the major influence on younger composers. His example was adapted in various ways, all of them related to his idea of continuous music drama, free of barriers between recitative and aria, or song and speech. Jules Massenet (nicknamed 'Mademoiselle Wagner') produced a long series of lushly coloured, erotically explicit melodramas. Gustave Charpentier presented a slice of real contemporary Parisian life in *Louise*. Inspired by the sonorities of *Parsifal*, Claude Debussy created a true masterpiece with *Pelléas et Mélisande*.

Twentieth-century opera in France has not been so lively. Maurice Ravel's short operas have charm and Francis Poulenc's *Dialogues des Carmélites* has a grim power and intensity. But the major composers of the last fifty years seem to have lost confidence in the form: Olivier Messiaen's massive *Saint François d'Assise* is more oratorio than opera, and Pierre Boulez has as yet failed to find a text which he considers theatrically viable.

Nor has modern France managed to produce many first-class singers, despite a high level of public spending on classical music and superbly equipped new buildings such as the Opéra Bastille.

Hector Berlioz (1803–69)
La Damnation de Faust

Four parts. First performed Paris, 1846.
Libretto by Almire Gandonnière and the composer

Berlioz never intended his adaptation of episodes and themes from Goethe's *Faust* to be staged as an opera, and for all its obvious theatrical and pictorial elements, this '*légende drama-tique*' (as the composer labelled it) continues to work best in the concert hall.

The text is based on Gérard de Nerval's translation of Goethe's epic poetic drama.

✵ Plot

In his study, the scholar Faust sings of his joyless isolation. He decides to kill himself, but as he reaches for the poison, the walls of his study part to reveal a church congregation cel-ebrating the resurrection. Faust is heartened to live, but then the devil Mephistopheles appears and offers to fulfil all his earthly desires. After carousing in Auerbach's beer cellar, Faust is enraptured by a vision of the beautiful village girl Marguerite. Through his magic, Mephistopheles arranges for the two of them to meet and fall in love.

Marguerite despairs when she is abandoned by Faust. In a mountain gorge, Faust addresses the majesty of Nature and is then carried off by demons to his damnation. Marguerite, on the other hand, is redeemed as angels usher her into heaven.

✵ What to listen for

An orchestral rather than vocal showpiece, whether in the swagger of the Hungarian March, the crash and bash of the Ride to the Abyss, or the beautiful accompaniments to the arias (for example: the desolate horn of Marguerite's 'D'amour l'ardente flamme' or the pizzicato guitar effect that underpins Mephistopheles's serenade).

The role of Faust lies high for modern tenors, but the chance to sing the rapturous invocation to Nature attracts them anyway; Marguerite can be sung by either mezzo-soprano or soprano, as long as the colour suggests girlish openness and vulnerability; likewise, Mephistopheles cannot be taken by a booming bass, since his arias demand a singer who can move fleetly in an almost baritonal register.

∾ In performance

Because this work was not truly conceived for the stage, producers have used it as an excuse for all sorts of extravagant visual fantasies of mayhem and apocalypse, many of them using film or video elements. Concert performances, in which the mind's eye is allowed to realize its own individual landscapes, are probably more cost-effective and aesthetically satisfying.

∾ Recording

CD: Nicolai Gedda (Faust); Colin Davis (cond.). Philips 416 395 2
DVD: Paul Groves (Faust); Sylvain Cambreling (cond.). Salzburg Festival production. Arthaus Musik 003

Les Troyens (The Trojans)

Two parts and five acts. First performed Paris, 1863 (incomplete). Libretto by the composer

Inspired by Virgil's *Aeneid* and the operas of Gluck, *Les Troyens* is an enormously ambitious work containing four hours of music. In Berlioz's lifetime, only a truncated version of the second half was ever performed and the first truly complete staging did not take place until 1969.

∾ Plot

Part One: La Prise de Troie (The Capture of Troy)

After years of a futile siege, the Greeks have apparently left their camp outside Troy, leaving behind only a large wooden horse. The Trojans are overjoyed, but King Priam's daughter Cassandra (Cassandre) prophesies doom. Her lover Chorebus (Chorebe) fails to console her. Celebrations are interrupted by Andromache, the grieving widow of Prince Hector, a casualty of war, and by news from Prince Aeneas (Enée) that a priest who threw a javelin into the wooden horse's flank has been devoured by two serpents. Aeneas thinks that the goddess Athena needs to be appeased, so the horse is dragged into her temple within the city walls.

Hector's ghost appears to Aeneas and tells him that Troy has fallen – Greek soldiers have disgorged from the belly of the wooden horse and set fire to the city. Hector commands Aeneas to leave Troy with his son Ascanius (Ascagne) and establish a new empire in Italy. In the Temple of Vesta, Cassandra discovers that Aeneas has fled and Chorebus has been killed in the fighting. Fired by a vision of the glory awaiting the Trojans in Italy, Cassandra and the temple virgins choose death rather than dishonour at the hands of the marauding Greeks.

Part Two: Les Troyens à Carthage (The Trojans at Carthage)

In Carthage, a new colony founded by fugitives from Tyre, citizens gather to hail the widowed Queen Dido (Didon) and celebrate their prosperity – threatened only by the king of neighbouring Numidia, who claims Dido's hand and Carthaginian territory. The Trojan fleet is blown to the shores of Carthage. Dido offers generous hospitality, remembering her own experiences as a refugee. Aeneas disguises himself and allows his son Ascanius to speak for the Trojans, but he throws off his disguise when Dido's minister Narbal announces that the Numidians have invaded and announces that he is ready to fight in Carthage's defence.

An orchestral interlude, the 'Royal Hunt and the Storm', depicts how Dido and Aeneas fall in love after they are forced to shelter in a cave when a storm interrupts their hunt. Back at the court, Carthage celebrates the success of Aeneas's war against the Numidians. After Dido and Aeneas rejoice in their mutual love, the god Mercury reminds Aeneas of his duty to establish a new empire in Italy.

Aeneas is torn, but after visitations from Trojan ghosts, he decides that he must do his duty and leave for Italy. Dido is enraged at Aeneas's desertion. Impelled by a mixture of remorse, vindictiveness and misery, she commands the construction of a pyre on which all relics of the Trojans are burnt. As the Carthaginians add their curses, Dido stabs herself. But before she dies, she is granted a disturbing vision of her descendant Hannibal, defeated by the glory of the empire that Aeneas is destined to establish – Rome.

∾ What to listen for

A score of astonishing richness, at its most relentlessly intense in the breathtaking Part One, dominated by the baleful figure of Cassandra, set against the extraordinary power of the choruses. Note the exquisitely melancholy clarinet solo which accompanies the widowed Andromache's mute appearance. Part Two blossoms into a more sensuous charm, grace and emotional variety: the elegant anthem 'Gloire à Didon' and the relaxed, expansive duet for Dido and Anna, the brilliant orchestral scene-painting of the 'Royal Hunt and the Storm', the wonderful way in which a quintet becomes a septet celebrating the glory of a starlit night and modulates into Dido and Aeneas's sublimely lilting love duet; the sailor Hylas's evocative aria of homesickness, 'Vallon sonore', and the alternating grief and fury to which the betrayed Dido gives vent before the solemn rituals of the final scene and the triumphant restatement of the Trojan March as it makes its way to its Roman destiny. Note also Berlioz's arrestingly sinister handling of the ghostly apparitions.

Aeneas lies both uncomfortably high and low for modern tenors and requires soft high notes that most of them simply can't produce. It is also a long role which explodes periodically rather than building steadily: of recent interpreters, only the wilfully individualistic Jon Vickers has been decisively successful with it, and even someone as versatile as Placido Domingo had to retire defeated before its demands. Cassandra and Dido should be strongly contrasted: Cassandra belongs in the Gluckian classical tradition – a fierce, strong character requiring a high mezzo-soprano with fire in her belly; Dido is a warmer mezzo-soprano of more Romantic hue, but she too must find the power for the emotional turmoil of the final scenes.

ᏉᎳ In performance

With its ballets, huge chorus, and massive set changes, *Les Troyens* presents a daunting challenge for an opera house, and only the bravest stage it on one evening – with intervals, a complete performance lasts well over five hours. Aside from whatever they make of the sheer spectacular possibilities (such as the appearance of the Trojan horse), directors can also point an interesting contrast between the doomed grandeur of the embattled, decadent, hierarchical Trojan civilization and the younger, more open, vulnerable and energetic colony of Carthage. To convey the latter, several productions have chosen to evoke images of New World Puritanism and clean-living, free-thinking rural Shaker settlements.

ᏉᎳ Recording

CD: Ben Heppner (Aeneas); Colin Davis (cond.).
LSO Live 0010

Béatrice et Bénédict

Two acts. First performed Baden-Baden, 1862.
Libretto by the composer

An adaptation of Shakespeare's *Much Ado about Nothing*, originally intended as a one-act divertissement and written almost as relaxation after the rigours of *Les Troyens*.

❧ Plot

Hero, daughter of the governor of Messina, loves Claudio. Bénédict and Béatrice pretend to despise each other, and engage in witty repartee. A plot is hatched by their friends to make them fall in love. The music master Somarone rehearses a local choir. Béatrice and Bénédict acknowledge their true feelings, and are married alongside Hero and Claudio.

❧ What to listen for

Berlioz described the score as 'a caprice written with the point of a needle' and it requires the lightest of touches from everyone concerned, not least the conductor. The tenor role of Bénédict has nothing much to offer, but Béatrice is a gift to a mezzo-soprano with wit and personality (though the last page of her Act II aria lies very high). Lyric sopranos singing Hero often stumble when it comes to the clumsily composed coloratura passage Berlioz writes at the end of her aria.

The highlight of this delicately orchestrated score is undoubtedly the sublimely simple nocturne for Hero and Ursula at the end of Act I.

❧ In performance

The drama is very feeble, with much of what makes Shakespeare's play complex and interesting (such as the figure of Don John) simply omitted and the focus firmly placed on the silly love-intrigue plot. The character of the music-master Somarone gives all too much room for a comic turn, with often extremely tiresome results. The spoken dialogue is generally an embarrassment to singers (passages from Shakespeare's text are customarily used in productions performed in English). But for all that, the opera has great charm.

❧ Recording

CD: Janet Baker (Béatrice); Colin Davis (cond.).
Philips 416 952 2

Charles Gounod (1818–93)
Faust

Five acts. First performed Paris, 1859.
Libretto by Jules Barbier and Michel Carré

Adapted from the first part of Goethe's *Faust* to suit the sentimental French taste. It is an opera which has never recovered the extraordinary popularity it enjoyed in the late nineteenth century, but audiences invariably respond to the richness of melody and theatricality whenever it is revived today.

∾ Plot

Longing to recover his youth, the elderly scholar Faust calls on the devil Mephistopheles, who shows him an alluring vision of the beautiful but humbly born maiden Marguerite. Faust agrees to a pact – in return for his immortal soul, Mephistopheles will restore him to youth and grant all his earthly desires.

In the town square, a summer fair is being celebrated. Faust and the disguised Mephistopheles appear, and encounter Marguerite's brother Valentin, just off to the wars, and her admirer, Siebel. Mephistopheles wreaks some demonic magic on the revellers, until Valentin uses his broken sword to make the sign of the cross. Faust meets Marguerite, who is passing on her way from church.

Siebel leaves a modest bunch of flowers for Marguerite in her garden. Mephistopheles replaces them with a casket of jewels: when Marguerite finds them, she is entranced by their glitter. Mephistopheles distracts the attention of Marguerite's friend Marthe, allowing Faust to declare himself to the susceptible Marguerite. They agree to meet the next day, but after a little resistance, Marguerite allows Faust into her bedroom – much to Mephistopheles's amusement.

Faust abandons Marguerite, leaving her with a baby. Siebel remains steadfast, but Marguerite continues to believe that Faust will return. She enters a church to pray, but

Mephistopheles taunts her. Valentin returns from the wars, discovers his sister's disgrace and challenges Faust to a duel. Helped by Mephistopheles, Faust wins the fight. With his dying breath, Valentin curses Marguerite.

Mephistopheles attempts to distract Faust with visions of famous courtesans, but he insists on returning to Marguerite, who is in prison awaiting execution, having gone mad and killed her baby. He begs her to escape with him, but she refuses. As she dies, a choir of angels is heard promising her redemption.

∾ What to listen for

Originally written with passages of dialogue, but now customarily performed with the sung recitatives which Gounod added – along with an elaborate 'Walpurgisnacht' ballet – for a later production.

A score which intellectuals scorn today, but which is full of rich, sweet Victorian melody – Faust's elegant 'Salut, demeure chaste et pure'; the Soldiers' chorus and Kermesse waltz; Marguerite's ballad of the 'Roi de Thulé', Jewel and Spinning Songs; charming numbers for the baritone Valentin ('Avant de quitter ces lieux') and light mezzo-soprano Siebel ('Faites-lui mes aveux'); and the show-stopping final trio.

Faust is a role for lyric tenor, with some very high notes (in the duet with Marguerite) that modern singers often omit or fudge. Marguerite is a grateful, well-paced role for lyric soprano which requires a light touch for the Jewel Song but no coloratura; the only real difficulty is the final trio, where the faint-voiced can run out of puff and end up drowned out by the orchestra.

The opera is long if performed complete, and cuts are often made to get the audience out in under four hours.

∾ In performance

The seduction of a peasant girl by a lubricious gentleman was a favourite Victorian theme, and contemporary productions like Frank Corsaro's for Chicago take the sexual politics seriously. A much-travelled production by Ian Judge, originally for ENO, presents the final scene in a lunatic asylum. Bad taste and bare breasts often come to the fore in the Walpurgisnacht ballet.

∾ Recording

CD: Richard Leech (Faust); Cheryl Studer (Marguerite); Michel Plasson (cond.). EMI 5 4624 2

Roméo et Juliette

Five acts. First performed Paris, 1867.
Libretto by Jules Barbier and Michel Carré

The most successful of some forty operatic adaptations of Shakespeare's play, focused on a series of lavish duets for the star-cross'd lovers. Hugely popular before the First World War, it has now become a vehicle for glamorous star couples like Roberto Alagna and Angela Gheorghiu.

∾ Plot

Broadly the same as Shakespeare's play, with the addition of a larger role for Roméo's page Stéphano, and less prominence given to Mercutio and the Nurse. The opera opens at the Capulets' masked ball.

∾ What to listen for

Giving the tenor (Roméo) and soprano (Juliette) four duets is probably a gesture unprecedented in operatic history: they develop in lyrical voluptuousness, culminating in the final scene where, unlike the play, Juliette wakes in good time to be reunited with Roméo. This fifteen-minute encounter is musically unusual for its time in its freedom of form and phrase-length.

Juliette's coloratura waltz song comes very early in the opera. It contains trills, chromatic runs and a top D and should brim with girlish verve and spontaneity – nervous sopranos find it difficult to sing before they have had a chance to warm up and settle down. The poison scene requires a much heavier voice, and is sometimes cut to spare the lighter soprano's cords.

Like so many French tenor roles, Roméo lies high for modern singers, and the aria 'Ah! lève-toi, soleil' is often transposed down a semitone to help them negotiate it. Stéphano offers a young mezzo-soprano a pretty aria, 'Que fais-tu', and the baritone singing Mercutio can take centre-stage in the virtuosic Queen Mab ballad.

∾ In performance

Irretrievably a piece of its period, and not one which benefits from ambitious directorial interpretation. The important thing is that the tenor looks good in tights and that Juliette makes a plausible object of amorous desire. As with *Faust*, the complete score is too long for the taste of a modern audience, and it generally benefits from a few cuts

∾ Recording

CD: Roberto Alagna (Roméo); Angela Gheorghiu (Juliette); Michel Plasson (cond.). EMI 5 56123 2
DVD: Roberto Alagna (Roméo); Charles Mackerras (cond.). Covent Garden production. Pioneer 425736 089 259

Ambroise Thomas (1811–96)
Hamlet

Five acts. First performed Paris, 1868.
Libretto by Jules Barbier and Michel Carré

Thomas was a successful composer of lighter works, who spent six years composing *Hamlet* in an attempt to rise to the grand style – with its spectacular processions and extended ballets – favoured by the Paris Opéra. Fine roles for coloratura soprano (Ophelia) and baritone (Hamlet) have ensured the opera's survival and in recent years the work's considerable dramatic merits have been increasingly appreciated.

∾ Plot

Broadly the same as Shakespeare's play, allowing for an enlarged role for Ophelia, the elimination of Hamlet's murder of Polonius and subsequent exile, and the deletion of minor characters such as Fortinbras, Osric and Rosencrantz and Guildenstern. The chief difference is the ending, in which Hamlet finally kills Claudius and is proclaimed King of Denmark.

∾ What to listen for

Heavily sugared in terms of its harmonic and melodic style, this opera can none the less exert considerable dramatic impact when sung by artists of the calibre of Simon Keenlyside and Natalie Dessay. The role of Hamlet is one of the first of several star parts which French opera offers to a high baritone rather than a tenor (who has to be content with the insignificant role of Laertes). His vocal opportunities include a bravura drinking song, red-blooded duets and encounters with the Ghost, Ophelia and Gertrude.

The other first-rate role is that of Ophelia. Her mad scene is among the most difficult in the repertory, with tricky intervals and chromatic scales. The section which begins 'Pâle et

blonde' is based on a Swedish folk song and was introduced
by the soprano Christine Nilsson, the first Ophelia.

✧ In performance

There is no use in pretending that the opera is comparable in
depth or complexity to Shakespeare's play, as over-enthusias-
tic directors have occasionally tried to suggest. Treating it as
a romantic Victorian melodrama, with good special effects
for the appearance of the Ghost, is a more satisfactory
approach.

✧ Recording

CD: Thomas Hampson (Hamlet); Antonio de Almeida
(cond.). EMI 7 54820 2

Georges Bizet (1838–75)
Les Pêcheurs de Perles

Three acts. First performed Paris, 1863.
Libretto by Eugène Cormon and Michel Carré

Composed at great speed when Bizet was only twenty-four, this opera did not enjoy initial success and was only revived, in a tastelessly edited version, after his death. Today, most of Bizet's original intentions are honoured again, although the tenor–baritone duet 'Au fond du temple saint' continues to overshadow its other fragrant charms.

∾ Plot

On a beach in Ceylon, the pearl fishers elect Zurga to be their king. His friend Nadir returns from his wanderings, and the two young men recall how they once simultaneously set eyes on a beautiful girl in a Hindu temple and both fell in love with her. But their friendship came first, and they vowed not to pursue her.

A veiled lady appears, accompanied by Nourabad, High Priest of Brahma. She has been selected to protect and pray for the pearl fishers as they dive for their dangerous trade. Nadir recognizes her as the beautiful girl from the temple. Her name is Leïla, and she has taken a vow of chastity. Nevertheless, she and Nadir fall deeply in love.

Nourabad spots this and denounces the lovers to the people. Zurga intervenes, but when he recognizes Leïla and realizes that Nadir has broken his oath of friendship, he orders their execution. Later, Zurga is filled with remorse. But when he sees how strong Leïla's love for Nadir remains, he refuses her clemency. As she leaves, Leïla asks a fisherman to take her necklace to her mother. Zurga recognizes this necklace as the one he once gave to a young girl who had saved his life.

Before the sacrificial pyre, Leïla and Nadir await their death. Just before the fatal moment, Zurga appears and distracts Nourabad and the bloodthirsty crowd with news that the camp which forms their home has been set on fire. As they all rush off to save their possessions, Zurga frees Nadir and Leïla, explaining that he is the man whose life Leïla once saved and that he deliberately started the fire to save her life in return. Nadir and Leïla flee, with Zurga's blessing.

ᕒ What to listen for

No less a personage than Berlioz thought that this opera contained 'a considerable number of beautiful, expressive pieces full of fire and rich colouring'. Today, it may seem dramatically pallid, and its pseudo-oriental harmonies and melisma merely quaint, but Berlioz was not wrong. A well-cast performance reveals much more than one memorable duet (the central tune of which, 'Oui, c'est elle, c'est la déesse', makes a couple too many thumping appearances in the opera as a result of posthumous editing of the score). Leïla is, like Gounod's Juliette, a role which starts with high, fleet coloratura and then descends in the duet with Zurga (baritone) to more dramatic territory which leaves lighter voices gasping. Bizet's markings for Nadir's evocatively orchestrated aria 'Je crois entendre' suggest that he intended Nadir to be sung by a sweet-voiced tenor with a clean, pure head voice. Today, it has passed to coarser, chestier types, and the aria sometimes has to be transposed down to accommodate them.

Bizet himself recognized the relative weakness of Act III.

ᕒ In performance

Few productions have succeeded in suggesting the oriental setting without descending into cardboard kitsch, but it is impossible to update or change the setting. One ingenious solution, adopted by Nicolas Joel in Chicago, was to present the action within the frame of a Victorian gentleman's club. Two of its members recline on divans and smoke hookahs, and the opera then unfolds like their opium dream.

∾ Recording

CD: Henri Legay (Nadir); André Cluytens (cond.).
EMI 565 266 2

Carmen

Four acts. First performed Paris, 1875.
Libretto by Henri Meilhac and Ludovic Halévy

Adapted from a superb short story by Prosper Mérimée, *Carmen* was considered shockingly obscene when it was first performed and Bizet tragically died three months later under the impression that the opera had failed. Within a few years, however, it had swept the world, even winning the admiration of the philosopher Friedrich Nietzsche, who favourably compared its 'light feet' and Mediterranean qualities to Wagner's decadent Teutonic gloom and pretension.

∾ Plot

The timid village girl Micaëla arrives in Seville with a letter from the mother of a young corporal, Don José, who is stationed outside a cigarette factory. José thinks that he loves Micaëla, until one of the factory girls, a gypsy called Carmen, flirtatiously throws a red flower at his feet and captivates him with her sexual allure. Later, Carmen is arrested after a brawl in the factory. When she is put under José's guard, he besottedly allows her to escape, thus earning himself time in jail and loss of rank.

A month or so later, in Lillas Pastia's low dive of a tavern, Carmen consorts with her friends Frasquita and Mercédès and some officers. Escamillo, a glamorous toreador, appears. He is attracted to Carmen, but she is still intrigued by José, who has just been released from prison. After Escamillo leaves, José enters the tavern and he confesses to Carmen that he is infatuated with her. Carmen taunts him seductively and he ignores the trumpet recalling him to barracks. Instead, he decides to become an outlaw, joining up with Carmen and a group of smugglers.

In the smugglers' mountain lair, Carmen's relationship with José is soon breaking up, and she sees her impending death in the cards. A frightened Micaëla appears in search of José with news that his mother is dying. Escamillo fights José over Carmen. She sides with Escamillo, and accepts his invitation to a bullfight. José remains determined to win Carmen back.

Outside the bullring, crowds hail Escamillo, who is accompanied by Carmen. Her friends warn that the enraged José is pursuing her, but she fatalistically stays her ground. Inside the bullring, Escamillo triumphs as José confronts Carmen and begs for her love. When she refuses, he kills her and gives himself up to the authorities.

❧ What to listen for

Familiarity with its marvellous tunes blinds us to the genius with which *Carmen* has been put together. It is a hugely original and influential work which combines the traditions of *opéra-comique* – the quintet in Act II and the smugglers, for example – with a stark emotional realism which is quite new to opera and which becomes most vivid in the duel of a duet between Carmen and Don José in Act IV. The scoring is brilliant (particularly in relation to the wind section), the flow of melody ceaseless and, despite some muddle in Act III, the cumulative dramatic impact enthralling – no wonder *Carmen* has been so widely and consistently popular.

The title role was originally written for the small, light voice of Célestine Galli-Marié, but today the tendency is to seek out bigger, fruitier mezzo-sopranos who end up blasting their way through the Habanera and Seguedilla at the cost of all its seductiveness and subtlety, even if they can let themselves go impressively in the no-holds-barred final scene. Because the role does not lie particularly low, it is also possible for sopranos – Emma Calvé, Maria Callas and

Victoria de los Angeles among them – to sing the role successfully. The same is true of Don José, evidently intended
for a light tenor but now the province of meatier singers, like
Placido Domingo, who need to cut the high-lying Act I duet
with Micaëla and ignore the instruction to end the Flower
Song with a B flat pianissimo. Micaëla is a deceptive role: the
character may be all girlish innocence in contrast to
Carmen's sexual knowingness, but her aria in Act III
demands a rich and womanly lyric soprano; Escamillo is
graced with the thumping hit of the Toreador's song, but
basses find the role lies too high and baritones find it lies too
low, and nobody has ever made his macho strutting anything
but faintly ridiculous.

✕ In performance

In an effort to leave behind tapas-bar, picture-postcard views
of southern Spain, directors have adopted various twentieth-
century proletarian settings – the Spanish Civil War and the
banana republics being prevalent. Other clichés of *Carmen*
productions include the image of the bullring, the flamenco
troupe and a figure representing *duende* or Fate.

Several versions have more radically adapted or cannibal-
ized the opera: Oscar Hammerstein, for example, located the
plot in a black American environment for a musical comedy
version, *Carmen Jones*; while in *La tragédie de Carmen*, the
director Peter Brook stripped the piece back and used the
music to illustrate something closer to Mérimée's original
and the realities of gypsy life.

There are some minor textual problems: until the 1970s,
Carmen was regularly performed in a version with sung
recitative (composed by Ernest Guiraud after Bizet's death) in
place of the original spoken dialogue. Since the publication of
Fritz Oeser's scholarly edition of the score in 1964, the dialogue has been generally restored, though scholars argue
over Oeser's inclusion of passages of music (notably in Act
III) which Bizet had himself discarded in his edition of the
vocal score.

Outstanding Carmens of recent years – all mezzo-sopranos – include Teresa Berganza, Agnes Baltsa, Maria Ewing and Denyce Graves.

∾ Recordings

CD: Victoria de los Angeles (Carmen); Thomas Beecham (cond.). EMI 5 67357 2

Video: Maria Ewing (Carmen); Bernard Haitink (cond.), Glyndebourne production. Warner 4509 9949 4

DVD: Agnes Baltsa (Carmen); James Levine (cond.). Met production. DG 073 000 9

Camille Saint-Saëns (1835–1921)
Samson et Dalila

Three acts. First performed Weimar, 1877.
Libretto by Ferdinand Lemaire

Originally classified as an oratorio because of its biblical subject (based on the story in the Book of Judges), *Samson et Dalila* is invariably regarded today as a banquet of a grand opera with all the spectacular trimmings.

∾ Plot

The Hebrews are held captive by the Philistines in Gaza. Their leader Samson leads them in prayer. When Abimelech, the Philistine governor, mocks the God of Israel, Samson kills him. The High Priest of Dagon curses Samson and enlists the Philistine maiden Dalila to seduce him. Despite warnings, Samson submits to her dazzling charms.

The High Priest goads Dalila to take revenge on Samson, whose amazing strength has just led to the defeat of the Philistines in battle. Dalila, a patriot, needs no encouragement. Samson appears, determined to put an end to his dalliance with Dalila and lead the Hebrews on to total victory, but again she seduces him, and ekes out the secret of his strength – his long hair. Philistine soldiers arrest Samson. His hair is shorn and he is imprisoned, blinded and forced to drive a mill-wheel. Overcome with remorse, he decides to sacrifice his life to save his people.

Inside the temple of Dagon, the Philistines exult in an orgy. Samson is led in to be mocked, and Dalila reveals the plot behind her treachery. But Samson finds his way to the two marble pillars which support the temple, and after a prayer to God, manages to muster enough strength to push the pillars down and destroy the temple, thus massacring the pagan revellers as well as putting an end to himself and Dalila.

∾ What to listen for

Samson et Dalila offers the tenor and mezzo-soprano taking the title roles a magnificent series of vocal opportunities: for Samson the virile declamation of his opening address to the Hebrews and his noble Act III mill-wheel lament; for Dalila, three gorgeously sensual arias, 'Printemps qui commence', 'Mon coeur s'ouvre' and 'Amour! viens aider'. Red-blooded voices are required to ride the sumptuous orchestration, but the only drawback is that the opera is in French, a language which few non-native speakers can enunciate with any eloquence or subtlety. Wagnerism manifests itself in the use of motifs and in the dramatic musical dialogue between Samson and Dalila in Act II.

The chorus is the opera's third principal character: as the Hebrews in Act I, it has been suggested, they sound under the austere influence of Bach, while as the Philistines in Act III they become more rumbustiously Handelian.

∾ In performance

Most productions have apparently been directed in the spirit of Cecil B. de Mille, with the Act III Bacchanal providing the perfect excuse for a display of cavorting flesh, floating veils and spangled jockstraps. Sadly, today's rigorous health and safety regulations generally prevent the final collapse of the temple being the *coup de théâtre* that Saint-Saëns must have envisaged.

One successful attempt to reinterpret the ideology of the opera's scenario was Barbara Mundel and Veit Volkert's production in Frankfurt in 1996. Here, the setting became Paris around the time of the Franco-Prussian War, and the Philistines were shown as the decadent bourgeoisie of the Second Empire confronted with the stern (Hebrew) socialists of the Commune.

∾ Recording

CD: Jon Vickers (Samson); Rita Gorr (Dalila); Georges Prêtre (cond.). EMI 7 475895 8

Jacques Offenbach (1819–80)

(*See also* Part Five, Operetta)

Les Contes d'Hoffmann
(*The Tales of Hoffmann*)

Five acts. First performed Paris, 1881.
Libretto by Jules Barbier

After the fall of the Second Empire in 1869 – the regime with whose spirit his operettas were so closely identified – Offenbach went out of fashion. He spent much of the last period of his life working at a grand opera, based on a play drawn from the short stories of the eccentric German writer, E. T. A. Hoffmann. But Offenbach died during rehearsals, leaving the score slightly incomplete, and subsequently the opera became a prey to scholars with radically different ideas of what form the opera should take. Manuscript discoveries in the 1970s and 1980s have continued to fuel the controversy, but most productions follow one of the two major new editions by Fritz Oeser and Michael Kaye.

᳁ Plot

In Luther's tavern in Nuremberg, the Muse of Poetry laments the time Hoffmann spends pursuing the prima donna Stella, when he should be writing verse. The Muse then transforms herself into Hoffmann's friend Nicklausse, who accompanies Hoffmann when he appears in the tavern in a desperate state. Hoffmann is further unsettled by the presence of Lindorf, his rival for the love of Stella, who is singing in *Don Giovanni* at the opera house next door. The drunken Hoffmann explains to his fellow-drinkers how his love-life has been thwarted by several Lindorfs, and proceeds to tell them three stories, which become the opera itself.

Hoffmann's first story concerns Olympia, the 'daughter' of the inventor Spalanzani. In fact, she is nothing but a mechanical doll, invented by Spalanzani in an attempt to recover from a financial disaster. Spalanzani is in dispute with his former partner Dr Coppelius, who has made the doll's eyes and a pair of magic spectacles through which everything seems beautiful. Spalanzani fobs Coppelius off with a worthless cheque, and presents Olympia to a fashionable crowd. Everyone is impressed by her singing and clockwork movements, but Hoffmann dons the magic spectacles and is bewitched into thinking her to be human. He dances with her and ends up hopelessly in love. Coppelius returns in a fury, having discovered that Spalanzani's cheque is worthless. In revenge, he breaks the doll and reveals – to Hoffmann's dismay – that she is nothing but a doll.

In Munich, the widowed violin-maker Crespel implores his lovely but physically enfeebled daughter Antonia not to exhaust herself by singing too much – she has inherited her mother's chest disease and must not be overexcited. For similar reasons, Crespel is also trying to keep Antonia away from her admirer Hoffmann, but the latter manages to sneak into the house to see her. Later, Hoffmann hides away and overhears a conversation between Crespel and the mysterious Doctor Miracle, who appears to have been responsible for the death of Madame Crespel and whose ministrations will either kill or cure Antonia. Hoffmann persuades Antonia to give up singing, but the charisma of Doctor Miracle is too much for her. Conjuring up the voice of her dead mother and playing his daemonic violin, Doctor Miracle goads her to sing until she drops dead.

The courtesan Giulietta draws up in a gondola at a Venetian palazzo, where an orgiastic party is in progress. Hoffmann is one of the drunken revellers, but he is entranced by her beauty. The sorcerer Dapertutto promises Giulietta a fabulous diamond if she will prise Hoffmann's reflection away from him – a bargain she has already executed over her current lover, Schlemil. In her chamber, Giulietta duly seduces Hoffmann and asks that he leaves his reflection behind for her to remember him by. He agrees, and discovers that he can no longer see himself in the mirror. Schlemil enters and challenges Hoffmann to a duel. But no sooner has Hoffmann triumphed and taken the key to Giulietta's chamber from the dead Schlemil, than he sees Giulietta falling into the arms of her servant, Pittichinaccio. Nicklausse drags Hoffmann away, as Dapertutto laughs in triumph.

We return to Luther's tavern. Having told his three tales of romantic humiliation, Hoffmann is now in a drunken stupor, and scarcely seems to register his current beloved Stella leaving the opera house on Lindorf's arm. Nicklausse transforms back into the Muse of Poetry and implores Hoffmann to draw on his sad experience and rededicate himself to his art.

ᦰ What to listen for

No two productions of Hoffmann will present precisely the same musical text, and the merits of putting the 'Giulietta' act before the 'Antonia' act, and vice versa, are still disputed. The Barcarolle is taken from an earlier Offenbach operetta, *Les Fées du Rhin* (*The Rhine Fairies*), and Dapertutto's 'Scintille, diamant', an aria first added to the score in 1904, was adapted from another obscure Offenbach operetta. Both are sometimes now omitted. Many other textual problems relate to the 'Giulietta' act, which was the least finished when Offenbach died, and which the first production omitted entirely.

Hoffmann is a glorious lead role for the tenor and mezzo-sopranos enjoy Nicklausse (especially now that a recently unearthed aria with beautiful violin accompaniment can be incorporated), but the modern preference for casting one singer as Hoffmann's three thwarted loves creates all sorts of difficulties: something invariably needs to be cut or transposed, and some conductors prefer to evade the problems by casting three different singers with three different vocal timbres. Olympia's coloratura aria is horribly difficult to sing with total needle-point accuracy, and some sopranos omit the even more hair-raising ensuing passage in which the doll is meant to fly out of control. An even more complex coloratura aria for Giulietta, also recently discovered, is

probably just too tricky and exhausting to catch on. For
Antonia, a full lyric voice is required for the climactic trio.
Offenbach seems to have wanted one singer for these three
roles (as he did for the three bass-baritone villains), but did
not live to make the necessary adjustments to range and
weight.

✍ In performance

An opera about the dreams, illusions and disappointments
which beset the artist, *Les Contes d'Hoffmann* presents a wide
range of theatrical possibilities. John Schlesinger's production at Covent Garden is a handsome, traditional pantomime
spectacle; for the Paris Opéra, Patrice Chéreau explored the
opera's darker side and interpreted its significance more alle-
gorically, culminating with a striking final image of the
scenery vanishing into the flies and leaving a completely bare
stage; in San Francisco, Christopher Alden took a more
bleakly expressionist line, his set dominated by a huge blank
page of manuscript paper and a quill dripping blood rather
than ink.

✍ Recordings

CD: Placido Domingo (Hoffmann); Joan Sutherland
(Olympia, Antonia, Giulietta); Richard Bonynge (cond.).
Decca 417 363 2
Video: Placido Domingo (Hoffmann); Georges Prêtre
(cond.). Covent Garden production. NVC Arts 0630 19392 3

Jules Massenet (1842–1912)
Manon

Five acts. First performed Paris, 1884.
Libretto by Henri Meilhac and Philippe Gille

Massenet's greatest success – perhaps the best of the many
operas to be based on Abbé Prévost's 1731 novel, *Manon
Lescaut*. It brilliantly combines rococo pastiche with sentimental romanticism and paints a strong portrait of the
contrary yet sympathetic heroine.

✎ Plot

In the courtyard of a provincial inn, two lecherous gentlemen,
Guillot and Brétigny carouse with local 'actresses'. Lescaut
greets his pretty young cousin Manon, who dismounts from the
coach that is taking her to a convent. Manon longs for a life of
fun and luxury, and is soon the recipient of Guillot's attentions.
He plans to abduct her, but instead she runs off to Paris in
Guillot's coach with des Grieux, an ardent and sincere young
nobleman she has met outside the inn.

Manon and des Grieux set up a modest home together. Des
Grieux writes to his father to ask permission to marry
Manon, but she seems reluctant to commit herself further.
Manon is told that des Grieux's father plans to remove him
from his dissolute life, and during des Grieux's absence,
Lescaut persuades her to throw her lot in with the wealthy
Brétigny, who will set her up as a fine lady. She prepares to
leave, bidding the apartment a tearful farewell. Des Grieux
returns and tells her of his sad dream, in which he was separated from her. When he answers a knock at the door, he is
seized by his father's agents. Manon is full of remorse for her
complicity in the plot.

Some months later, Manon is the toast of fashionable
Paris. She visits the thronging pleasure gardens of Cours-la-
Reine on Brétigny's arm. Guillot is still smarting from the

way Manon tricked him at the inn and plots revenge on her. Manon overhears des Grieux's father tell Brétigny that des Grieux is about to enter the priesthood and will preach his first sermon at St Sulpice that day. She resolves to visit him.

After his sermon, des Grieux's father vainly persuades him to marry respectably and settle, but he expresses himself determined to enter the priesthood. Alone, he prays for peace of mind. Then he confronts Manon: his anger at the way she treated him melts when she ardently begs him for forgiveness and they soon reassert their love for each other.

In a disreputable gambling hall, Lescaut, Guillot and the actresses play cards. Manon enters with des Grieux, who needs cash to compensate for the exhaustion of his inheritance. Des Grieux accepts a challenge from Guillot, but when he repeatedly wins, Guillot vindictively accuses him of cheating and sees his chance for revenge. He turns des Grieux over to the police, and Manon is charged with prostitution.

Des Grieux's father intervenes to ensure his son's release, but Manon has been sentenced to deportation. Lescaut and des Grieux's plot to rescue Manon fails, but on the road to Le Havre, Lescaut manages to bribe the guards to allow him some time with Manon. He leaves her alone with des Grieux, and the lovers remember past happiness before Manon dies, begging des Grieux's forgiveness for the shame she has brought on him.

ও What to listen for

The opera is too long and slow to get started (almost every performance is cut to some degree), but none the less irresistible for its sensitive, touching and delicately coloured characterization of the joys and tribulations of young love. The contrast between romantic passion and rococo pastiche is brilliantly handled. Note the use of rhythmically accented spoken dialogue over orchestral accompaniment – a device known as *mélodrame*.

For any lyric soprano with some coloratura facility, Manon will rank as one of the great roles. At a technical level, it is cunningly paced, with the short, dainty and wistful arias ('Je suis encore' and 'Adieu, notre petite table') tactfully spaced between Acts I and II, and the coloratura fireworks exploding in the central Cours-la-Reine scene, by which time the voice is well warmed for the big emotional guns of Acts IV and V. Massenet and his librettist also provide her with a trio of girls – the giggling and chattering 'actresses' Javotte, Poussette and Rosette – who constitute her backing group and support act. Des Grieux is a less richly drawn figure, but the tenor is offered plenty of gratifying music to sing. Sadly, there are very few first-class French tenors today, and what you are likely to hear is a one-size-too-large Hispanic or American substitute who will be happier with the ardour of Acts IV and V than the gentle, heady sweetness called for in Acts I and II.

ᐳ In performance

Although *Manon* is a pretty and touching opera rather than a front-rank masterpiece, it does not have to be staged as a chocolate-box fantasy. The central emotional situation is strong, and a director like David McVicar at ENO can emphasize its darker undercurrents, subtly reminding an audience that Manon is as much the victim of prurient pimping as she is the venal coquette.

ᐳ Recording

CD: Victoria de Los Angeles (Manon); Pierre Monteux (cond.). EMI 7 63549 2

Werther

Four acts. First performed Vienna, 1892.
Libretto by Edouard Blau, Paul Milliet and Georges Hartmann

Adapted from Goethe's epistolary novel, *The Sorrows of Young Werther*.

↝ Plot

A small town in Germany in the 1780s. Charlotte, daughter of a widowed magistrate (known in the opera as Le Bailli), is betrothed to the sensible Albert, but during his absence she has come to know the melancholy young poet Werther, who is visiting the town. Werther is enchanted by Charlotte's simplicity and sincerity as she looks after her younger siblings, and delights in their shared taste for the poetry of Klopstock.

Following a ball which they have both attended, Charlotte and Werther walk home through the moonlight. After she tells him of the tragedy of her mother's early death and the responsibilities she has been left with, Werther declares his love for her. Then news comes that Albert has unexpectedly returned and, to Werther's dismay, Charlotte reveals that on her mother's deathbed she promised that she would marry him.

Charlotte and Albert duly marry. Werther is plunged into despair, and despite the efforts of Charlotte's chirpy younger sister Sophie, he leaves the town contemplating suicide. Charlotte begs him not to return until Christmas. Albert guesses that Charlotte is still in love with Werther.

On Christmas Eve, Charlotte secretly rereads Werther's letters. Sophie pleads with her to cheer up, but she breaks down in tears. Werther duly returns and, after a vain attempt at ordinary conversation, Charlotte cannot resist falling into his arms. She hurriedly leaves the room, insisting that they should never meet again. Albert is suspiciously questioning his wife when a message comes from Werther asking to borrow Albert's pistols, ostensibly to protect himself on a journey he is about to take. Albert orders his wife to hand the pistols over. After her husband has left, Charlotte rushes out to find Werther.

But it is too late: when Charlotte arrives at Werther's house, she finds that he has indeed shot himself. They remember their first meeting and Charlotte admits that she has always loved him. As Werther dies, children are heard singing a carol outside.

❧ What to listen for

For all its occasional vulgarities (such as the overuse of the melodramatic device of the *sforzando*, or sudden fortissimo blast of orchestral noise), *Werther* is a coherent, effective music drama which provides two superb leading roles. For the tenor, Werther is pure joy, with a glorious aria ('Pourquoi me réveiller' in Act III) fewer of the problematic high-lying or soft passages that so many French operas require. Charlotte is a strongly drawn personality, whose voyage towards self-discovery is movingly and perceptively drawn through her great scene in Act III. The orchestration is dark in hue, with a striking use of the saxophone to accompany Charlotte's 'Les larmes qu'on ne pleure pas' in Act III.

Massenet also wrote a version which transposed Werther's role for baritone – this was recently revived at the Met for Thomas Hampson – and Charlotte can also be sung by a darker-coloured soprano such as that of Angela Gheorghiu.

❧ In performance

The opera does not move easily out of its original period (though in Amsterdam, Willy Decker tried an admired abstract approach) and the success of a performance depends less on imaginative production than on securing two principal singers who can strike the necessary sparks off each other and rise to the high drama of Act III with life-or-death intensity.

❧ Recording

CD: Angela Gheorghiu (Charlotte), Roberto Alagna (Werther); Antonio Pappano (cond.). EMI 556820 2

Claude Debussy (1862–1918)
Pelléas et Mélisande

Five acts. First performed Paris, 1902.
Libretto by Maurice Maeterlinck, edited by the composer

Debussy toyed with many ideas for operas, including an adaptation of *As You Like It*, but eventually settled on a successful contemporary play in the fashionable Symbolist vein. Initially received with hostility and bafflement, *Pelléas* is now acknowledged as one of the masterpieces of modern opera, though the subtlety of both music and text means that its great underlying emotional power is not always evident on a first hearing.

❧ Plot

In the mythical kingdom of Allemonde, Prince Golaud meets a mysterious girl when he is wandering in a forest. Her name is Mélisande, but she does not know where she has come from and seems possessed by some deep sadness. As related to his grandfather, the blind King Arkel, in a letter read aloud by his mother Geneviève, Golaud subsequently marries her.

Pelléas, Golaud's stepbrother, returns from his travels. Mélisande remains uncommunicative but evidently unhappy in the dark and gloomy castle; she is befriended by Pelléas and loses her wedding ring when they are out walking together. Golaud questions Yniold, his son by his first marriage, about relations between Pelléas and Mélisande, but gets no clear answer. Golaud becomes increasingly jealous and attacks the pregnant Mélisande, to the dismay of Arkel.

Pelléas feels he must leave the castle. He secretly meets Mélisande for the last time in the park outside the castle. Finally, they quietly declare their love for each other. Golaud, who has been spying on them, kills Pelléas.

Mélisande lies dying, having been delivered of a premature child. Golaud is full of remorse and begs Mélisande to tell

him the truth about her relations with Pelléas, but she is inco-
herent. Arkel laments the sadness of life, as Mélisande, mysterious to the last, passes away.

∾ What to listen for

More purely a play set to music than any opera previously
written, *Pelléas* uses a fluent vocal line which embodies the
rhythms and accents of ordinary speech rather than their lyrical expansion. Although the opera contains no obvious set
pieces, certain episodes do stand out – Geneviève's reading of
Golaud's letter, for instance (so exposed for the contralto that
it sternly tests her ability to stay in tune); the hauntingly
beautiful modal folk-song which Mélisande sings as she lets
her hair fall from the window of her tower; or the enthralling
love duet in which Pelléas's shy confession seems about to
blossom into a tune ('On dirait que ta voix') only to be
drowned by the tension of the situation. Note also how, in its
final scene, the opera, like Mélisande herself, seems to die
away rather than conclude.

The opera is often described as Wagnerian. But although
one can certainly sense the anterior influence of *Tristan* and
Parsifal, Debussy's use of melodic motifs is much more spar-
ing than Wagner's, and the score does not have the overall
cumulative structure of Wagner's late operas – instead,
Debussy uses the orchestra to evoke an atmosphere and a
visual impression, most notably in the breathtaking transformation of the sounds which accompany Pelléas and Golaud
as they move out of the vaults into the sunlight in Act III.

At one level, Mélisande is relatively easy to sing – there are
no high notes, nothing sustained or long-breathed – but less
easy to interpret. The range of notes required is so narrow
that the role can comfortably be sung by either soprano or
mezzo-soprano; the orchestration which underlies her music
is not heavy either. What makes a great performance is the
subtlety with which the singer colours or inflects words and
phrases, suggesting the evasiveness of the girl. Pelléas lies
most comfortably for a high-lying, light-timbred baritone,

but is also often taken by light tenors. As bass-baritone, Golaud is more challenging, at least in terms of riding orchestral storms. Arkel is a bass, with a long, noble monologue in Act IV; Yniold can be sung either by a boy treble or a very light, flat-chested and boyish-sounding soprano.

∾ In performance

Initially associated with the sub-culture of homosexuals, decadents and Symbolists, *Pelléas* was first staged in a medieval fairy-land which kept the emotional drama obscured. Today's directors have seized on the opera with relish, and it has received several radically different interpretations. At the Met, for instance, Jonathan Miller set it in a Victorian country-house and gave the opera the feel of a late Henry James novel, in which what the repressed inhabitants don't say becomes more interesting than what they do; in Amsterdam, Peter Sellars presented the action in and around a crumbling, isolated mansion on the Atlantic or Pacific seaboard, populated by four generations of a wealthy but dysfunctional American upper-class family; for Opera North, Richard Jones suggested that Arkel's castle was something like a prison, in which the characters were confined to whitewashed cells and much was made of the image of a locked door and what happens behind it; for WNO, Peter Stein's wonderfully musical and visually beautiful production returned to the piece's roots, presenting a *fin-de-siècle* fairy-tale setting (and faithfully representing all Maeterlinck's stage directions, including a flight of doves and a flock of live sheep) without any loss of psychological complexity or human reality.

∾ Recordings

CD: Irène Joachim (Mélisande): Roger Désormière (cond.). EMI 7 61038 2
Video: Alison Hagley (Mélisande); Pierre Boulez (cond.). WNO production. DG 072 431 3

Maurice Ravel (1875–1937)
L'Enfant et les sortilèges
(*The Child and the Magic Spells*)

One act. First performed Monte Carlo, 1925.
Libretto by Colette

An opera originally conceived as a ballet, which in its vein of surrealist fantasy and scenic fluidity also bears the marks of Ravel's fascination with the cinema. Often performed in a double bill with Ravel's other one-act opera, *L'Heure Espagnole*, a farce about a Spanish clock-maker with an adulterous wife.

∾ Plot

A recalcitrant little boy is scolded by his mother over his failure to finish his homework. In a rage, he sets about attacking everything in his room – he kicks the cat, upsets a kettle, smashes a teapot, pulls strips off the wallpaper and breaks the pendulum on a grandfather clock. But suddenly the assaulted objects and animals decide to speak back and teach the child a salutary lesson. A chair recoils when he tries to sit in it; the teapot challenges him to a boxing match, the fire spits back at him and so forth.

Finally, two cats leap out into the garden. The child follows them, only to face further criticism from the objects of the child's destructiveness – including a tree, a dragonfly and a squirrel who pleads for another of his kind to be released from captivity in the child's room. The child feels lonely and unloved, and the animals begin to batter him and then each other. The child escapes from the fray and binds the paw of a wounded squirrel. The animals are delighted by this act of kindness. They forgive the chastened child and help him to call for his mother.

∿ What to listen for

Ravel's richly coloured and inventive score offers the cast only short cameo roles but also demands some virtuoso singing. Ravel enjoyed writing for the extremes of the vocal ranges: for example, Fire, the Nightingale and the Princess (which the composer specifies should be sung by the same soprano) demand trills and a Queen-of-the-Night top F – a note which the character tenor playing Arithmetic also has to touch. The Child should be performed by a slight-figured mezzo-soprano.

The opera is full of delicate pastiche and dances – a minuet for two armchairs, a nonsense Chinese pentatonic foxtrot for the cup and teapot, a pastorale for the wallpaper shepherd and shepherdess, and an extended orchestral waltz for the frogs. The squirrel's lament is vocally perhaps the most pure-ly beautiful section of the score, though the final fugal chorus of farewell runs it a close second. Note the elements of jazz, blues, ragtime and American popular music, especially in the piano part.

∿ In performance

An enchanting fantasy with a moral, which doesn't allow directors much room for interpretation, but which has given artists such as David Hockney (at the Met) and the children's books illustrator Maurice Sendak (at Glyndebourne) a chance to let their whimsies rip. Ravel is reported to have enjoyed Walt Disney's early cartoons and to have believed that the medium could have animated the opera as he had always dreamed.

∿ Recording

CD: Colette Alliot-Lugaz (L'Enfant); Charles Dutoit (cond.). Decca 44 333 3

Francis Poulenc (1899–1963)
Dialogues des Carmélites

Three acts. First performed Milan, 1957.
Libretto by the composer

One of the most successful of post-war operas – startlingly dramatic, profoundly moving and rich in psychological complexities. The story is broadly based on historical fact: the actual libretto is adapted from a play by George Bernanos, itself based on a German novel drawn from Mother Marie's memoirs of the episode.

ᐎ Plot
Shortly before the outbreak of the French Revolution in 1789, there is a violent attack outside the mansion of the Chevalier de la Force. His neurotic daughter Blanche wants to joins a Carmelite convent. The elderly Prioress, Madame de Croissy, questions Blanche's motivation sceptically, but admits her as a novice.

Blanche befriends cheerful Sister Constance. The Prioress dies in agony, and a new Prioress, Madame Lidoine, is appointed. As the Revolution intensifies, Blanche's brother attempts to persuade her to leave the convent, but she refuses – although it is not clear of what she is fearful, or what she is evading.

The nuns are expelled from the convent and take a vow of martyrdom. Blanche flees the convent in terror. She returns home and discovers that her father has been guillotined. Mother Marie, the Prioress's deputy, arrives to take Blanche back to the convent, but she is too afraid to leave.

The Carmelites are condemned to death for supporting the royalist regime. Because of her visit to Blanche, Mother Marie is separated from her sisters, and she is dismayed that she cannot join them in their ordeal: her confessor suggests that it is the will of God. The remaining nuns mount the scaffold one by one, singing the 'Salve regina'. Constance, the last to be executed, is overjoyed when a spiritually resolved Blanche finally appears to join her sisters in their martyrdom.

ᔥ What to listen for

The vocal line contains no formal arias and little easy melody. It is largely couched as lyrical solo declamation, and the influence of Monteverdi's operas, Mussorgsky's *Boris Godunov* and Debussy's *Pelléas et Mélisande* is evident throughout. Communicating the text to the audience is paramount: Poulenc was a great composer for the human voice, and the opera was carefully written to be sung with verbal clarity. The score is unfailingly dramatic in the way it creates an ever-thickening atmosphere of imminent menace and anxiety, contrasted with the calm and certainty implied by the nuns' chants and rituals.

Women's voices dominate – the male roles are all small and peripheral – and the five central characters are all carefully contrasted in vocal colour and type. Blanche, written for lyric soprano, is the most psychologically complex role, her personality a fascinating mixture of neuroses and hysteria; Constance is designed for a fresh, youthful soubrette, and her music contains the opera's only element of sweetness and charm; Madame Lidoine is for a high-lying Straussian soprano, Mother Marie for dramatic soprano and the Old Prioress, contralto. This latter role is usually taken by an elderly prima donna who may compensate for her vocal shortcomings by falling back on ham: the effect will be much greater, however, if Poulenc's notes are as potently interpreted as they are by singers of the class of Rita Gorr or Felicity Palmer.

ᔥ In performance

Poulenc's memories of the persecutions attendant on the Nazi occupation of France, as well as the drawn-out and painful death of Poulenc's lover, colour this opera, the underlying theme of which is fear – the fear bred by political terror, Blanche's fear of commitment to God, and the fear of the agony of death, as suffered by the old Prioress. The drama is also rich in the erotic element in Catholic mysticism, but its attitude to marytrdom is entirely unsentimental and the nuns' final march to the guillotine, singing the 'Salve regina' is more stomach-churning than uplifting.

Outstanding productions of this magnificently theatrical and emotionally devastating work – one of the masterpieces of the second half of the twentieth century – include those by John Dexter at the Met and by Phyllida Lloyd for ENO, both of them visually austere and sharply focused on the intense psychological drama of Blanche's spiritual pilgrimage.

ᐁ Recording

CD: Denise Duval (Blanche); Pierre Dervaux (cond.).
EMI 7 67135 2

PART FIVE

Operetta

Operetta grew out of the eighteenth-century French *opéra-comique*, the German *Singspiel* (both of which employed spoken dialogue between musical numbers) and the Italian *opera buffa*, as well as various national traditions of popular entertainment involving songs and satire. It tends to fit more happily into theatres than large opera houses, and uses lighter voices and smaller orchestras than those required for Verdi and Wagner.

Beyond that, operetta is difficult to define. The key figure in its development is Jacques Offenbach. Like Meyerbeer, Offenbach was a German-born Jew who settled as a young man in Paris. Hugely prolific and versatile, he produced a long series of short, saucy and piquant comedies, full of little tunes and wry jokes, which delighted the cynical, pleasure loving society of Second Empire Paris.

Offenbach's lightness of touch made its mark on the Anglo-Irish composer Arthur Sullivan and his librettist William Schwenck Gilbert. Together they developed their own distinctively English version of Offenbach's operetta style – devoid of French salaciousness, shot through with a vein of sentiment, and hitting a wide range of satirical targets, from the Houses of Parliament (*Iolanthe*) to the Aesthetic Movement (*Patience*) and Italian opera (*The Sorcerer*).

Offenbach was hugely popular in Vienna, too, but in *Die Fledermaus* and *Der Zigeunerbaron* (*The Gypsy Baron*), the 'Waltz King' Johann Strauss made something rather more musically substantial of the operetta concept than was customary in Paris: dance sequences played a prominent role, and story-lines were more romantic and realistic than satirical or fantastic. For the Edwardian era, Franz Lehár's sensuous and sumptuous *The Merry Widow*, with its cosmopolitan sophistication and Ruritanian intrigues caught the mood of Europe on the brink of the catastrophe of the First World War.

Following Lehár's lead, twentieth-century operetta lost its satirical edge and became even more romantic in tone: from the USA came *Kismet*, *The Student Prince* and *The Desert Song*; from England, Ivor Novello's *Perchance to Dream* and Noel Coward's *Bitter Sweet*. But since the Second World War, operetta has virtually died, superseded by the vigour of American musical comedy. This tradition first flourished in the 1920s in the glamorous and urbane, if flimsily plotted, entertainments composed with a jazzy touch by George Gershwin, Cole Porter and Richard Rodgers in collaboration with the lyricist Lorenz Hart.

A landmark is the 1927 première of Jerome Kern's *Show Boat*, which boldly dealt with issues of interracial marriage, presaging the greater dramatic coherence and darker themes introduced in the 1940s by Richard Rodgers and his second major collaborator Oscar Hammerstein in *Oklahoma!*, *Carousel* and *South Pacific*. In their wake came a series of shows which have already established themselves as classics: *My Fair Lady* and *Camelot*, with music by Frederick Loewe, a composer who was Viennese in origin and whose father had sung in the first performance of *The Merry Widow*; Frank Loesser's comic *Guys and Dolls* and Leonard Bernstein's tragic *West Side Story*, both quintessentially New York in character; John Kander and Fred Ebb's brilliant *Cabaret*, set in Berlin during the rise of Nazism. Latest and perhaps last in the line of great musical comedy composers is Stephen Sondheim, whose shows have great artistic ambition and complexity. One of his most charming works is *A Little Night Music*, a true operetta harking back to the elegant waltz and schmaltz of Strauss and Lehár. Several of Sondheim's shows have been successfully presented by opera companies.

From the late 1970s, elements of rock music have been used to vivify and extend the possibilities of musical comedy. Andrew Lloyd Webber's *Evita* and Claude-Michel Schönberg's *Les Misérables* went one stage further, with their serious themes and highly emotional scores uninterrupted by dialogue, indirectly influenced by opera composers such as Meyerbeer, Wagner and Puccini. Such works also lean heavily for their effectiveness on electronic amplification and spectacular staging.

Jacques Offenbach (1819–80)

(*See also* Part Four, French Opera)

Orphée aux Enfers
(*Orpheus in the Underworld*)

Two acts. First performed Paris, 1858.
Libretto by Hector Crémieux and Ludovic Halévy

Offenbach, a German Jew who emigrated to Paris, had enjoyed some success with his smaller-scale operettas, but it was the saucy and irreverent *Orphée*, with its irresistible '*galop infernal*' in the can-can style, which won him sensational fame and which stands as the first great operetta. A good-humoured satire on the pomposity and corruption of Napoleon III's Second Empire, it was revised and expanded in 1874: this provides the basis for the versions performed today.

✎ Plot

The fiddle-playing Orpheus and his flirtatious wife Eurydice are tired of each other. Orpheus lays a trap for Eurydice's disguised lover Pluto, but it is Eurydice herself who falls for it – with the happy result of her being dragged off to the Underworld by its king, Pluto himself. In the interests of respectability, Public Opinion advises Orpheus to retrieve his wife.

The gods on Mount Olympus are bored with their heavenly life and complain about Jupiter's autocratic ways. Mercury brings news of Pluto's abduction of Eurydice, which causes a furore. Jupiter calms everybody down by proposing a trip to the Underworld, aimed at forcing Pluto to return Eurydice to Orpheus.

Eurydice languishes in the Underworld and decides she wants to return to earth. She is locked up to prevent her escaping. Jupiter arrives and falls in love with Eurydice, transforming himself into a fly in order to gain admittance to the locked room. When Eurydice catches the fly and kisses it,

Jupiter is transformed and promises to take Eurydice with him to Olympus.

Pluto throws a party for the visiting gods. Jupiter and the disguised Eurydice are about to depart, when Orpheus and Public Opinion arrive. Orpheus is told that he can rescue his wife so long as he does not look behind him on their way back to earth. But Jupiter launches a thunderbolt which shocks Orpheus into doing just that. Eurydice is sent back to the Underworld – to the satisfaction of everyone except Public Opinion.

∾ What to listen for

Offenbach never overplays his hand – his music remains 'light' in the sense of orchestral texture as well as mood and pace. Nothing is over-egged or pretentious, none of the numbers lasts longer than a pop single, and many are barely a minute long. Apart from the pounding can-can of the *galop infernal* in the last scene, highlights include the captivating hummed 'slumber' chorus and the gods' martial 'rebellion' chorus, both in the second scene, and the buzzing fly duet for Eurydice and Jupiter in the third scene. Much of the best solo music is accorded to Eurydice, a role which demands virtuosic coloratura and rises to a high E – innocent musical-comedy soubrettes, beware. The quotation from Gluck's 'J'ai perdu mon Eurydice' ('What is life to me without thee?') as Orpheus announces that he wishes to redeem Eurydice from Hades is made with an *élan* typical of Offenbach.

∾ In performance

For ENO, the satirical cartoonist Gerald Scarfe provided sets dominated by huge, monstrous caricatures of Victorian respectability; the effect was perhaps overwhelmingly grotesque for such a drily witty opera. Teutonically intellectualized productions have been offered by Herbert Wernicke in Brussels and at Berlin's Komische Oper by Harry Kupfer, but the most successful recent version has been that of Laurent Pelly, first seen in Geneva in 1998, in which the humour is understated and the sexiness Gallically alluring rather than coarsely semaphored.

❧ Recording

CD: Natalie Dessay (Eurydice); Marc Minkowski (cond.).
EMI 5 56725 2 0

La Belle Hélène

Three acts. First performed Paris, 1864.
Libretto by Henri Meilhac and Ludovic Halévy

Another satire on the pleasure-loving, materialistic France of
the Second Empire, full of digs at the political shenanigans of
the day and the pretensions of grand opera.

❧ Plot

In Sparta, before the outbreak of the Trojan War, the priest
Calchas laments the lack of interest in his temple and the
public's obsession with Venus ever since she won the golden
apple from Paris by promising to deliver him Helen, the most
beautiful girl on earth. Helen is bored with her dull husband
Menelaus, and is delighted when the handsome shepherd
Paris comes to claim her. Menelaus's allies, the Greek kings
Agamemnon, Achilles and the two Ajaxes, organize a game of
charades; when Paris wins, he reveals his true identity as a
Trojan prince, much to everyone's consternation. Calchas
announces that Menelaus has been banished to Crete for a
month, leaving the field clear for Paris and Helen.

Helen dallies with Paris for a month without actually making love to him. But while Helen is dreaming in bed, Paris
takes advantage of her – just as Menelaus returns to discover
them in a clinch. Everyone departs for a seaside holiday. On
the beach, Menelaus confronts Helen with her adultery, but
she insists that she was tricked into surrendering her virtue.
Her sincerity may be doubted. When others blame the
ubiquitous influence of Venus for this state of affairs,
Menelaus demands a visit from her High Priest. The High
Priest duly appears, announcing that he will make amends by

taking Helen away to participate in a ritual sacrifice. But this High Priest is none other than Paris in disguise, and as he and Helen sail off to Troy, the Greek kings vow that they will avenge the wrong done to Menelaus by declaring war.

∾ What to listen for

A more graceful, lyrical score than that of the fizz-pop *Orphée aux Enfers*. Two of its best solo numbers occur in the first scene: Paris's jaunty, 'Au Mont Ida' and Helen's wistful 'Amours divins' show two aspects of Offenbach's genius at their best. Other highlights include Helen's seductive 'Dis-moi, Vénus'; the duet for Helen and Paris, 'Oui, c'est un rêve'; and the affectionate parody of patriotic marches by Rossini and Wagner. Paris's Tyrolean yodelling in the final scene never fails to win a laugh. Unlike the stratospherically high-lying role of Eurydice, Helen lies happily in the mezzo-soprano range. Paris requires a tenor with more beef than operetta usually demands.

∾ In performance

In 1932, *La Belle Hélène* was rewritten as *Helen*, a West End musical by the composer Erich Korngold and librettist A. P. Herbert; it had enormous success, but dated quickly. In 1995, the management of ENO commissioned the playwright Michael Frayn to try again: he stripped away the mythological trappings and came up with *La Belle Vivette*, located in Second-Empire Paris with Vivette–Hélène played as a courtesan-cum-operetta-star and Menelaus as her elderly protector. Result: an abysmally unfunny disaster. Much better, as Laurent Pelly at the Châtelet and Patrice Caurier and Moshe Leiser for Scottish Opera have proved, to stick with Meilhac and Halévy's original libretto and simply insert a few well-placed topical references. The charades played in Act I refers to a game popular at the court of Napoleon III.

∾ Recording

CD and DVD: Felicity Lott (Hélène); Marc Minkowski (cond.). Virgin 545 477 2 (CD); DVO PLBH (DVD)

Johann Strauss (1825–99)
Die Fledermaus (*The Bat*)

Three acts. First performed Vienna, 1874.
Libretto by Karl Haffner and Richard Genée

Based on a French farce, this musically rich and vocally challenging operetta has found a firm foothold in conventional
opera houses, and many great singers (among them Lotte
Lehmann, Elisabeth Schumann, Elisabeth Schwarzkopf, Kiri
Te Kanawa, Hermann Prey, Thomas Allen) and conductors
(Bruno Walter, Herbert von Karajan, Carlos Kleiber) have
been among its finest interpreters.

Ꮼ Plot

Eisenstein, a Viennese gentlemen, is about to spend a day in
prison after being convicted of a tax dodge, thus giving his
wife Rosalinde a chance to dally with her lover, the operatic
tenor Alfred. Her maid Adele asks for the evening off to visit
her aged aunt, but permission is refused – much to her fury, as
she was in fact hoping to attend Prince Orlofsky's exotic ball
with her sister Ida. Eisenstein's friend Dr Falke reminds
Eisenstein of a night when Eisenstein made Falke walk home
after a fancy-dress ball, dressed as a bat. Meanwhile, he
encourages Eisenstein to accompany him to Orlofsky's ball for
an evening of naughty fun before he begins his day in prison.
Rosalinde is dining secretly with Alfred when the police arrive
and arrest him, mistaking him for Eisenstein. To avoid scandal, Rosalinde does not offer the obvious explanation.

At the ball, Falke tells Orlofsky how he plans a comical
revenge on Eisenstein for the bat episode. He has orchestrated what follows, much to Orlofsky's amusement. Eisenstein
appears, disguised as 'Monsieur Renard', followed by Adele,
who has managed to escape her domestic duties, and is
accompanied by her sister Ida. Adele denies her identity to
Eisenstein, who flirts with her. 'Monsieur Renard' is then

introduced to Frank the prison governor, himself disguised as another French gentleman, and then to a mysterious Hungarian countess – in fact Rosalinde, also in disguise. Unaware that she is his wife, Eisenstein flirts with her too, and she goes off with his watch. Eisenstein boasts to everyone about the jape he played on Falke, and at dawn leaves to start his prison sentence.

In the prison, the idiotic jailor Frosch tries to stop Alfred singing. Adele and Ida appear in search of the 'French nobleman' whom they had met at the ball – Adele's real hope being that he might help her to become an actress. Eisenstein appears with Falke to give himself up, only to find that Alfred is serving his sentence for him. He disguises himself as a lawyer in order to interrogate both Alfred and Rosalinde, who has come to the prison to secure Alfred's release. Eisenstein is outraged by Rosalinde's deceit, until she produces the tell-tale watch as evidence of his own misbehaviour. Everybody finally reveals their true identity, and Falke is delighted at the mayhem he has provoked. All ends in good humour, however, and a general toast to champagne, on whose inebriating effects all the confusion is blamed.

∾ What to listen for

Strauss's style was influenced by Offenbach, but his idiom stretches into more lush and sentimental territory, with longer numbers and a more symphonic attitude to orchestration. The superb overture is more than a pot-pourri of the best tunes: it is a display of Strauss's wonderful command of dance rhythms – polka, waltz, march and mazurka. Act I contains some sparkling duets and trios, but it is Act II, the party scene, presided over by the spirit of champagne, which provides a forty-minute unbroken string of hit numbers (only broken when gala performances introduce special-guest star turns half-way through): the 'laughing' song for Adele (coloratura soubrette soprano), the sly 'Ich lade gern' for Orlofsky (usually played by a mezzo-soprano with a taste for camping it up in drag, but sometimes taken by counter-tenors or tenors), the 'ticking watch' duet for Eisenstein and Rosalinde (lyric soprano), the brilliant and taxing Czardas for the disguised Rosalinde, and the chorus 'Brüderlein und Schwesterlein', the quintessence of maudlin Viennese schmaltz, which leads into the effervescent waltz finale. Eisenstein is a gift for a lively high baritone, while Alfred parodies the ardour of the operatic tenor.

✎ In performance

Hysterically gag-filled, surrealist productions like Richard Jones's at ENO or Hans Neuenfels's at Salzburg do not make *Die Fledermaus* any more amusing – in fact, they detract from what is essentially a boulevard farce which works best when played 'for real', with a cast whose members avoid the fatal temptation to fall over themselves trying to be funny. Several attempts have been made to update the scenario and adapt the score into a musical-comedy style, substituting new titles like *Gay Rosalinda*, *A Wonderful Night* and *Champagne Sec*; and there have also been frequent, if less drastic, redraftings of the libretto the Met recently employed the veteran Broadway writers Betty Comden and Adolph Green, to little effect.

Every performance suffers from the weakness, both musical and dramatic, of the brief third act. This weakness is often exacerbated by the tedious antics of the actor who plays the spoken role of the drunken jailor Frosch and who is traditionally allowed to spin the anticlimax out by ad libbing.

✎ Recording

CD: Julia Varady (Rosalinde); Carlos Kleiber (cond.).
DG 415 646 2

Arthur Sullivan (1842–1900)
The Pirates of Penzance, or The Slave of Duty

Two acts. First performed New York, 1879.
Libretto by W. S. Gilbert

The Pirates of Penzance was completed and first performed in New York, where Gilbert and Sullivan were presenting *HMS Pinafore*, their first surviving full-scale collaboration. Its score is more operatic in character and ambition than that of *Pinafore*, but in recent years has also been successfully translated into a rock idiom.

✎ Plot

Having completed his apprenticeship and come of age, Frederic is ready to join the distinctly unfearsome pirates of Penzance and to marry his nursemaid Ruth – the only woman he has ever seen. Instead, he decides to turn the pirates and their swashbuckling King over to justice and falls in love with Mabel, one of the daughters of Major-General Stanley, who is taking a holiday in the area. The pirates' plan to kidnap Major-General Stanley's daughters is foiled when the Major-General tells the pirates that he is an orphan – a word that always sends the pirates into paroxysms of maudlin tears.

The police prepare to arrest the pirates. Through Ruth, Frederic discovers that because he was born on 29 February in a leap year, he is legally only five and his apprenticeship will not lapse for another sixty years. A 'slave to duty' and honour, Frederic is therefore bound to desert Mabel and return to his pirate indenture. The pirates outwit the police, but yield when Queen Victoria's name is invoked. It then transpires that the pirates are in fact 'all noblemen who have gone wrong'. All is forgiven and Mabel and the under-age Frederic are united, as the pirates pair off with the rest of Major-General Stanley's daughters.

ᖇ What to listen for

The most famous number – in fact, only added at the very
last minute – is Mabel's gracefully Frenchified waltz song,
'Poor wand'ring one', a charming showpiece for coloratura
soprano. The Stanley girls' chorus, 'Climbing over rocky
mountain', is lifted from Gilbert and Sullivan's first – and
now otherwise totally lost – collaboration *Thespis*. Sullivan
exploits his rare gift for counterpoint in Act II, where Mabel
and Edith's 'Go, ye heroes, go to glory' is matched against
'When the foeman bares his steel'; the noble unaccompanied
chorus 'Hail, Poetry' in Act I reminds one that Sullivan was
also celebrated as the Victorians' laureate composer of sacred
anthems; and the passionate duet for Frederic and Mabel in
Act II suggests that he was already aching for the broader
emotional pastures of grand opera.

Major-General Stanley's patter-song, 'I am the very model
of a modern Major-General', has been much adapted over
the years, including a brilliant version by the cabaret satirist
Tom Lehrer, which incorporated the entire chemical table.

ᖇ In performance

The Pirates of Penzance has always ranked as one of the most
consistently popular of the G and S operettas, but it gained a
new lease of life in 1980 when the American director Joseph
Papp devised a brilliant rock version using synthesized
instruments and turning the pirates into camply swashbuckling Errol Flynn types. It proved a big hit on Broadway and in
the West End. Interestingly, Papp remained pretty faithful to
Gilbert's dialogue and avoided the temptation to introduce a
lot of ephemeral contemporary gags. Conventional D'Oyly
Carte productions still provide plenty of innocent pleasure,
however. A little-known fact: Prince Charles played the
Pirate King in a production at Gordonstoun School in 1967.

ᖇ Recording

CD: Valerie Masterson (Mabel); John Reed (Major-
General); Isidore Godfrey (cond.). Decca 425 196 2

Iolanthe, or *The Peer and the Peri*

Two acts. First performed London and New York, 1882. Libretto by W. S. Gilbert

Iolanthe was simultaneously premièred in London and New York. Resistance among peers to Gladstone's Liberal reforms made the satire of the House of Lords highly topical at the time, and its political edge is still cutting. Sullivan's score is one of his most delightful and sophisticated.

∾ Plot

After twenty-five years of banishment for the crime of marrying a mortal, the fairy Iolanthe is readmitted to Fairyland. She reveals that her half-mortal son Strephon is in love with Phyllis, a ward of court who requires the Lord Chancellor's permission in order to marry. This he refuses to give, as he wishes to marry her himself. Phyllis is also courted by the silly-ass Lord Mountararat and Earl Tolloler. The fairies arrange for Strephon to stand for parliament, where he proves enormously successful. When the Lord Chancellor persists in his desire to marry Phyllis, Iolanthe reveals that she is his long-lost wife and Strephon their son. Fairy law requires that she dies as a result of this confession, but the Lord Chancellor's simple amendment – 'every fairy shall die who *doesn't* marry a mortal' – solves the problem. Strephon marries Phyllis, the Queen of the Fairies marries Private Willis, the sentry outside the Houses of Parliament, and the rest of her brood all marry peers.

∾ What to listen for

One of Sullivan's strongest scores, and one which has much to offer a company of opera singers. The overture is no mere medley, but a textbook example of sonata form, with a tune which does not recur when the curtain rises. Some Wagnerian influence (via the Rhinemaidens) can be detected in the daintily sensuous music for the fairies and the brassy march of the peers (via *Meistersinger*), while Iolanthe's aria pleading for her son's life, written a few days after Sullivan's beloved mother had died, is perhaps the most heartfelt melody he ever composed. The sparkle and vivacity of the long finale to Act I is pure operetta genius, with fourteen melodic episodes matched to some of Gilbert's most deliciously silly rhymes: for example, 'I ought to be more chary,/It seems that she's a fairy,/From Andersen's library,/And I took her for/The proprietor/Of a ladies' seminary'.

ᐒ In performance

It is a comment on either Gilbert's genius or the inertia of the British political system that with only a little rejigging, the satire in *Iolanthe* continues to lend itself happily to the controversies of our own day: recent productions have managed to incorporate references to matters such as the 'Thatcher effect', the abolition of the Greater London Council, spin-doctoring and the reform of the House of Lords.

ᐒ Recording

CD: John Reed (Lord Chancellor); Isidore Godfrey (cond.). Decca 414 145 2

The Mikado, *or The Town of Titipu*

Two acts. First performed London, 1885.
Libretto by W. S. Gilbert

A rage for all things Japanese swept London in the early 1880s, and the great joke in *The Mikado* is that behind all its comic orientalism, the tone of the proceedings remains thoroughly British. Gilbert's original inspiration is said to have been a Japanese sword, hung on the wall of his study, which crashed to the ground as he was pacing up and down. He also visited the Japanese village set up near his home in South Kensington.

∾ Plot

The Mikado's son, Nanki-Poo, has fled from the court and the amorous clutches of the hideous Katisha. Disguised as a wandering minstrel he arrives in the town of Titipu, where he has fallen for the ingenuous Yum-Yum, fresh out of school. Yum-Yum, however, is engaged to her guardian Ko-Ko, Lord High Executioner, who has been ordered to perform a decapitation. Nanki-Poo offers himself, in exchange for a month of marriage to Yum-Yum. Katisha arrives in search of Nanki-Poo.

Yum-Yum is dismayed to discover that the law decrees that all widows must be buried alive. Ko-Ko lies to the Mikado and tells him that he has executed Nanki-Poo. When Nanki-Poo's identity is revealed, it emerges that the death penalty is exacted for killing the Mikado's heir. Further muddles – also involving Pooh-Bah, Titipu's Lord High Everything Else, and Yum-Yum's friend Pitti-Sing – are finally resolved when Ko-Ko agrees to marry Katisha and it emerges that Nanki-Poo has not been executed after all.

∾ What to listen for

Following a quarrel with Gilbert, Sullivan was reluctant to write *The Mikado* – a fact belied by the score's melodic freshness. There is an element of pastiche of Japanese music in the pentatonic opening chorus and the chorus which precedes the Mikado's entry is a genuine Japanese army anthem, but the score is otherwise as English as Yorkshire pudding. Among the score's highlights are the graceful chorus 'Comes a train of little ladies' which precedes the mercurial 'Three little maids', and in Act II, Yum-Yum's 'The sun whose rays', a tune in which the influence of the music for the Woodbird in Wagner's *Siegfried* has been detected, and the madrigal 'Brightly dawns our wedding day'.

∾ In performance

Like *Hamlet* or *Carmen*, *The Mikado* is inexhaustible. We've had *The Swing Mikado* and *The Hot Mikado*, both with all-black casts. Groucho Marx and Frankie Howerd are among many great comedians who have played Ko-Ko. It has been performed in Catalan and Croatian. Mike Leigh made a marvellous film, *Topsy-Turvy*, which explored the opera's genesis and first performance, and its great numbers, like 'Three little maids from school' and 'I've got a little list', pop up in any number of odd contexts. Perhaps the most brilliantly daft and totally irresistible modern version is Jonathan Miller's production for English National Opera at ENO, set without a hint of japonaiserie in the foyer of a 1920s grand hotel, redolent of the novels of P. G. Wodehouse.

❧ Recording

CD: Marie McLaughlin (Yum-Yum); Charles Mackerras (cond.). Telarc 80284 1

Franz Lehár (1870–1948)
Die Lustige Witwe
(*The Merry Widow*)

Three acts. First performed Vienna, 1905.
Libretto by Victor Léon and Leo Stein

Based, like *Die Fledermaus*, on a *risqué* French farce, *Die Lustige Witwe* boasts a wonderful succession of schmaltzy melodies, richly orchestrated for a band much larger than operettas customarily employ. To the Edwardians, it seemed exotically sexy and sophisticated, but it also hit a topical nerve in the years before the First World War because of the way it touched on the Balkan question. A huge and immediate international success, it spawned many inferior imitations, as well as 'Merry Widow' fashions and merchandise.

❧ Plot

In the Paris embassy of the impoverished Balkan state of Pontevedro, the envoy Baron Mirko Zeta is worried that that the millions belonging to the wealthy widow Hanna Glawari will be lost to the nation if she remarries a Frenchman. He hatches a plot to pair her off with a Pontevedrian bachelor, Count Danilo. The two of them have previously been amorously entangled, but Danilo now avoids her, not wishing to look like a vulgar fortune-hunter. Meanwhile, Baron Zeta's wife Valencienne is being pursued by a French aristocrat, Camille, who is widely suspected of courting Hanna Glawari.

Hanna holds a glamorous party. Valencienne has an assignation with Camille in a summerhouse, but leaves him only with a fan inscribed 'I am a respectable wife'. Confusion follows when Hanna is mistaken for Valencienne, and Hanna deliberately provokes Danilo by announcing her engagement to Camille. Danilo storms off to Maxim's in a rage. Once she is confident that Danilo still truly loves her, Hanna explains all to Danilo, and they declare their love for each other.

Pontevedro is saved – and the discovery of Valencienne's inscribed fan reassures Baron Zeta that his wife's honour has not been besmirched.

✍ What to listen for

The most glamorous and subtle of operetta scores, notable from its hectically exhilarating prelude for its rich and full orchestral scoring, Slavic musical effects (tambourine and guitar being among the instruments used) and seductively erotic tinge, embodied in the haunting refrain of Hanna Glawari's 'Vilja', and the matchless 'Lippen schweigen' waltz – surely one of the most suavely perfect melodies ever composed. All three of its acts have masterly finales. The summerhouse duet between Camille and Valencienne has been labelled Wagnerian, and there is indeed an emotional depth and intensity here that one finds nowhere else in operetta.

✍ In performance

An operetta said to have received over a quarter of a million performances, in twenty-five languages. Producers today seem to be left very uncomfortable by this romance, and don't know whether to send it all up rotten or take its background in pre-First World War Balkan politics seriously. The casualty of both approaches is any sense of the Edwardian café-society glamour which made the opera so popular in the first place. As with so many other operettas, *Die Lustige Witwe*'s sensual charm dissipates in large opera houses, and recent star-studded productions at the Metropolitan and Opéra Bastille have been unenthusiastically received.

Several pleasantly escapist film adaptations of the operetta have been made – with Jeanette Macdonald and Lana Turner among those taking the title-role – and a balletic version became a vehicle for the last years of Margot Fonteyn's career.

✍ Recording

CD: Cheryl Studer (Hanna Glawari); John Eliot Gardiner (cond.). DG 439 911 2

PART SIX

English Opera

English opera grew out of the theatrical tradition of the court masque and the custom of introducing songs and dances into spoken plays. John Blow's *Venus and Adonis* (*c.*1683) is probably the first true opera in English, 'through-composed' on the Italian model, followed shortly afterwards by Henry Purcell's *Dido and Aeneas*.

With the arrival of Handel in London in 1710, Italian operas became all the rage – a vogue satirized by *The Beggar's Opera* (1728), an old-style play with songs, written by John Gay with music culled from popular ballads and folk tunes. Throughout the eighteenth and early nineteenth centuries, opera in England continued to be largely an Italian import, though composers like Thomas Arne continued to produce works in the native tongue, often pastoral in subject-matter and, like *The Beggar's Opera*, drawn from music taken from a variety of sources (such operas were known as *pasticcios* or pastiches).

More sophisticated in their musical language and more dramatically ambitious were hugely successful operas on romantic themes by two Irish-born composers – Michael Balfe's *The Bohemian Girl* (1843) and Vincent Wallace's *Maritana* (1845), often linked in a trilogy with Julius Benedict's *The Lily of Killarney* (1862). With *Ivanhoe*, a romantic opera first performed in 1891, Sir Arthur Sullivan made his sole, unsuccessful attempt to produce something in a similarly grand style.

Composers of the early twentieth century struggled to find a satisfactory operatic form. Edward Elgar left only sketches; in *Sir John in Love*, *Hugh the Drover* and *The Pilgrim's Progress*, Ralph Vaughan Williams composed beautiful and lyrically evocative music that lacks theatrical punch; in *Savitri* and *At the Boar's Head*, Gustav Holst made interesting experiments in a post-Wagnerian idiom that led nowhere.

It was only with Benjamin Britten – and in particular, *Peter Grimes* – that English opera found a truly confident and distinctive voice. As a young man, Britten honed his craft writing songs, film and radio scores before moving into the theatre. His early operas contain elements of the old ballad style, filtered through the influence of Berg's *Wozzeck* and Gershwin's *Porgy and Bess*, but by the time of *Billy Budd* and *Gloriana* (written for the coronation of Elizabeth II in 1953) he had found a way of writing full-scale grand operas in a twentieth-century idiom. He also relished the challenge of working with the English Opera Group, a company which made a virtue of its limited resources to perform outside conventional opera houses. A trilogy of one-act works, written in the early 1960s and known as the 'Church Parables' (*Curlew River*, *The Burning Fiery Furnace* and *The Prodigal Son*) demonstrate an increasing fascination with East Asian music and theatrical devices. Britten's other great gift was an almost flawless instinct for holding an audience's attention and making opera a vivid and immediately communicative dramatic experience.

Britten's great contemporary, Sir Michael Tippett, was more of a maverick. He wrote his own libretti, and many find his poetic prose baffling and pretentious. But Tippett had blazing musical inspiration and his operas address profound human issues. Following the mystical and ecstatic *The Midsummer Marriage*, his next opera, *King Priam*, is a complex exploration of the havoc that a state of war plays on the human heart, and in *The Knot Garden* and *The Ice Break* he made brave if confused attempts to bring crises of the modern world into the opera house.

The outstanding figure among Britten's and Tippett's successors is Harrison Birtwistle: *Punch and Judy*, his violent, parodic and ritualistic first opera scandalized Britten at its first performance in 1966. Later Birtwistle operas such as *The Mask of Orpheus*, *Gawain* and *The Last Supper* have all been musically preoccupied with variation within repetition – an idea expressed theatrically by recourse to elements of religious ritual. This ruggedly independent and uncompromising composer also explores the possibilities presented by electronically produced sound. Another significant experimenter is Alexander Goehr, whose *Arianna* constructs a new work around surviving fragments of an otherwise lost work by Monteverdi.

Younger British composers have been brilliantly diverse and inventive. Oliver Knussen's *Where the Wild Things Are* is a rumbustious children's opera, full of charm and energy. Judith Weir's *A Night at the Chinese Opera* and *Blond Eckbert* are weird and sinister fantasies. Thomas Adès's *Powder her Face* is a poignant satire on the scandalous life story of Margaret, Duchess of Argyll. Most impressive of all is Mark Anthony Turnage, whose funky, jazz-coloured style and demotic edge has animated both the dark surrealist nightmare of *Greek*, a reworking the Oedipus legend in a setting of modern urban desolation, and *The Silver Tassie*, an adaptation of Sean O'Casey's moving play about the victims of the First World War trenches.

Henry Purcell (1659–95)
Dido and Aeneas

Three acts (normally performed without an interval).
First performed London, ?1689.
Libretto by Nahum Tate

It is often said that the first performance of this opera was
given in 1689 at Josias Priest's boarding school for girls, but it
seems likely that it was composed some four years earlier and
perhaps performed like a masque on some ceremonial royal
occasion.

∾ Plot

Dido, the widowed Queen of Carthage, is reluctant to declare
her love for Prince Aeneas, a fugitive from ruined Troy. Belinda,
her lady-in-waiting, and the court urge her on, and when
Aeneas presses his suit, she yields, amid general rejoicing.

Malevolent witches plot havoc. They raise a storm, and
one of the coven, disguised as Mercury, reminds Aeneas that
he must sail on to Italy. To the witches' delight, Aeneas heeds
the injunction and leaves Carthage. Dismayed at his betrayal,
Dido bids farewell to life.

∾ What to listen for

In its modest way, this opera is a model in terms of its dramatic pace, contrast and development. It also contains a
wealth of richly charged and supple melody, set to the text
with an unforced grace and ease which avoids predictable
emphases and subtly shades the implication of particular
words with the genius of a poet. All the numbers are short,
based on the principle of a solo aria followed or answered by
a chorus, with danced interludes in each of the three acts.
The most substantial number comes in the last scene – Dido's
lament, 'When I am laid in earth', sung over a repeated five-
bar phrase (or ground bass) and culminating in cries of

'Remember me' which can seem as heart-rending as anything in Wagner or Verdi.

The Sorceress is a boldly melodramatic character, who declaims recitative rather than singing arias; Aeneas, in contrast, seems stiff and weak, the mere victim of her unexplained malevolence. The scene for the witches ends very abruptly, and some music is thought to have been lost at this point.

✎ In performance

One of the most refreshing removals of this opera from the standard baroque or neo-classical context was made by the American choreographer Mark Morris. His version was sung in the pit and danced on stage, Morris himself doubling as Dido and the Sorceress, with only the simplest of costumes and barest of settings. The expressive power of this production reminded one that in Purcell's conception of opera, dance played as important a role as song.

✎ Recordings

CDs: Janet Baker (Dido); Anthony Lewis (cond.). Decca 425 720 2

Anne-Sofie von Otter (Dido); Trevor Pinnock (cond.) Archiv 427624 2

Benjamin Britten (1913–76)
Peter Grimes

Three acts. First performed London, 1945.
Libretto by Montagu Slater

Britten famously found a copy of George Crabbe's long narrative poem *The Borough* (first published in 1810) in a second-hand bookshop while he was in the USA during the early part of the Second World War. Reading Crabbe made him feel homesick for his native Suffolk, where *The Borough* is set, and introduced him to the characters of Peter Grimes and Ellen Orford. The opera was largely written on the composer's return to England and was first performed shortly after VE Day, thus making it the signal of a new era for English opera.

∾ Plot

In a Suffolk village (clearly Aldeburgh, but referred to in the opera only as the 'Borough', perhaps because Aldeburgh is not an easily singable word), an inquest is held into the dubious circumstances behind the death of a boy apprenticed to the fisherman Peter Grimes, a man of poetic temperament, capable of great sensitivity as well as outbursts of rage. A verdict of accidental death is upheld, but Grimes remains under suspicion. Only the widowed schoolteacher Ellen Orford stands by him: Grimes hopes to prosper and marry her. Ellen collects a new apprentice for Grimes from the workhouse and hands the boy over to Grimes in the local pub during a terrible storm. The villagers ostracize and demonize Grimes, who is incapable of normal social communication.

Some weeks later, on a Sunday morning outside the church, Ellen discovers that Grimes has been ill-treating his new apprentice. She confronts Grimes with his cruelty, and at the end of a terrible quarrel, he hits her and runs off distraught. Villagers emerging from a service witness this scene, and set off in a grim posse to Grimes's hut. Meanwhile, in the course of some over-hasty preparations for a fishing expedition, Grimes is party to another accident which causes the apprentice to lose his footing and fall to his death. When the posse arrives at Grimes's hut, they find it empty and assume he has gone out to sea.

Some days later, Grimes has not been seen again. Ellen finds a jumper she had knitted for the apprentice washed up on shore and realizes that the boy must have drowned. At night, Grimes's boat is seen in the harbour: with renewed venom stimulated by the malicious gossip of the neurotic Mrs Sedley, the villagers gather and again set out to the hut, this time as a lynch-mob. Ellen and Captain Balstrode, a kindly old merchant skipper, find Grimes wandering on the shore, out of his mind. Balstrode gently orders him to take his boat out to sea and scuttle her. Numbly, Grimes agrees. As the daily routines of the village begin again at dawn, somebody spots a boat sinking on the horizon.

✧ What to listen for

One of the elements which had crucially held English opera back since Purcell was its failure to find a form of dramatic recitative appropriate to the English language which did not sound merely 'churchy'. Already experienced as a song writer, Britten solves this problem brilliantly, and from the opening scene, one is aware of how 'naturally' the stresses fall, and how clearly every word can be articulated.

Which is not to say that the score lacks lyrical highlights – for example, Grimes's eerie evocation of the night sky after the storm, 'Now the Great Bear and Pleiades', its opening pitched on a repeated E, a note which had a uniquely distinctive sound in the tenor of Britten's partner Peter Pears, who created the role; or Ellen's soprano outburst down a simple descending scale, 'Let her among you without sin', or her reverie over the abused apprentice's jumper, 'Embroidery in childhood'. The slithering silken harmony of the quartet for women's voices in Act II owes something to the final trio of Strauss's *Der Rosenkavalier*.

Note also how sharply Britten characterizes individual members of the Borough: Ned Keene, the flirtatious apothecary; the hysterical Methodist preacher Bob Boles; the neurotic and snobbish widow, Mrs Sedley; the bluff pub landlady, Auntie, and her two silly nieces (who appear to act as the local prostitutes and duet in a style drawn on Gilbert and Sullivan). The stunning choruses – indeed, the chorus's central role in the whole opera – show the influence of Mussorgsky's *Boris Godunov*.

The four richly coloured orchestral interludes depicting various moods of the sea (in the manner of Debussy's *La Mer*) are often played separately as a concert suite.

✍ In performance

An opera of immense theatrical strength, which has been staged in several different idioms. At Covent Garden, Elijah Moshinsky was inspired by the early Victorian photographs of the Suffolk coast taken by P. H. Sutcliffe to present the opera on an almost bare stage, animating it with evocative lighting and unsentimentalized, uncaricatured performances dominated by Jon Vickers's Grimes, the embodiment of the visionary outsider turned maniac. John Copley in Chicago and Trevor Nunn at Glyndebourne evoked the community with more naturalistic detail and architecture, bringing the opera close to the world of the Victorian novel. Several productions, notably Willy Decker's in Brussels, have made Grimes's homosexuality explicit rather than implicit (showing him, for instance, repelled by Ellen's affectionate physical advances), while at the Opéra Bastille, Graham Vick interpreted it in even more specific terms of modern tabloid-style hysteria about child abuse. Tim Albery's production for ENO was more expressionistic, setting the story in the context of the prejudices and anxieties which haunted British society at the end of the Second World War and showing the chorus acting *en masse* like so many pre-programmed zombies.

❧ Recordings

CD: Anthony Rolfe Johnson (Grimes); Bernard Haitink (cond.). EMI 754 8322

Video: Philip Langridge (Grimes); David Atherton (cond.). ENO production. Decca 071 428 3

The Rape of Lucretia

Two acts. First performed Glyndebourne, 1946. Libretto by Ronald Duncan

Britten's first chamber opera, a remarkable contrast in scope, mood and subject-matter from its precursor, *Peter Grimes*. Superbly constructed in dramatic terms, it employs an instrumental ensemble of thirteen players to astonishing effect and offers fine opportunities for its eight vocal soloists. Only some pretentious passages in its generally over-poetic libretto mar its haunting power and austere beauty.

❧ Plot

Two figures, presented as a Male and Female Chorus, frame the story for the audience and comment from their different moral perspectives on its implications.

Some five hundred years before the birth of Jesus Christ, Rome suffers under the harsh rule of the Etruscan prince Tarquinius, who sits in a tent outside the city drinking in the company of two Roman generals, Collatinus and Junius. Together, they bemoan the general infidelity of women. Only Collatinus's wife Lucretia escapes their mockery – she is known to be chastely loyal to her husband. Hearing this, Tarquinius resolves to ride back to Rome and do his worst. He finds Lucretia and her servants living in domestic tranquillity and they modestly grant his request for a bed for the night. Later, he slips into Lucretia's room. After she wakens in terror, he rapes her and leaves. Next morning, the servants blithely welcome the sunshine, until an ashen-faced Lucretia enters and coldly commands them to summon Collatinus. When he arrives, she tells him what has happened and, overwhelmed by shame, kills herself. The Male and Female Chorus lament the tragedy and look forward to the arrival of a superior Christian morality of tolerance and forgiveness.

∾ What to listen for

Tautly composed around two melodic themes (one associated with Lucretia, one with Tarquinius) and the sonorities of a chamber ensemble – flute (doubling piccolo and alto flute), oboe (doubling cor anglais), clarinet (doubling bass clarinet), bassoon, horn, percussion, harp, two violins, viola, cello, double bass – which deliberately excludes the brighter brass instruments and gives the opera an extraordinarily tense and haunting atmosphere, as if a thunderstorm is about to break into a clammy evening. The score is particularly rich in arresting effects (the harp which depicts the rustling of the cicadas outside the generals' tent, for example, the cor anglais which bleakly embodies Lucretia's grief and shame, or the depiction of Tarquinius's furious horseback Ride to Rome, in which different instruments are used to represent different terrain). More generally, strings and drum are associated with the men, harp, flute and clarinet with the women, and the listener is always conscious of the separation between their two spheres.

∾ In performance

In line with modern sexual psychology, most modern productions suggest that Lucretia (mezzo-soprano), sexually unawakened by her beloved husband Collatinus (bass), is aroused by Tarquinius (baritone) and feels herself to be in some sense complicit in the rape – hence the sense of guilt that feeds into her shame. Should the opera more properly be called *The Seduction of Lucretia*? For the director, an even trickier question is the presentation of the figures of the Male and Female Chorus (tenor and soprano). Should they be physically involved in the action, moving up close to the characters like ghosts, as they did in David McVicar's production for ENO; or detached from it, as in Graham Vick's production – also for ENO – in which they observe the stage from a gantry? How seriously can one take the Male Chorus's final assertion of Christian perspective, and to what extent are the Male and Female Chorus hostile to each other? Another possibility is that Junius is the true villain of the piece. It is he who goads and manipulates the unabashedly lust-driven Tarquinius into acting as he does.

∾ Recording

CD: Janet Baker (Lucretia); Benjamin Britten (cond.). Decca 425 666 2

Albert Herring

**Three acts. First performed Glyndebourne, 1947.
Libretto by Eric Crozier**

Based on a Maupassant short story, 'Le Rosier de Madame Husson', but like *Peter Grimes*, deeply rooted in Britten's native Suffolk and the problems faced by those who defy its narrow social codes. It can also be regarded as a pendant to *The Rape of Lucretia* (see above), as an exploration of the crisis of sexual initiation. This was the first opera to be performed at the Aldeburgh Festival, in its inaugural season of 1948.

∾ Plot

Local dignitaries, dominated by the pompous Lady Billows, gather to elect the village of Loxford with its Queen of the May. When no suitable female virgin presents herself, it is decided to elect a male instead. The fey, put-upon Albert Herring, who works in the greengrocer's owned by his widowed and nagging mother, is approached. Reluctantly, he accepts the dubious and embarrassing honour.

At a starchy tea-party in a marquee, Albert is crowned.

After making a monosyllabic speech, he drinks a glass of lemonade, laced with rum by his well-meaning friend Sid, a butcher's lad in love with Nancy from the bakery. That evening, Albert returns to the shop quite drunk and decides it is time for him to break out and sow a few wild oats.

The next day, Albert has vanished. Mrs Herring is distraught, especially when his King of the May garland is found crushed by a cart on the roadside. He is assumed dead, but after everybody has joined in the greengrocer's to mourn him, he pokes his head round the door and without going into details, makes it plain that he has been on the tiles and up to no good. He blames his mother's mollycoddling for the 'wild explosion', expresses a certain discomfort at what he experienced and announces that he now wishes to return to ordinary life. Sid and Nancy are delighted by Albert's self-assertion.

✎ What to listen for

A lively and largely conversational score, notable for its witty characterization of the village worthies – a slow march for Lady Billows, palpitatingly romantic arpeggios for the susceptible Miss Wordsworth, bumbling double bass accompanying the incompetent policeman Sergeant Budd. Note the sly quotation from Wagner's *Tristan und Isolde*, when Sid laces Albert's lemonade with rum. The one sustained number is the long and complex threnody in the third act as Albert's death is prematurely mourned – over a ground bass, to different themes, the characters voice their various reactions before combining in one polyphonic ensemble. One critic, Patricia Howard, has asked whether it 'dangerously inclines towards being too funny about death or being too tragic for the ludicrous circumstances and the light-hearted mood of the rest of the opera'. But that ambivalence of tone is also what makes *Albert Herring* so intriguing.

✎ In performance

The brilliant parody and caricature of the first scene, focused on the pompous and pontificating Lady Billows (written for older soprano), surrounded by her hangers-on, should not deceive one into thinking that *Albert Herring* is just farce: it is better described as a comedy on the verge of turning tragic. Albert himself (tenor) should not be interpreted as a half-wit. He may be put-upon and repressed, but he is not stupid, and a good performance will communicate the pain and uncertainty of a young man's initiation into the world of adult experience – whether homosexual or heterosexual.

∾ Recording

CD: Peter Pears (Albert); Benjamin Britten (cond.).
Decca 421 849 2

Billy Budd

**Four or two acts. First performed London, 1951.
Libretto by E. M. Forster and Eric Crozier**

Based on the novella by Herman Melville, this was Britten's first 'grand' opera, also notable for its exclusively male cast. Broadly speaking, E. M. Forster was responsible for the monologues in the libretto, while Crozier worked on the dialogues and stage directions.

In 1961, Britten revised the score, compressing the original four acts into two – the major changes included the elimination of the finale to Act I and a new finale to Act II. In recent years, however, the original four-act version has been successfully revived, and the gains and losses are now regarded as being equally spread between the alternatives. The opera has enjoyed an extraordinary surge in popularity over the last decade, and is now virtually standard repertory in many major houses throughout Europe and North America.

∾ Plot

The action takes place on board the *Indomitable*, a British man o' war, during the early years of the war against Napoleon.

Billy Budd is one of several press-ganged recruits: a handsome, enthusiastic lad with a stammer, he is delighted to serve a great cause under the noble, reflective and highly civilized Captain Vere. But Claggart, a sinister officer with a psychotic grudge against innocence and beauty, resolves to bring about Billy's downfall. Billy refuses to heed warnings against Claggart's malevolence and fails to understand the significance of an attempt, set up by Claggart, to bribe him to join a mutiny.

A French ship is sighted, but, to the crew's frustration, mists fall and prevent an engagement. Claggart blackens Billy's name. The sceptical Vere summons Billy, who believes he is about to be promoted. When he hears Claggart's accusations, Billy stammers and instinctively lashes out at Claggart, who is killed by the blow. Under naval law, Vere is obliged to sentence Billy to death, even though he knows in his heart that Billy was good and Claggart evil. Billy accepts his fate uncomplainingly, but when he is hanged from the yardarm, the ship's crew rises in spontaneous mutiny, which the officers quell. In an epilogue, the elderly Vere looks back and reflects on Billy's redemptive example.

∾ What to listen for

The libretto's moral ambiguities are embodied in the way in which the music constantly vacillates between two keys or two notes a semitone apart – a movement which also suggests the ship rocking on the sea. Although there are some fine set-pieces for the principals – a monologue in which Claggart exposes his need to destroy 'beauty, handsomeness, goodness', for example, or Billy's touchingly ardent and sincere aria as he awaits hanging – it is for its big ensembles that the opera is most notable. These may be relatively simple (the sea shanties) or more dramatically tense and complex, as in the scenes of the failed engagement with the French which open the second half of the opera, or the scene of Billy's hanging and its aftermath. Note the way that the melodic motif associated with the 'Rights' o' man' motif recurs throughout the opera, and also the extraordinary sequence of thirty-four simple chords, all based in one key, which through their modulations of dynamics and harmonic and instrumental colour graphically tell the inner and outer story of Vere's final interview with Billy.

Ꮛ In performance

Billy Budd touches on large metaphysical issues – the unmotivated existence of good and evil, the incompatibility of human and divine justice, the paradoxical guilt of the innocent and innocence of the guilty – and on the printed page can look pretentious. On stage, however, the sheer theatricality of the plot and the conflicts it embodies carries it along, and one notices how teenagers and those with no prior interest in opera invariably find it enthralling, especially when the different levels of the ship are presented as spectacularly as they are in John Dexter's production at the Met. It's important that the characters all look physically convincing – a handsome blond Billy (baritone), a sinister, spidery Claggart (bass) and a Vere (tenor) whose fine upstanding demeanour disguises his vacillating conscience. Productions sometimes fall down by their failure to drill the cast into giving a convincing impression of naval discipline, and Vere's disguise as an old man for the prologue and epilogue can cause unintentional hilarity.

This is the most blatantly homosexual of Britten's operas, and several directors, homosexual themselves, tend to camp up the infatuation of Claggart and Vere with the beautiful but unattainable Billy.

Ꮛ Recordings

CD: Simon Keenlyside (Billy); Philip Langridge (Vere); Richard Hickox (cond.). Chandos CHAN 9826
Video: Thomas Allen (Billy); Philip Langridge (Vere); Mark Elder (cond.). ENO production. Universal 079 2213

The Turn of the Screw

Two acts. First performed Venice, 1954.
Libretto by Myfanwy Piper

Based on the novella by Henry James, this immaculately composed and dramatically gripping chamber work is one of the most admired of post-war operas and has some claim to be the supreme masterpiece among Britten's theatrical works.

ᴼᵛ Plot

A nameless Governess arrives at a remote country house to look after two orphaned children, Flora and her younger brother Miles. She is apprehensive, having been specifically asked by their guardian not to consult him under any circumstances once she has taken up the post. At first the children seem delightful, and the Governess befriends the sensible housekeeper Mrs Grose. But then news comes that Miles has been disgracefully expelled from school – quite why is not clear. The Governess is incredulous. One evening, walking alone in the grounds, she sees an eerily vanishing man on the roof of the house. Later she describes the figure to Mrs Grose, who identifies him as the sinister Peter Quint, formerly a servant in the house, whose violent love affair with the Governess's predecessor, Miss Jessel, resulted in both their deaths and who was suspected of a malign influence over the children. The Governess passionately vows to protect the children from the ghosts who seem to want to possess them.

Miles becomes worryingly dreamy and *distrait*, and the Governess is further alarmed when she sees the apparition of Miss Jessel watching Flora from the other side of a lake. At night, the voices of Quint and Miss Jessel summon the children – until they are interrupted by the arrival of the Governess and Mrs Grose.

The Governess comes face to face with the ghost of Miss Jessel in the schoolroom and decides that she must risk breaking the terms of her employment by writing of her concerns to the children's guardian (with whom she may be infatuated). The Governess then attempts to wring the truth out of Miles, but he resists, still haunted by Quint's alluring voice and its injunctions. Quint also persuades Miles to steal the Governess's letter before it is posted. The Governess becomes convinced that Flora, bewitched by Miss Jessel, has grown to hate her, and Mrs Grose reports how Flora has poured out shocking profanities in her sleep. The Governess agrees that Mrs Grose should take Flora to her guardian, leaving the Governess alone with Miles. A final battle for Miles's soul ensues. The Governess questions him about the theft of the letter, and as he is on the verge of a confession, he shouts out 'Peter Quint, you devil!' (the first time he has uttered his name). The Governess is briefly exultant, believing that his cry indicates that she has triumphed, but then realizes it has cost the boy his life – he lies dead in her arms.

✒ What to listen for

A twelve-note theme – fifteen variations on which link each scene to the next like so many 'turns of the screw' – forms the musical basis of this taut and schematic opera. Britten draws an astonishing range of colour and sonorities out of a chamber ensemble similar to that used in *The Rape of Lucretia*.

The requisite spookiness is created by the ironic use of cheerful nursery songs (such as 'Tom, Tom, the Piper's Son' and 'Lavender's Blue'), lullabies, twittering bird-song, prayer-book chants and primer piano pieces, set against the exotic and eerie sounds of celesta, gong, harp and glockenspiel. Nothing in the opera is more haunting or haunted than the way that, in the fifth scene of Act I, Miles suddenly modulates into a Latin classroom mnemonic, 'Malo, malo' – a serene yet sinister melody that heralds the melismatic cry of 'Miles, Miles' that Quint alluringly keens at the end of Act I.

✒ In performance

The question in James's short story as to whether the ghosts are figments of the Governess's cabin-fevered imagination does not arise in the opera: Britten's ghosts undoubtedly exist, and the question becomes whether it is they or the Governess who are the more destructive of Miles's and Flora's innocence.

Among many superb productions that this eminently theatrical opera has received, that of Deborah Warner for the Royal Opera stands out for the creation of an uneasy moral atmosphere, suggesting the possibility that the children may find the influence of the ghosts more benign and liberating than that of the Governess's hysterical paranoia. A great practical difficulty is finding a young soprano who can impersonate Flora convincingly – few children are capable of singing the role, and adults tend to be either too tall or too bosomy to give the right impression! The use of mirrors by the designer as a means of creating ghostly effect has become a cliché.

ᛒ Recording
CD: Robert Tear (Quint); Colin Davis (cond.).
Philips 446 325 2

A Midsummer Night's Dream

Three acts. First performed Aldeburgh, 1960.
Libretto by William Shakespeare, edited by the
composer and Peter Pears

Written in haste, with only one non-Shakespearean line – 'Compelling thee to marry with Demetrius' – added to the text. Although not as innovative as other Britten operas, its delightful musical creation of the fairy world, as well as its wit and good humour, serve as a rebuff to all those who persist in thinking that a twentieth-century opera must be grim and unenjoyable.

ᛒ Plot
Broadly the same as Shakespeare's play, omitting the opening Athenian scenes.

ᐁ What to listen for

From the opening bars, with their glassy string glissandi evocative of deep-breathed sleep and night-time forest murmurs, this is an opera full of magic of an unexpected kind. It contains three distinct sound worlds: fairy, mortal and rude mechanical. The fairy king Oberon, sung by a counter-tenor, is both sensual (as in the gorgeous aria 'I know a bank') and commanding, in contrast to his high-pitched (in both senses) wife Titania, with her extravagant soprano coloratura skittering, the treble choir of attendants, and the perky spoken rhymes of Puck, whose acrobatics are accompanied by a pealing trumpet and drum which bring the opera to an end. In comparison, the mortal lovers sound distinctly earthbound, though their lovely canonic quartet when they awake from the spell shows that they have been touched by the wonder of their comically nightmarish experience. The 'rude mechanicals', led by Quince and Bottom, are perhaps too bluntly mocked by their music (underlined by the use of a blundering solo trombone), though their version of *Pyramus and Thisbe* contains a hilarious parody of several of the sillier conventions of Italian opera. The final scene is perhaps the most magical of all, as Oberon and Titania arrive to bless Theseus's palace, with the 'Scotch snap' of 'Now, until the break of day'.

ᐁ In performance

Robert Carsen's chic production, first seen at the Aix Festival, covered the stage with a giant bed, symbolic of the underlying innocent eroticism to the proceedings, and presented Puck as a dirty old man in a flasher's raincoat. But the most enchanting production is surely Peter Hall's at Glyndebourne, designed by John Bury. Costumes suggested a lavish Jacobean masque, and the trees of the forest seemed truly alive, their branches moved by actors who sat inside their trunks. Elsewhere, it has become common to see the lovers presented as silly toffs from a Noel Coward drawing-room comedy and to take a sophisticated, even satirical view of the pantomime magic.

Ꮖ Recording

CD: Brian Asawa (Oberon); Colin Davis (cond.).
Philips 454 122 2

Death in Venice

Two acts. First performed Snape, 1973.
Libretto by Myfanwy Piper

Britten's last major work, completed shortly before he under-
went an operation for the heart condition which eventually
killed him. *Death in Venice*, based on the novella by Thomas
Mann, is a sombre and intense work, on a theme painfully close
to aspects of Britten's own emotional life. Aschenbach is the
last operatic role he wrote for his partner, the tenor Peter
Pears, who also created the roles of Peter Grimes, Albert
Herring, Vere in *Billy Budd* and Quint in *The Turn of the Screw*.

Ꮖ Plot

Failing in health and inspiration, the celebrated novelist
Gustav von Aschenbach arrives for a recuperative holiday in
Venice. At his hotel, he is struck from a distance by the beauty
of a young teenage boy who belongs to a Polish family.
Without ever speaking to him, Aschenbach begins to watch
the boy – whose name is Tadzio – with what he believes to be
disinterested platonic pleasure. Slowly, however, as the rot-
tenness and corruption of the city closes in on him, he realizes to his wonder and horror that he is deeply and carnally in
love with Tadzio. Although the emotion in some respects
revitalizes him, Aschenbach's situation becomes increasingly
abject. Venice empties as rumours of an outbreak of cholera
spread, and Aschenbach realizes that the Polish family are
about to leave. He sits on the beach, gazing adoringly at
Tadzio for one last time. Finally, he calls Tadzio's name out
loud for the first time and then dies.

❧ What to listen for

The grimmest and most austere of Britten's operas, focused on Aschenbach's interior monologue, conveyed through a recitative that can often seem like little more than rhythmic speech, much of it underpinned by raw piano chords. In contrast stands the exotic, percussive and pseudo-oriental music associated with Tadzio, symbolic of the spirit of the Greek god Dionysus, whose cult originated in India. A Venetian barcarole, a series of choral dances (accompanying Aschenbach's fantasy of Tadzio playing the games and sports of Ancient Greece) and the banal popular songs of a group of strolling players give relief from the brooding, death-directed intensity.

❧ In performance

The opera involves twenty-four short scenes and a host of minor characters (played by a small number of singers doubling up), necessitating simple flexible settings or projections and a lot of teamwork. The show will nevertheless stand or fall by the ability of the mature tenor playing Aschenbach to make the vocal line expressive and the man's inner torments externally palpable. Tadzio is a silent role, usually played by a professional dancer.

❧ Recording

CD: Peter Pears (Aschenbach); Steuart Bedford (cond.).
Decca 425 669 2

Michael Tippett (1905–98)
The Midsummer Marriage

Three acts. First performed London, 1955.
Libretto by the composer

Tippett's first full-scale opera owes much to *Die Zauberflöte*, the poetry of T. S. Eliot and the philosophy of Jung. Shrouded in complex mysticism and a clumsy plot, the details of the libretto may be hard to follow or fathom, but the score has a radiant lyricism and energy which is immediately enthralling. Since its initial hostile reception, the opera has increasingly been recognized as one of the masterpieces of the post-war repertory.

❧ Plot

Midsummer morning, during 'the present time': Jenifer and Mark are about to be married, but, outside a temple, they quarrel and separate – she up a staircase (towards disinterested enlightenment), he down into a cave (of his own sensuality and egotism). Jenifer is pursued by her father, the businessman King Fisher, who is accompanied by his secretary Bella and her mechanic boyfriend, Jack. Jenifer and Mark return, and Jenifer persuades him to accompany her on another, upward spiritual journey.

Afternoon: With their more ordinary aspirations, Bella and Jack discuss the prospect of their wedding. From the temple, dancers enact rituals symbolic of the male pursuit of the female.

Evening: King Fisher enlists the clairvoyant Madame Sosostris to help him bring Jenifer back. Instead, she declaims an oration on the nature of inspiration and creativity, and Jenifer and Mark reappear, transfigured in a blaze of light. The enraged King Fisher tries to shoot Mark, but he is blinded by the light and falls dead himself. Following another ritual dance, embodying images of sacrifice and rebirth, the marriage of Jenifer and Mark is finally celebrated in triumph.

❧ What to listen for

Rapturously lyrical in its vocal lines and richly chromatic in its harmonic language, this is a score which seems quite literally to burst into life, and has often been labelled Beethovenian. Highlights include the youthful ecstasy of Mark and Jenifer's music in Act I, the blazing colours and energy of the ritual dances in Act II, and the long visionary scene in Act III of Madame Sosostris – a character like Sarastro in *Die Zauberflöte* or Erda in the *Ring* whose music does seem to embody some deeper wisdom. The choral writing throughout has a peculiar radiance.

❧ In performance

An opera which deals with the immanence of marvels and wonders just one step behind the surface of the ordinary, everyday world. Perhaps best understood as a foreshadowing of the sixties hippie movement, and its fascination with transcending visible reality to reach into other states of consciousness and modes of social life – this, at least, was the line followed by Tim Albery at ENO, Graham Vick at Covent Garden and Richard Jones in Munich, the latter in particular providing a funny, touching, inventive and ultimately uplifting production which evoked the dawning of a new age of higher spirituality without sentimentality or corniness.

❧ Recording

CD: Joan Sutherland (Jenifer); John Pritchard (cond.). Gala GL 100 524

Harrison Birtwistle (1934–)
Gawain

Two acts. First performed London, 1991.
Libretto by David Harsent

Loosely based on the anonymous medieval poem known as *Sir Gawain and the Green Knight*, this is probably Birtwistle's most popular work to date. Its subject matter embodies his consuming interest in pagan ritual and mythology. For the opera's 1994 revival, Birtwistle substantially cut a long 'masque of the seasons', and it is this latter, shorter version which is now considered definitive.

✎ Plot

The court of King Arthur celebrates Christmas, when an unknown knight, clad in green, appears unexpectedly. He issues a challenge – he will submit to having his head severed with an axe, on the condition that whoever does so will accept a similar blow after a year and a day have passed.

Sir Gawain accepts the challenge and strikes off the Green Knight's head. The body of the Green Knight picks up the severed head, which continues to speak, summoning Gawain to a green chapel. As a masque of the seasons is enacted, Gawain prepares himself for his quest.

Gawain travels forth into the unknown forest and arrives at the castle of Sir Bertilak and Lady de Hautdesert, who tell him that the green chapel is close by. For three successive days, Bertilak goes out hunting, leaving his wife to attempt a seduction of Gawain. Every evening, the two men exchange the day's winnings: a stag, a boar and a fox for three kisses. On the third day, a frightened Gawain also accepts from Lady de Hautdesert a magically protective sash. At the appointed time, Gawain presents himself at the green chapel where the Green Knight awaits him. Gawain bows his head, but two blows of the axe do not injure him at all, while a third only draws a little blood. It transpires that the Green Knight is in fact Sir Bertilak and the plot has been hatched by the enchantress Morgan le Fay, who has a grudge against Arthur. The blood was drawn as payment for his deceit in secretly keeping and wearing the magic sash.

Gawain returns to Arthur's court. He refuses to play the hero, and the knights turn from him with contempt. Gawain has gained self-knowledge, but at the price of being left an outsider.

❧ What to listen for

Once described as a 'sonic battering ram', *Gawain* contains several recurrent short refrains and blocks of musical material repeated with variations – in parallel with the plot's emphasis on the passage of time and the seasons. It also uses complex parodies of medieval musical forms, such as the Marian choral motet, and some obvious onomatopoeia (for example, the 'clip-clop' representation of horses' hooves). The role of Gawain is for baritone, that of the Green Knight for bass.

Birtwistle's music deliberately favours orchestra over voice, and is therefore extraordinarily hard for humans to sing and to articulate verbally (especially for the soprano who sings Morgan Le Fay). The composer has therefore sanctioned the use of surtitles.

Gawain may lack the delicacy, wit and grace for which the original medieval poem is notable, but the sheer physical power of the music is undeniably impressive.

❧ In performance

Gawain has to date received only one staged production, directed by Di Trevis at Covent Garden. It used a circular stage, reflecting the circular nature of the music and the action, and cleverly managed the illusion of the speaking severed head.

❧ Recording

CD: François Le Roux (Gawain); Elgar Howarth (cond.). Collins 70412

PART SEVEN

Slavic Opera

Imported Italian opera dominated in Russia until 1836, when Mikhail Glinka paved the way for a native school with *A Life for the Tsar* – a piece rooted in Russian history and folk music, with a peasant as its hero and the chorus, representing the Russian people, playing a major role. Glinka's second opera *Ruslan and Ludmila*, a fantastic if rambling fairy-tale, drawn from a poem by Alexander Pushkin, contains dazzling orchestration and exotic oriental inflections. These two operas served as inspiration to a younger breed of patriotic composers determined to forget the Italians and cultivate a distinctively Russian style. Thus Alexander Borodin's *Prince Igor* and Modest Mussorgsky's *Boris Godunov* and *Khovanshchina* have grand historical and social sweep, while operas like *The Snow Maiden* and *The Golden Cockerel* show their composer Nikolai Rimsky-Korsakov saturated in the bright colours of Russian myth and legend. Igor Stravinsky was a pupil of Rimsky-Korsakov: his early one-act operas such as *The Nightingale* and *Renard* follow his master's example in several respects, but are also notable for using dancers as well as singers to tell the story on stage. After Stravinsky left Russia, he deserted the music of his country too: *Oedipus Rex*, with its Latin text, reinterprets the Handelian opera-oratorio, while *The Rake's Progress* contains artful parody of western European opera of the eighteenth century, from Gay's *The Beggar's Opera* to Mozart's *Così fan tutte*.

Under the Stalinist regime, opera was obliged to conform to socialist ideology: Shostakovich's *Lady Macbeth of Mtsensk* had an electrifying impact when first performed in 1934, but its tone was much too dangerous, cynical and subversive to survive a repressive censorship. A more superficial and versatile composer, Sergei Prokofiev, survived with more aplomb, producing less ambitious operas in a variety of genres before devoting his final years to *War and Peace*, a patriotic epic which looks back to Glinka and Mussorgsky. Prokofiev also inherited the exuberantly lyrical gifts of another great master of Russian opera, Pyotr Ilyich Tchaikovsky. Although belonging to the same generation as Mussorgsky and Rimsky-Korsakov, Tchaikovsky stands apart from them, and his attempts at public drama like *Mazeppa* and *The Maid of Orleans* are not as convincing as *Eugene Onegin* and *The Queen of Spades*, operas which focus on intimate and even neurotic emotions of the individual psyche.

The great majority of Russian operas created in the Soviet era amount to crude and simplistic efforts to play by the rules and are of no lasting value. Since *glasnost*, however, Alfred Schnittke's *Life with an Idiot* has made some international impact – its bitter absurdism recalls the spirit of Shostakovich, as well as the more nightmarish fictions of Gogol, Dostoevsky and Kafka.

The Russian opera scene is currently suffering devastating impoverishment caused by the abrupt withdrawal of the massive subsidies allocated by the culture-respecting Communists. But Russia continues to produce magnificent voices of a matchless power and amplitude, and the foreign travels of Moscow's Bolshoi and St Petersburg's Maryinsky (or Kirov) Operas prove that the great nineteenth-century traditions survive and even flourish.

In Eastern Europe, national schools of opera have fought to establish their own space between the culturally invasive might of the German, Russian and Austro-Hungarian empires which dominate their political history.

Poland boasts Stanislaw Moniuszko's *The Haunted Manor* (1865), with its richly amusing plot and lively score, as well as Karol Szymanowski's *King Roger* (1926), an austere but impressive exploration of a medieval Christian drawn back to the pagan cult of Dionysus. From Hungary comes the sombre, gripping allegory of Béla Bartók's *Bluebeard's Castle* (1918) and György Ligeti's scabrous *Le grand Macabre*, first performed in Stockholm in 1978 and one of the few successful comic operas of the century.

Perhaps the most fertile operatic grounds in this region have been the Czech, Slovak and Moravian lands. Prague hosted the first performance of *Don Giovanni*, as well as those of familiar masterpieces of Bedřich Smetana and Antonin Dvořák. Brno has the honour of being home to Leoš Janáček, a genius whose reputation has grown over the last fifty years to the point at which he ranks among the very greatest of twentieth-century operatic composers.

On a more northerly Russian border, one should also note the importance of opera in Finland, a young country with a small population in which music has been an important factor in the consolidation of national identity. Aulis Sallinen's *The Horseman* (1974) and *The Red Line* (1979) are essays in direct and involving music drama of a sort that Glinka and Mussorgsky would have appreciated.

Modest Mussorgsky (1839–81)
Boris Godunov

Prologue and four acts, or seven scenes.
First performed St Petersburg, 1874.
Libretto by the composer

Based on Pushkin's five-act drama, much influenced by Shakespeare's *Macbeth* and imaginatively drawing on actual historical events which took place between 1598 and 1605, the opera has a complex genesis. An original version in seven scenes was rejected unheard by the management in St Petersburg. Mussorgsky subsequently revised and expanded the score into nine scenes, adding the episode in Poland.

After Mussorgsky's death, Rimsky-Korsakov produced two editions, which softened some of Mussorgsky's rough edges and enriched the orchestration: it was Rimsky's second version, with the great Russian bass Feodor Chaliapin, which made the opera popular in the west, but it is now only favoured in Russia. In 1939–40, Shostakovich made another version, restoring some of Mussorgsky's intentions – a process continued in the scholarly edition prepared by David Lloyd-Jones in 1975. The original 1869 version has been revived several times in recent years; partly because it is shorter (and therefore cheaper to mount), it has gained some ground, but despite some problems with the ordering of the scenes, the merits of the 1874 version, in whatever edition, are undoubtedly superior.

✥ Plot

The authorities threaten the people of Moscow, urging them to save Russia from anarchy by electing the boyar Boris Godunov as tsar. Boris is duly crowned, appearing before the people and humbly dedicating himself to his responsibility. But Boris fails to bring peace or prosperity to Russia, and in his cell the scholarly old monk Pimen, formerly a soldier at the tsar's court, tells the young novice Grigory how years earlier Boris had secretly ordered the murder of the young tsarevitch Dmitri in order to open his path to the throne. Grigory is the same age as the tsarevitch, and decides to impersonate him and claim the throne for himself. He sets out to Poland with two drunken monks Varlaam and Missail, hoping to gain support for his claim. In an inn on the border, he narrowly escapes arrest.

Boris has never been convinced that the tsarevitch actually died, and is racked by guilt and hallucinations. In Poland, Grigory–Dmitri falls in love with the noble Marina, who is persuaded by the wily Jesuit Rangoni to use his infatuation to win him to the cause of spreading the Catholic faith into Russia. The treacherous Shuisky brings Boris news of Grigory–Dmitri's campaign in Poland. In the street, Boris is accosted by a truth-telling Holy Fool who unnerves him further. Shuisky conspires with the monk Pimen, and when Boris hears his false tale of the tsarevitch's miracles, he collapses with horror and dies. Grigory–Dmitri, accompanied by Varlaam, Missail and a crowd of peasants from the Kromy forest, advances on Moscow. The Holy Fool laments Russia's misery.

✂ What to listen for

From its extraordinary opening scene, in which the police brusquely taunt and goad the wretched, terrified people of Moscow, there is an overwhelming directness about the way this music communicates. There may be few extensive or hummable melodies in *Boris Godunov* (and most of those, such as the 'Slava' anthem in the Coronation scene or the little song sung by the Hostess of the border inn, are adapted or invented folk-tunes), but every note is dramatically expressive and vividly characterful, and for all their harmonic crudity and instrumental rawness, Mussorgsky's scores are rich in marks specifying precisely how the words should be inflected and coloured (Boris's monologues provide the most obvious example of this). A more conventionally operatic episode is the 'Polish' act, with its graceful Polonaise, luscious love duet and elegant choruses: the figure of the scheming Jesuit Rangoni is a masterpiece of characterization. Most exciting of all, however, is the scene in the Kromy forest, as the chorus turns into a frenzied vengeful mob, lynching the chanting Jesuit priests and hailing Grigori–Dmitri's arrival, before the stage is left to the Holy Fool, lamenting the sufferings of the Russian people.

❧ In performance

Modern productions like to emphasize the opera's relevance not just to the course of Russian history and the tyrannies which have dogged it, but also to the universal problem of authoritarian regimes which oppress peoples and lead to armed dissent and revolution: Herbert Wernicke's Salzburg production, for instance, presents Boris and the boyars as black-suited Mafia thugs, and many others have updated their setting to the Stalinist era. But Mussorgsky does not take sides in a facile way, and it is important that Boris' nobility is felt: in his remorse, he has a greater soul than those scheming self-interestedly around him.

❧ Recordings

CD: Anatoly Kotscherga (Boris); Claudio Abbado (cond.). Sony S3K 58977
Video: Robert Lloyd (Boris); Valery Gergiev (cond.). Kirov production. Decca 071 139 3

Khovanshchina
(The Khovansky Affair)

Five acts. First performed St Petersburg, 1886.
Libretto by the composer

Like *Boris Godunov*, this is an epic of Russian history, based on actual events and historical sources. Mussorsgky died, riddled with alcoholism, before he had completed the score or marked up the orchestration. A performing edition was prepared by Rimsky-Korsakov for the opera's first posthumous production. It involved much recomposition, and has now been universally replaced by Shostakovich's more 'faithful' realization of the composer's intentions and style. In detail, the plot may be hard to follow, but in a strong performance its impact is immense.

∾ Plot

The action takes place during the early years of the reign of Peter the Great, who supported religious reform and the Orthodox church. In the name of the Old Believers, Prince Ivan Khovansky and his son Andrei, supported by the troop of élite musketeers known as the Streltsy, are plotting against Tsar Peter's enlightenment. The boyar Shaklovity alerts the tsar to the conspiracy by means of an anonymous letter. Andrei pursues a German girl, to the dismay of his former lover, Marfa. Dosifei, the pious leader of the Old Believers, calls for prayer.

Prince Vassily Golitsin, an ally of the Khovanskys, summons Marfa to foretell the future. She predicts only disaster, and he throws her out, ordering a henchman to drown her. Ivan Khovansky quarrels with Golitsin, until Dosifei appears and urges them to reconcile. Marfa returns, having been saved from drowning by Tsar Peter's bodyguard. The conspirators realize that Peter has learned of their scheming against him, and soon the Tsar's troops have routed the Streltsy.

Ivan Khovansky withdraws to his estate, where he is entertained by Persian dancers. He is murdered by the two-timing boyar Shaklovity; Golitsin, meanwhile, is exiled. Dosifei and Marfa realize that their cause is lost. Andrei continues to pursue Emma, but Marfa tells him that she has been sent away and that his father has been murdered. Peter pardons the Streltsy on the verge of their mass execution, but the old Believers will not make their peace with him. In a forest, led by Dosifei, Andrei and Marfa, they set fire to themselves.

✎ What to listen for

Khovanshchina is as difficult to grasp musically as it is dramatically, not least because Mussorgsky was struggling through his drunkenness and depression to compose something hugely original – in the words of the scholar Gerard McBurney, the opera is 'constructed from small (melodic) bits which are constantly reshuffled and reordered to create the illusion of a grand unfolding line'. *Khovanshchina* lacks the Shakespearean variety of atmosphere and character which animates *Boris Godunov*: although the melodic style is lusher and less jaggedly violent, the overall tone is harsher – this is an opera without heroes or even much in the way of good behaviour. Two beautiful orchestral passages, the opening 'Dawn over the Moscow River' and the 'Dance of the Persian Slaves' in Act IV are often played as concert items.

✎ In performance

Even more than *Boris Godunov*, *Khovanshchina* exists in grey moral and political areas. Whose side are we meant to be on? The Old Believers Marfa and Dosifei represent stern and fatalistic beliefs and values, the Khovanskys back-stabbing political treachery. A third element is the westernizing reformer Peter the Great, a character who (because of contemporary censorship restrictions) never appears on stage. Are we meant to think that the Old Believers achieve a sort of apocalyptic transcendence when they immolate themselves? Or are we witnessing the death of an old order and the birth of a new, as we do at the end of *Götterdämmerung*? Perhaps it is best to think of the opera not as a fully shaped drama so much as chapters from an old historical chronicle, from which one can draw one's own conclusions. For a director, it is much easier to stage each scene convincingly than to make the overall narrative clear.

✎ Recording

CD: Marjana Lipovšek (Marfa); Claudio Abbado (cond.). DG 429 758 2

Bedřich Smetana (1824–84)
The Bartered Bride (*Prodaná nevěsta*)

Three acts. First performed Prague, 1866.
Libretto by Karel Sabina

An opera originally performed in two acts with spoken dialogue, but today almost always performed in a revised three-act version with sung recitative. Very much a 'national' opera which embodies a certain view of Czech culture. Smetana rather despised the piece, which he regarded as no more than a *jeu d'esprit*, and longed for his more serious historical dramas to share its popularity.

✎ Plot

In a Bohemian village, Mařenka is in love with Jeník, but her parents and the wily marriage broker Kecal want her to marry the son of the wealthy Tobias Micha. The latter is thought to have two sons, but Kecal claims that the elder vanished long ago and is presumed dead. The younger one, Vašek, turns out to be a stuttering fool, and Mařenka makes every effort to put him off. Kecal offers Jeník money to withdraw, but he agrees to do this only in favour of Micha's elder son – who, unknown to anyone, is in fact none other than Jeník himself. The villagers are shocked to hear that Jeník has renounced love for money.

Vašek is entranced by the dancer Esmeralda, a member of a visiting circus, who persuades him to dress up as a performing bear. Mařenka hears of Jeník's bargain with Kecal and, in a rage, agrees to marry Vašek after all. The village gathers to celebrate the marriage of Mařenka to 'the son of Tobias Micha'. Then Vašek's parents recognize Jeník as their long-lost son, and Mařenka is delighted at Jeník's clever ploy. Kecal storms off in a rage and, despite some confusion caused by the appearance of Vašek in his performing-bear costume, Jeník and Mařenka are happily united.

❧ What to listen for

The sparkling overture and energetic opening chorus get the opera off to a cracking start. Much of what follows is grounded in Czech folk-rhythms, especially the fast polka. Some of the tunes may sound like traditional melodies, but they are in fact almost all Smetana's original compositions. Each act contains one danced section (polka, *furiant* and *skočná*): these were not part of the opera's original scheme, but part of the process by which Smetana bulked up the score after its initial frosty reception. The arias are not complex or elaborate, and it is for its feisty duets that the opera is most admired. The role of Mařenka is the most substantial, requiring a soprano who can ride over the heavy scoring of her Act III aria.

❧ In performance

Productions in Frankfurt and at Opera North and Glyndebourne have tried livening up the rather genteel nature of the comedy by updating the opera to the Communist era – influenced, perhaps, by satires of modern Czechoslovakia like Forman's movie *The Firemen's Ball* – but the idea of arranged marriages doesn't make much sense in a modern social context. Left in a folksy Czech setting, however, it can seem awfully twee and toytown: one solution, first attempted by Walter Felsenstein in East Berlin in 1951 and subsequently successfully adopted by both Rudolf Noelte for WNO and Thomas Langhoff in Munich, is to underplay the sunny farce and contextualize the farcical plot with a realistic portrait of a hard-working, mean-spirited rural community against which Mařenka and Jeník are busily rebelling.

❧ Recording

CD: Gabriela Beňačková (Mařenka); Zdeněk Kosler (cond.). Supraphon 103511 2

Pyotr Ilyich Tchaikovsky (1840–93)
Eugene Onegin

Three acts. First performed Moscow, 1879.
Libretto by the composer and Konstantin Shilovsky

Based on Pushkin's verse novel, though the opera's romantic tone is very different from the wryly satirical literary source. Tchaikovsky began composing the opera shortly after receiving an unsolicited letter from the woman who briefly and disastrously became his wife. This has obvious parallels with the situation of Tatyana, a figure with whom the homosexual Tchaikovsky must also have identified from his own perspective of amorous frustration and unspoken yearning.

✦ Plot

On a modest country estate in early nineteenth-century Russia, the widowed Madame Larina lives with her daughters, the outgoing Olga and the introspective Tatyana. Visitors are announced – the poet Lensky, who is courting Olga, appears with the jaded and urbane aristocrat, Eugene Onegin. Tatyana is smitten with his glamour, and in the course of a sleepless night, writes and sends him an impassioned love letter. The next morning, Onegin kindly but firmly rebuffs her and urges her to more self-restraint.

Madame Larina holds a modest party to celebrate Tatyana's name-day. Irritated at being forced by Lensky to attend such a dull event at which he is the focus of much gossip, Onegin perversely decides to flirt with Olga. Lensky is furious and rashly challenges Onegin to a duel, causing a furore at the party. At dawn the next morning, Lensky reflects on his love for Olga. After all the proprieties are observed, Onegin shoots Lensky dead and leaves Russia.

Several years later, Onegin returns from years of foreign travel to discover that Tatyana has become the wife of Prince Gremin and a great lady of St Petersburg society. Full of remorse and regret, he realizes that he loves her. He begs her for a private meeting, which she reluctantly grants. Alone together, Tatyana confesses that she still loves Onegin, but as a happily and respectably married woman, she cannot yield to his ardent entreaties. Onegin is left alone in despair.

ᖇ What to listen for

The first performance was given by students, and the opera presents no great vocal challenges: all the roles are attractively singable, and opera houses find it relatively easy to cast, though it is important to find a Tatyana (soprano) who can grow convincingly from the fragile, vulnerable girl of Act I to the passionate woman of the final scene. In the course of its seven scenes, the score moves from gentle rustic simplicity to melodramatic intensity, but its emotional centre comes early on, in the second scene, when Tatyana spends the night writing her fateful letter to Onegin (baritone). Here, the music vividly embodies over a twelve-minute span all the girl's anxieties, hesitations and ardour, crowned by a wonderful orchestral crescendo and a piping oboe which heralds the dawn. As Richard Taruskin put it, 'we can "see" and "feel" Tatyana – her movements, her breathing, her heartbeats – in her music'.

Other highlights of the score include the rapturous parlour duet sung off-stage by Tatyana and Olga (mezzo-soprano) at the beginning of the opera in counterpoint to the more down-to-earth recollections of Madame Larina and the old babushka Filipyevna; Lensky's aria, the quintessence of Russian melancholy, sung just before his fatal duel (preferably by a tenor who can bring some rich-toned plangency to it); the telling contrast of the jolly waltz at Tatyana's name-day party with the stately polonaise at the St Petersburg ball; and the no-holds-barred confrontation between Onegin and Tatyana in the final scene.

ᖇ In performance

Lovers of Pushkin's poem may find the opera falls short of the original's wit and subtlety – 'undeniably notable music,' wrote Turgenev to Tolstoy when he heard the opera, 'but what a libretto!' Yet Tchaikovsky makes something emotionally true and sincere from what on paper might look rather novelettish, and productions which take the drama and characters at face value rarely fail to make an effect with it. Notable among recent stagings is Graham Vick's spare yet evocative version at Glyndebourne, which gently charted Tatyana's sexual awakening and growth from adolescence to maturity. Thomas Allen, Thomas Hampson and Simon Keenlyside are among the handsome baritones who have recently enjoyed tremendous success in the title role; among many wonderful Tatyanas, Ileana Cotrubas, Mirella Freni and Elena Prokina have been particularly memorable.

❧ Recordings

CD: Mirella Freni (Tatyana); James Levine (cond.).
DG 423 959 2
Video: Elena Prokina (Tatyana); Andrew Davis (cond.).
Glyndebourne production. Warner 0630 1401 4 3

The Queen of Spades
(Pique Dame, Pikovaya Damu)

Three acts. First performed St Petersburg, 1890.
Libretto by the composer and Modest Tchaikovsky

Tchaikovsky initially showed little interest in his brother Modest's idea of adapting Pushkin's novella for the stage, but by the time he had finished composition (it took him less than two months) he judged the opera 'a masterpiece' – a judgment with which posterity generally concurs. The libretto changes the story's original ending: Pushkin shows Lisa happily married and Herman confined to a lunatic asylum.

❧ Plot

St Petersburg, late in the eighteenth century. Herman, a strange, intense and penniless young officer who is a mystery to his friends, loves Lisa, ward of an elderly Countess. Lisa, however, is engaged to the urbane Prince Yeletsky. Herman's friends tell him the story of the Countess: once a great beauty at the court of Versailles, she lost all her money at the gaming tables. In exchange for a sexual favour, she was told the secret of three cards which would unfailingly trump in any game. A ghost subsequently warned her that she would die at the hand of a man, crazed by love and desperate to learn her secret. Herman becomes obsessed with the story, and sees the formula of the three cards as the key to his fortunes and Lisa's love. He breaks into her apartment and declares his love to her. She is entranced by his ardour.

At a ball, Herman's friends tease him over his growing obsession. Lisa gives Herman a key to the Countess's apartments, through which he can enter hers. Later that night, the Countess disrobes in her bedroom and reminisces alone about her glory days in Versailles. Herman appears and begs her to reveal the secret of the cards. Horror-stricken at his intrusion, she dies, thus fulfilling the ghost's prophecy. Lisa enters and is appalled to realize that the secret of the cards has become more important to Herman than his love for her.

Back in his room at the barracks, Herman receives an imploring letter from Lisa and a visitation from the ghost of the Countess. She tells him to marry Lisa and reveals the formula – three, seven, ace. When he meets the distraught Lisa, he appears insane and can think only of trying out the secret of the three cards. In despair, Lisa drowns herself. In the gaming house, Yeletsky consoles himself for the loss of Lisa amid drunken carousing. Herman enters and feverishly begins to play. He wins on the three and seven, but when Yeletsky vengefully challenges him to another round, he turns up not the ace, but the queen of spades. As the ghost of the Countess appears to him again, Herman kills himself.

ᴥ What to listen for

From the orchestral introduction onwards, the score is woven through with various three-note figures, presumably intended to symbolize the fateful three cards. Tchaikovsky also offsets the increasingly gloomy and nightmarish drama with episodes of rococo elegance – the centre-piece of the splendid ballroom scene is a dainty pastoral interlude, and Herman's confrontation with the Countess is all the more chilling for being preceded by her sleepy, mumbled singing of a pretty old eighteenth-century tune (lifted straight from an opera by the composer Grétry). Note how the tension of this astonishingly powerful episode – surely the most original in all of Tchaikovsky's theatrical output – is maintained without any descent into musical histrionics: everything is tense, whispered, fragmentary and lightly scored until the very last bars, when the horror of what has happened strikes home to both Herman and Lisa and the orchestra bursts mightily forth. Equally, the opera ends not with the expected crashing blast of obvious cadences but a short, hauntingly soft chorus of lament.

Herman is an extremely heavy and demanding role for heroic tenor. The singer also needs the acting skills to manage the descent into madness without appearing ludicrous. With two highly charged, broadly phrased and uninhibitedly erotic arias, Lisa is a grandly scaled role for a full-voiced soprano. Yeletsky has a gracious aria in the ballroom scene which also serves as a standard concert item for every Russian baritone; more important to the narrative is the bass Tomsky's narrative of the story of the three cards, cast in ballad form. Long after they have otherwise retired, elderly divas relish playing the small but show-stealing role of the Countess, but it is not as easy to sing as it looks, and lies too low for most sopranos with ambitions to do anything more than croak.

❧ In performance

Thirty years ago, this opera was generally staged as a Gothic melodrama, but the fashion now is to read it as a Dostoevskian study of mental decline, obsession and isolation focused on the figure of Herman. Superb surrealistically tinged productions by Graham Vick at Glyndebourne and Richard Jones for WNO have won enormous critical and popular acclaim, as has Elijah Moshinsky's handsome but more conventional version at the Met. Vick used the idea of a blank white wall being gradually covered by the obsessive inky scribbles of a lunatic; Jones made a subtle but convincing updating to mid-twentieth-century Communist Russia, presenting the Countess as a survivor of pre-revolutionary Tsarist society.

❧ Recordings

CD: Gegam Grigorian (Herman); Valery Gergiev (cond.). Philips 438 141 2
Video: Yuri Marusin (Hermann); Andrew Davis (cond.). Glyndebourne production. Warner 079 2023

Antonín Dvořák (1841–1904)
Rusalka

Three acts. First performed Prague, 1901.
Libretto by Jaroslav Kvapil

Drawn from various literary stories about water-nymphs and mermaids in tragic contact with earthly human life, this is the only one of Dvořák's ten operas to have survived in the regular repertory. Its popularity is greatly enhanced by its hit number, Rusalka's 'Song to the Moon'.

❧ Plot

Rusalka the water-nymph has fallen in love with a Prince and wants to become human. Ignoring the warnings of the Spirit of the Lake, she enlists the help of the witch Ježibaba, who tells her that if she is to be transformed into mortal shape, she must agree to remain dumb, and that both she and the Prince will be damned if he is unfaithful to her. Rusalka is undeterred and she becomes human. The Prince is enchanted by her beauty and decides to marry her, but he soon tires of her speechlessness and transfers his attentions to the cunning Foreign Princess who wants the prince for herself. By this betrayal, Rusalka is condemned to wander for ever as a will-o'-the-wisp: Ježibaba offers her the chance of breaking the curse by shedding human blood. She refuses, but then finds that her sister water-nymphs reject her. The Prince arrives, begging forgiveness. Rusalka tells him why she was silent and explains that she can be released by his embrace, although it will cost him his life. The Prince nobly sacrifices himself, and dies in her arms. Rusalka returns to the waters.

❧ What to listen for

A score which shows the influence of Wagner's *Ring*, not only in its use of melodic motifs attached to particular characters and its 'through-composed' structure, but in the contrast between the magical spirit world and the earthier splendours of the prince's court, marked to great dramatic effect in Act II. The water spirits are clearly cousins to the Rhinemaidens, and throughout there is a Wagnerian sumptuousness to the orchestral texture and harmony.

One of its few detachable numbers, Rusalka's haunting 'Song to the Moon' occurs in Act I, but her much grander and more openly emotional aria in Act III is equally impressive. It's a long role, in which the soprano must compete with Dvořák's heavy scoring. Also striking are the one-voiced love duet with the Prince (tenor) at the end of Act I, in which Rusalka's part is taken by the orchestra, the light relief provided by the Gamekeeper and Kitchen Boy at the Prince's court who sing a bagpipe song, and the flamboyantly sinister utterances of Ježibaba (contralto). The Foreign Princess is a fine cameo role for a budding dramatic soprano, with her two short but very striking scenes.

☙ In performance

Rusalka is all the more remarkable if one considers that at the time of its composition it was the gritty realism and lurid melodrama of verismo that was operatically fashionable. In his celebrated production for ENO, however, David Pountney noted its relation to another contemporary classic – J. M. Barrie's *Peter Pan*. He took the opera away from the usual medieval fairy-tale landscape and interpreted it as a parable of adolescence, setting it in an Edwardian nursery, over which Ježibaba presided as a grim governess or housekeeper in black bombazine and the Spirit of the Lake was a kindly old man in a wheelchair. The imagery was Freudian and surrealist, with mechanical toys suddenly coming to life and Rusalka sealed off from the real world inside a translucent perspex box.

☙ Recordings

CD: Renée Fleming (Rusalka); Charles Mackerras (cond.). Decca 460 568 2
Video: Eilene Hannan (Rusalka); Mark Elder (cond.). ENO production. Universal 079 2823

Leoš Janáček (1854–1928)
Jenůfa

Three acts. First performed Brno, 1904.
Libretto by the composer

Janáček based this opera on Gabriela Preissová's *Her Foster-daughter*, a naturalistic drama itself based on a true story. It used to be performed in a version which smoothed down the brazen orchestration and made several small cuts, but since the pioneering work of the conductor Sir Charles Mackerras, Janáček's stunningly powerful original has now been firmly re-established.

ᴥ Plot

Jenůfa is pregnant by her feckless cousin Števa and worries that if he is conscripted into the army, she will not be able to marry in time to save herself from disgrace. In the event, Števa is not called up, but celebrations are interrupted when Jenůfa's fearsomely respectable and widowed foster-mother, the Kostelnička (translated as 'the wife of the Sexton') insists that Števa must stay sober for a year before she will allow the marriage. Števa's half-brother Laca is in love with Jenůfa and mightily jealous of Števa. In a spasm of rage, Laca slashes Jenůfa's face with his knife.

The Kostelnička discovers Jenůfa's pregnancy and hides her away to save her reputation, telling villagers that she has gone to Vienna. A sickly baby son is born: the Kostelnička hopes that it will die. She sends Jenůfa to bed with a strong sleeping draught. Števa appears, and the Kostelnička now begs him to marry Jenůfa as soon as possible. But since she has been scarred by Laca's attack, he has lost interest in her and instead plans to marry the mayor's daughter. Laca arrives next, asking permission to marry Jenůfa. The Kostelnička tells him about the baby, at which he is so appalled that she goes on to tell him that the baby has already died. Alone, the Kostelnička wrestles with her conscience and finally decides

that the only way to ensure her beloved Jenůfa has the chance
of a decent life will be to kill the baby. She takes it away and
drowns it in the river. Jenůfa awakes from her sleep and wonders where the baby has gone: when the Kostelnička returns
from her terrible mission, she tells Jenůfa that she has been
lying delirious for two days, during which time the baby died
naturally. The Kostelnička also tells her about Števa's forth-
coming marriage and advises her to look kindly on Laca.
When he arrives, Jenůfa meekly consents to marriage and
the Kostelnička, already haunted by guilt, gives them her
blessing.

Some months later, preparations for the wedding are under
way, though Jenůfa's mood is sombre and villagers remark
how haggard the Kostelnička looks. Števa and his new wife
arrive to pay their respects, and he and Laca are reconciled. A
wedding song is sung, when news comes that a dead baby has
been found under the ice: when pieces of its clothing are
brought in, Jenůfa cries out that the child was hers. The villagers are appalled – doubly so, as they assume that Jenůfa is
the murderer – and call for her to be punished. Then the
Kostelnička confesses all. Jenůfa is stunned, but realizes that
the deed was done out of love for her and forgives her foster-
mother. The Kostelnička is taken off to face trial. The devastated Jenůfa tells Laca that he must abandon her – how can he
possibly marry anyone associated with such disgrace? But
Laca insists that he will stand by her, and together they
resolve to face whatever the future holds.

❧ What to listen for

Janáček was fascinated by the 'naturalistic' school of Italian
verismo (Mascagni's *Cavalleria rusticana*, for example), but
Jenůfa, in a sense his own 'verismo' opera, has a power and
depth that takes it way beyond the Italians' lurid sensational-
ism. At the heart of the opera is the intense intimacy of Act II,
set inside the Kostelnička's cottage. The good-night which
Jenůfa bids to the Kostelnička is set to music of profound tenderness, orchestrated with violas and clarinets, and illustrative

of the depth of the love between the two women; in stark contrast is the Kostelnička's histrionic monologue in which she decides to kill Jenůfa's sickly baby, and Jenůfa's long lyrical reverie and prayer to the virgin after she has woken to find her baby missing. The final episode of the opera, as the Kostelnička makes her terrible confession and Jenůfa forgives her before bravely setting out with the loyal Laca to make of life what she can, is both desperately tragic and triumphantly uplifting. If it doesn't move you, then nothing in opera ever will.

The grimness of the story is lightened by the enchantingly graceful choric folk-songs in the first and third acts. Note also how alert Janáček's orchestra is to the drama: obvious examples being the recurrent use of a xylophone (often played invisibly on stage) in Act I to indicate both the inexorable rolling of the mill and the fateful nature of the unfolding action; the chaotic chord which is blurted out by the brass after the Kostelnička lies to Laca about the death of Jenůfa's baby; or the braying horns which herald the blasphemy of the Kostelnička's self-justifying idea that by killing the baby she will be returning it to God.

Janáček is not particularly comfortable to sing: he scores heavily, and Czech is dense with consonants. A lot of the musical success of a performance will therefore depend on a conductor who can allow the singers room to enunciate and project.

࢞ In performance

So concentrated and harrowing is the central emotional situation of *Jenůfa* that some directors feel they can ignore its setting in nineteenth-century rural Moravia and present the drama as universal. But a naturalistic production like Nikolaus Lehnhoff's at Glyndebourne shows how specifying a social milieu can enhance an audience's sense of the reverence in which the Kostelnička is held in the tightly knit, inward-looking community and the narrowness of the moral values which govern it. Act II also needs to convey the claustrophobic nature of Jenůfa's confinement and the freezing winter weather into which the Kostelnička takes the baby. For an audience to feel that, the set must show doors and windows which open to let in the icy blast.

The Kostelnička is a great role for an ageing dramatic soprano with presence, though the temptation to sing it approximately and overact in compensation must be avoided; in the original play, one hears much more about why she is so severe and her maltreatment at the hands of her late husband. Jenůfa, written for a younger lyric soprano, also presents great dramatic opportunities to a singer who can convey the character's burgeoning moral strength and compassion. Although the Kostelnička domineers, it is Jenůfa who gives her name to the opera and it is her inner journey that is central.

Both Laca and Števa are sung by tenors – tough roles both, hard to make sympathetic. But there are some good cameo roles: Števa's grandmother, his fiancée Karolka, and the pompous Mayor and his wife among them.

ꙮ Recordings

CD: Elisabeth Söderström (Jenůfa); Charles Mackerras (cond.). Decca 414 483 2
DVD: Anja Silja (Kostelnička); Andrew Davis (cond.). Glyndebourne production. Arthaus 208

Kát'a Kabanová

Three acts. First performed Brno, 1921.
Libretto by the composer

Based on Ostrovsky's play *The Storm*, but inspired by Janáček's great (though unconsummated) love for Kamila Stösslová, to whom the opera is dedicated. Perhaps the simplest and most unmitigatedly tragic of all Janáček's operas, with a uniquely rich, poignant and tender portrait of the eponymous heroine.

✎ Plot

Mid-nineteenth-century Russia, in a village on the banks of the Volga. Káťa is unhappily married to Tikhon, a feeble character under the thumb of his martinet mother, Kabanicha, in whose dreary house the couple live. Káťa confides to the cheerful Varvara, Kabanicha's foster-daughter, that she and Boris, another man in the village, are secretly in love. Tikhon leaves on a business trip and Káťa is afraid that in his absence, she will yield to temptation.

As the hypocritical Kabanicha receives the attentions of Boris's father, Dikoy, Varvara helps Káťa to arrange an assignation with Boris, and at the same time meets her own lover, Kudrjas. Káťa and Boris are impassioned but full of guilt; Varvara and Kudrjas, on the other hand, are love's young dream.

A storm breaks out in the village, and the superstitious peasants take it as a sign of God's wrath. Varvara warns Boris that Káťa's husband Tikhon has unexpectedly returned, and that Káťa has had a nervous collapse. Káťa then appears in a hysterical state and publicly confesses her adultery, before rushing off into the storm. Boris pursues her along the banks of the Volga, and tells her that his father is sending him away to a trading post. Káťa bids him farewell and then, bereft of hope and self-respect, drowns herself. A search party recovers her body. Tikhon rails at his mother, but Kabanicha can only stand stiffly over the corpse, thanking the gawping villagers for their help.

✎ What to listen for

No opera is more replete with the sheer sadness of human existence, and all its tragedy is embodied in the opening bars of its prelude, with its slow and achingly mournful initial theme, developing into an outburst of raging despair and a fierce assertion of fate, underpinned by drumbeats. The music for Káťa herself (lyric soprano), underpinned by warm string and woodwind, is swathed in a delicate sweetness and gentleness rare in Janáček's work, as well as a fleeting but soaringly rapturous lyricism which is pulled inexorably back to earth – reflecting Káťa's aspirations and the grim reality of her situation. Her final monologue and mad scene, its two parts divided by a moment of shattering silence, is almost unbearable in its bleak intensity. Although the opera proceeds with lightning concentration – it can be performed without an interval in less than two hours – its terrible underlying sadness is relieved by the grotesque comedy of Kabanicha (contralto) and her admirer Dikoy (bass), and the charm and innocence of Kudrjas (light tenor) and Varvara (light soprano), a love which will survive Kát'a's suicide. Note also the sleigh bells which recurrently symbolize the dream of escape from the village, the use of a violent ostinato drumbeat to indicate the hopelessness of that dream, and the evocative use of a haunting wordless chorus. The opera is heavily scored, and singers can find it hard to project the text over the orchestration.

❧ In performance

As with *Jenůfa*, it is crucial for a production to convey a specific social milieu in which Kát'a's imprisonment by the conventions of a narrow rural community, and the impossibility of her making her own choices or changing her circumstances are made plausible. A staging like Katie Mitchell's for WNO, transplanted to a mid-twentieth-century context in which adultery is no longer horrifying or exceptional, fails to address the obvious question as to why Kát'a doesn't simply run off with Boris and to hell with the rest of them. A brief but telling episode of the opera is the scene in which the villagers respond so superstitiously to the thunderstorm that they will not even consider the use of a lightning conductor.

At the Met, Jonathan Miller's production showed clapperboard houses suggestive of New England puritanism; Trevor Nunn's production at Covent Garden showed the whole stage embedded in swirls of mud, evocative of Munch's *The Scream* and symbolic of the forces which hold love and liberty back, as well as graphically representing the sheer dreariness of village life; Christoph Marthaler in Salzburg and Neil Armfield for Opera Australia have both transported the opera into the concrete desert of modern urban tower-blocks.

❧ Recordings

CD: Elisabeth Söderström (Káťa); Charles Mackerras
(cond.). Decca 421 852 2
DVD: Nancy Gustafson (Káťa); Andrew Davis (cond.).
Glyndebourne production. Arthaus 158

The Cunning Little Vixen
(Příhody Lišky Bystroušky)

Three acts. First performed Brno, 1924.
Libretto by the composer

This unique comic opera, with its underlying pantheistic
philosophy and wonder at the natural world, is based on some
popular cartoon characters published in a Brno newspaper.
Act III, Bystrouška's death and the final assertion of the glory
of natural renewal are Janáček's own invention.

❧ Plot

The Forester catches a spirited young vixen cub, Bystrouška.
Captive in the farmyard, she endures taunts from a Dog, con-
verts the Hens to feminism and makes a dashing escape.
Bystrouška evicts a Badger and sets up home in the forest. In
a nearby inn, a Parson and Schoolmaster lament their lost
loves; the Forester meanwhile becomes obsessed with pursuing Bystrouška.

Bystrouška falls in love with a handsome Fox, and they
marry in front of all the creatures of the forest. Bystrouška
then produces a huge number of offspring. The Forester
confronts a Poacher (who is about to marry a gypsy girl once
loved by the Schoolmaster) and puts down a trap for
Bystrouška. Bystrouška mocks the trap and goads the
Poacher, who finally shoots her dead.

The Forester is inspired by the beauty of nature and the

sight of young vixens reminds him of the unstoppable renewal of life.

∾ What to listen for

Janáček's fascination with notating the rhythms and cadences of speech in musical form extends in this opera into the world of animal cries and noises. Children's voices are sensitively used for the vixen's cubs and the insects. There are some enchanting dances, such as the little waltz for the cricket and grasshopper in the opening scene.

The opera is full of lively and imaginative orchestral scene painting, evocative of the richness and variety of forest life, but it only offers one extended lyrical passage for the human voice: the (baritone) Forester's exultant peroration to the glory of the nature. Bystrouška is a delightful role for a light soprano with the requisite feisty personality and the capacity to project over a full orchestra. Desire for contrast and a more mannish timbre often leads to the role of the Fox being assigned to a mezzo-soprano, but it is clearly written for a soprano.

∾ In performance

There is always the danger of sentimentalized, Disneyfied tweeness infecting stagings of this opera, but the pantomime element has to be there somewhere. David Pountney's much-travelled production skilfully treads the fine line. Some directors eschew animal costumes altogether; others have used film as a means of representing the splendour of the forest. A famous production of the 1950s was that of Walter Felsenstein in Berlin, rehearsed over several months, which drew extraordinarily vivid animal impersonations from the singers. More recently, an edge of natural savagery was strongly emphasized in a production by Nicholas Hytner for the Châtelet.

∾ Recording

CD: Lilian Watson (Vixen); Simon Rattle (cond.).
EMI 7 54212 2

The Makropulos Case
(The Makropulos Affair, Věc Makropulos)

Three acts. First performed Brno, 1926.
Libretto by the composer

This extraordinary story – both ironic comedy and profound tragedy – is drawn from a play by Karel Čapek, premièred only months before Janáček began his operatic adaptation.

∾ Plot

Prague, 1922. The glamorous prima donna Emilia Marty has a secret: she is over three hundred years old. In 1585, as Elina Makropulos, she was given an elixir of eternal life by her father, and since then she has continued to exist under a series of identities, retaining only the initials E. M.

The outcome of a long-running inheritance lawsuit, Gregor v. Prus, is expected imminently. Emilia shows remarkable knowledge of details of the case a century previously, including facts relating to Prus's mistress Elian MacGregor and the existence of a crucial will. After a performance at the opera house, Emilia holds court backstage. Both Prus and Gregor, still arguing over the case, are infatuated with her, and Prus agrees to bring her a Greek document in his possession if she spends the night with him. She agrees and after Prus has had his way with her, she then reveals her extraordinary story. A century ago as 'Elian MacGregor' she passed the document, detailing the formula of the elixir, to her lover, Prus's ancestor. Now she needs to take the elixir again in order to renew herself, but she has decided that life holds no more joy or meaning for her. She offers to pass the formula to Kristina, a girl who craves Emilia's stardom and beauty. But Kristina burns the document, and Emilia falls dead.

❧ What to listen for

On first hearing, *The Makropulos Case* is not an easy opera to appreciate or enjoy: the setting is modern and urban, and the score's idiom is therefore appropriately short-winded, edgy, dry, dissonant and modernist. Until Emilia Marty's ecstatic final monologue, almost everything is couched in quick-fire dialogue, allowing Janáček to pursue his fascination with rendering in music the melodic patterns of speech. This makes it a text-heavy opera, and perhaps its only shortcoming is that the brilliant but heavy scoring makes it difficult in the theatre to follow the words.

Although her character is in many respects repellent, Emilia Marty offers a great role for a soprano like Anja Silja who can radiate the prima-donna mystique and open another dimension in the final scene capable of suggesting that only death gives beauty and purpose to life. The overture, which paints a graphic picture of urban anxiety counterpointed against Emilia's isolation, is the longest of any of Janáček's operas.

❧ In performance

Perhaps the harshest of Janáček's operas, *The Makropulos Case* asks why humanity should crave immortality and proposes that only a normal lifespan can have meaning – eternity would actually be a hell of sheer monotony. It is in such a hell that Emilia Marty is trapped, leaving her beyond both emotion and morality, cold, contemptuous and ruthless. The characters surrounding her constitute a gallery of morally crooked fools, chasing their own tails in pursuit of their venal desires, and she despises them.

Nikolaus Lehnhoff's fine production for Glyndebourne was dominated by a set which moved constantly but with almost imperceptible slowness, symbolizing the inexorable passage of time which governs human existence.

∾ Recordings

CD: Elisabeth Söderström (Emilia Marty); Charles
Mackerras (cond.). Decca 430 372 2
Video: Anja Silja (Emilia Marty); Andrew Davis (cond.).
Glyndebourne production. Warner 0630 14016 3

From the House of the Dead
(Z mrtvého domu)

Three acts (normally performed without an interval).
First performed Brno, 1930.
Libretto by the composer

Janáček's last work, not quite finished when he died at the age of
seventy-four in 1928. Adapted from Dostoevsky's early novel –
libretto and music appear to have been written simultaneously –
it is distinguished from the composer's other major operas by its
almost exclusively male cast (there are only two tiny female
roles). In accordance with its subject-matter, the score is harsh,
angular and percussive, as well as ecstatically lyrical and passionately imbued with Janáček's Christian humanism.

∾ Plot

There is no plot in the ordinary sense: the opera consists of a
series of episodes in the harsh life of the inmates of a Siberian
prison camp in the mid-nineteenth century. Goryanshikov
arrives, having been convicted for political offences, and is
flogged. Prisoners tend an eagle with a wounded wing.
Goryanshikov offers to teach a Tartar boy to read. Amid
much squabbling and fighting, various prisoners tell their
stories, and plays are performed. Owing to a change in political circumstances, Goryanshikov is released. The remaining
prisoners symbolically set free the eagle, before returning to
their harsh daily routine.

❧ What to listen for

For all its grim setting and the absence of conventional aria or melody, this is an opera rich in all the variety and colours of human life. In form, it has been described as an orchestral poem over which the text is played out – 'take away Janáček's words', as the critic John Tyrrell suggests, 'and, very often, you have a symphonic continuity which is virtually self-sufficient'. It is also remarkable in having no single narrative focus, and no central characters: prisoners emerge to tell their stories and then disappear again into the mass.

The musical language is harmonically stark, built from the contrast and combination of short motifs, and austerely orchestrated. Janáček uses instruments at the extreme ends of their registers (notably the top of the piccolo and the bottom of the trombone), as well as a wide range of percussion instruments, including an anvil and clanging chains.

❧ In performance

The opera is less than two hours long, and best performed without an interval. What a production should communicate is best conveyed by something written by Janáček himself: 'I go into the minds of criminals and there I find a spark of God. You will not wipe away the crimes from their brows, but equally you will not extinguish the spark of God.' Several stagings have transplanted the action to the era of the Stalinist Gulag, but the setting really makes no difference – the implications of this opera are universal.

❧ Recording

CD: Ivo Zidek (Skuratov); Charles Mackerras (cond.). Decca 430 372 2

Béla Bartók (1881–1945)
Bluebeard's Castle (*Duke Bluebeard's Castle, A kékszakállú herceg vára*)

One act. First performed Budapest, 1918.
Libretto by Béla Balázs

Bartók's only opera, composed in 1911 and based on the fairy-tale by Charles Perrault and Maeterlinck's play *Ariane et Barbe-Bleue* (adapted into a fine opera by Paul Dukas in 1907). Like his two ballets *The Miraculous Mandarin* and *The Wooden Prince*, *Bluebeard's Castle* is a sinister and opaquely allegorical treatment of the mysteries of the relations between human beings.

Bartók dedicated the opera to his new wife Marta – it was not, one might suppose, the most endearing or encouraging of wedding presents.

∾ Plot

Bluebeard ushers his new wife Judith into his castle. It is dark and gloomy, and Judith craves some light. She sees seven doors and asks Bluebeard for their keys. Reluctantly, he hands over the first two: behind them lurk a torture chamber and an armoury, both of them stained with blood. Then he allows her a third and fourth key – these open on to a treasury and a garden, both bloodstained too. A fifth door opens to reveal a blaze of light, and the vast expanse of Bluebeard's kingdom. Bluebeard begs Judith to stop there, but her curiosity is irresistible. The sixth door reveals a lake of tears. Judith now insistently asks Bluebeard questions about his past loves and the seventh door. She soon realizes that he has murdered them all, and that it is their blood that she has seen. Bluebeard hands over the final key, and from the seventh door emerge the ghosts of three of his dead wives. Bluebeard hails them as the loves of dawn, noon and evening, but tells Judith that she is his love of night, and the most beautiful of them all. She takes her place alongside the other dead wives. The seventh door closes and Bluebeard is left alone in the darkness.

∾ What to listen for

The text is written in the poetic metre of old folk ballads, and the score seems mistily archaic as well as aggressively modernist. It radiates a uniquely sinister atmosphere, the result of Bartók's fascination with the exotic modes of Hungarian folk music and the kaleidoscopic colours and harmonies of Debussy's *Pelléas et Mélisande*. The casual listener will not notice, but through its episodes, the score follows a cycle of keys and esoteric harmonic correspondences. Note the 'dripping blood' motif (the interval of a minor second), and the way that Bluebeard's vocal line seems limited in range and melodic variety, whereas Judith's is constantly volatile and excitable. Whose side are we meant to take in this psychological battle?

Judith can be taken by either soprano or mezzo-soprano, Bluebeard by either bass or baritone.

∾ In performance

Although this is an opera which works magnificently in the mind's eye and is often played as a concert piece, it also offers great opportunities for imaginative staging and design: a celebrated production by Robert Lepage in Toronto made much from the simple idea of a blank wall and gradually increasing levels of light; others have exploited more obvious images of Austro-Hungarian decadence and art nouveau.

A problem this opera poses is the Hungarian language's peculiar system of stresses, un-Latinate roots and propensity for long portmanteau words make the text intractable to any translation. A spoken prologue, explaining that what follows is a parable of mankind's inner nature, is often omitted.

∾ Recording

CD: John Tomlinson (Bluebeard); Bernard Haitink (cond.). EMI 5561 622 2

Dmitri Shostakovich (1906–75)
Lady Macbeth of Mtsensk
(Katerina Ismailova)

Four acts. First performed Leningrad, 1934.
Libretto by Alexander Preys and the composer

This opera enjoyed huge success in Soviet Russia (and internationally) until in 1936 an article in *Pravda*, commissioned
by Stalin, condemned it as tuneless, coarse, primitive and
contrary to the dictates of the socialist realist aesthetic. It was
then withdrawn, only re-emerging in 1963, during the more
liberal Krushchev era, in a version retitled *Katerina Ismailova*,
shorn of its harder and more cynical edges. Over the last
thirty years, however, the magnificent original version has
been universally reinstated.

❧ Plot

In the Russian provinces in the mid-nineteenth century,
Katerina is unhappily married to the boorish merchant Zinovy.
Her father-in-law Boris berates her for her failures as a wife.
Zinovy goes away on business, and Boris humiliates Katerina
further. Sergei, a handsome new worker, arrives and gets
involved in an attack on Zinovy's housekeeper. When Katerina
attempts to quell the disturbance, Sergei challenges her to wres-
tle with him. Boris is appalled to discover Katerina in this com-
promising situation. That night, Sergei knocks on the door of
Katerina's bedroom and asks to borrow a book. He then proposes a resumption of their wrestling and soon seduces her.

Boris catches Sergei as he leaves the bedroom and beats him
up. He then demands food from Katerina – she gives him some
mushrooms that she has laced with rat poison. After revealing
his murderer, he dies in agony, and Sergei and Katerina resume
their love-making, interrupted only by the appearance of
Boris's louring ghost. When Zinovy returns, Sergei and
Katerina murder him too, hiding the body in the cellar.

Katerina and Sergei are about to be married when Zinovy's body is discovered by a peasant hunting for alcohol. They are arrested at the wedding by some pompous police. Katerina and Sergei are sent to Siberia. On the road, they quarrel and Sergei, resentful of the way Katerina has ruined his life, goes off with another woman, Sonyetka. Katerina pushes Sonyetka into the river and jumps in after her. Both of them are drowned, and the convicts continue on their way.

❧ What to listen for

A *tour de force* for the orchestra, as one might expect from one of the century's great symphonic composers. The overall tone is garish, brilliant and aggressive, and the pace swift, with the level of excitement intensified by the use of pounding ostinato and the 'Keystone Cops' scene in the police station providing grotesque comic relief. Katerina is a tremendous role for a strong soprano who can keep the audience's sympathy for a desperate woman. Note the graphic eroticism of the sex scene at the end of Act I (conveyed by sliding trombones), the gloomy passacaglia in Act II and the fierce dignity which elevates the final scene. The influence of Mussorgsky's *Boris Godunov* and its Shakespearean ability to modulate from comedy to tragedy and back again is omnipresent.

Shostakovich originally conceived the opera as the first of four treating the theme of the sufferings of modern womanhood, but was too demoralized following the attack in *Pravda* to pursue the project.

❧ In performance

Although Shostakovich was one of the twentieth century's great cynics, this opera is only incidentally a satire – for all its mockery, it is not heartless and the music makes it clear that we should see Katerina as a sort of heroine.

An obvious ploy for a modern producer is to transplant the action to the Stalinist era. For ENO, David Pountney provided a hugely impressive constructivist set, using the imagery of an abattoir and emphasizing collectivist, conform-ist behaviour by providing elaborately choreographed synchronized movements for the chorus. At the Met, Graham Vick presented it in a modern strip-cartoon setting, with surrealist touches. Russian productions have been less exaggerated, and perhaps more moving in consequence.

∾ Recording

CD: Galina Vishnevskaya (Lady Macbeth); Mstislav Rostropovich (cond.). EMI 49955 2

Sergei Prokofiev (1891–1953)
War and Peace

Thirteen scenes. First performed incomplete, Moscow, 1944; First performed complete, Moscow, 1959.
Libretto by the composer and Mira Mendelson

A series of tableaux, lasting about four hours, drawn from Tolstoy's epic novel and much influenced by Tchaikovsky's *Eugene Onegin* and Mussorgsky's *Boris Godunov*. It was largely composed in Russia during the terrible years of 1941–2, but despite Prokofiev's best efforts to create an 'accessible' piece that would help the war effort, the opera was disliked by the Stalinist authorities and it was not heard in anything like a complete version until some six years after the composer's death.

∾ Plot

Part One: Peace
Russia, during the Napoleonic wars. Prince Andrei Bolkonsky falls in love with young Natasha Rostov. Andrei's crusty father disapproves of the match and sends Andrei away: in his absence, the impressionable Natasha falls for the scheming Kuragin, but their elopement is foiled. Pierre tries to help Natasha, but he is trapped in an unhappy marriage and in love with her too. News comes of Napoleon's invasion of Russia.

Part Two: War
In despair at Natasha's betrayal, Andrei enlists. Napoleon receives bad news from the front and marvels at the strength of Russian resistance. Field-Marshal Kutuzov yields Moscow, in order to regroup. Pierre learns that Natasha and the Rostov family have fled, taking with them some Russian soldiers, among them Andrei – he and Natasha are reconciled on his deathbed. The French retreat and the Russians acclaim Kutuzov.

✎ What to listen for

Prokofiev is the most noble failure among twentieth-century opera composers. Like so many of his compatriots, he was deeply influenced by Mussorgsky's insistence on a continuous dramatic flow, uninterrupted by formal arias, but Prokofiev was not greatly gifted as a writer for the human voice and his operas seem dramatically and emotionally superficial, even though the adaptation of Dostoevsky's tale *The Gambler* (1917), the comic fantasy *The Love for Three Oranges* (1921) and the drama of devil-possession *The Fiery Angel* (1923, revised 1927) all have impressive aspects and memorable tunes. *War and Peace*, his most ambitious operatic project, is likewise more notable for its ballroom dances, patriotic choruses and scenes of mayhem and destruction (such as the burning of Moscow) than for its sustained or focused drama. Among a cast of nearly seventy characters, only Andrei has anything of much note to sing – both his opening paean to Natasha's beauty and his death scene are gratifying to a lyric baritone. Perhaps Prokofiev should rank as a greater composer for the cinema than for the opera house.

✎ In performance

A challenge for the resources of any opera company, requiring an enormous cast of soloists and enlarged chorus, as well as four hours of the audience's attention. A showpiece for Russian companies like the Bolshoi and Kirov, it has also been successfully staged throughout Europe and the USA, as well as being chosen for the opening of the Sydney Opera House in 1973. Budgetary restraints mean that productions will be visually austere rather than spectacular – both Colin Graham and Tim Albery have turned this to the work's advantage at ENO, giving the action a fluidity that isn't dependent on changes of scenery.

✎ Recording

CD and video: Gegam Grigorian (Pierre); Valery Gergiev (cond.). Philips 434 097 2 (CD); 070 427 3 (video)

Igor Stravinsky (1882–1971)
Oedipus Rex

Two acts (normally performed without an interval).
First performed Paris, 1927.
Libretto by Jean Cocteau

Described as an 'opera-oratorio' and often presented in concert form. The text of the drama, based on Sophocles' play, is sung in Latin, with a connecting narration spoken in the audience's native language. With its simple harmonies, austere orchestration and rigid separation of recitative and aria, the music embodies Stravinsky's neo-classical style in its purest form.

✎ Plot

Thebes is stricken with plague and its citizens beg their king Oedipus to free them from the curse that appears to have caused it. Oedipus's father-in-law Creon announces that the Delphic oracle blames the murderer of old King Laius, who is still at liberty within the city walls. Oedipus angrily accuses the seer Tiresias, but Tiresias insists that it is another king who is guilty. Oedipus's wife Jocasta stops the ensuing quarrel, and reminds them of the prophecy that Laius would be killed by his own son, and the fact that he was murdered by robbers at a crossroads between Daulia and Delphi. Oedipus is horror-struck, recalling that he once killed a stranger at those very crossroads. A messenger arrives, bearing news of the death of Oedipus's father, Polybus. It transpires that Polybus was not Oedipus's biological father at all, and that the infant Oedipus was recovered from a hillside by a shepherd. Jocasta leaves, appalled, and is later discovered to have hanged herself. The truth is out: Oedipus is the son of Laius and Jocasta, abandoned at birth, and he has both killed his father and married his mother. The humiliated Oedipus pierces his eyes with Jocasta's golden pin and the Thebans sadly banish him from the city.

❧ What to listen for

Stravinsky wrote *Oedipus Rex* at the height of his neo-classical phase, during which he chose to abandon the Wagnerian–Mussorgskian–Debussyan quest for continuous dramatic flow and revert instead to the eighteenth-century model, in which every number was discrete and song clearly separated from recitative. *Oedipus Rex* recalls Handelian oratorio and Italian opera, though its style is monumentally severe and emotionally unambiguous, with angular vocal lines, hard, static rhythms, lucid orchestration and clearly defined keys. Oedipus is written for a lyric tenor (Stravinsky specifically insisted that the singer 'must exploit dynamic contrasts, and his gradations in volume are extremely important'), Jocasta for a mezzo-soprano. Stravinsky had a particular soft spot for the 'early 20th-Century Fox' trumpet fanfares which herald the arrival of the Messenger.

❧ In performance

Stravinsky was accused of writing 'a waxworks opera', and he certainly specified that the soloist should be masked and that there should be no acting in the normal sense – 'the people in the (opera) relate to each other not by gestures, but by words,' he said. 'They do not turn to listen to each other's speeches but address themselves rigidly to the audience.' But this does not mean that the opera has no emotional impact. Recent productions, however, have often ignored the composer's instructions and 're-dramatized' the opera, taking the characters out of masks and suggesting the imagery of totalitarian oppression, terror and social crisis.

Stravinsky came to detest the device of the narrator and his supercilious tone, but felt that the pace of the whole work was too closely constructed around the hiatuses of his speeches to eliminate him.

❧ Recording

CD: Peter Schreier (Oedipus); Seiji Ozawa (cond.). Philips 438 865 2

The Rake's Progress

Three acts. First performed Venice, 1951.
Libretto by W. H. Auden and Chester Kallman

An opera inspired by Hogarth's series of eight engravings which the composer saw in Chicago in 1947. The English libretto incorporates references to other Hogarth engravings as well as neo-classical poets such as Pope and Dryden, and the score is rich in allusions to Mozart operas and English music (the ditties of *The Beggar's Opera*, for example, and the brilliance of Gilbert and Sullivan). Miraculously, from such a self-consciously assembled patchwork, there emerges a beautifully coherent and deeply touching work of art.

∾ Plot

England, in the eighteenth century. Trulove worries that his angelic daughter Anne is in love with a man, Tom Rakewell, who does not wish to work for his living. His suspicions are confirmed when the mysterious Nick Shadow appears with news that Tom has unexpectedly inherited a fortune from a long-lost uncle. Tom leaves for London at once, engaging Shadow as his valet with an agreement that wages will be paid after a year and a day of service.

Tom soon forgets Anne and loses all constraint: he visits Mother Goose's brothel and takes to a life of vice. When he confesses himself tired of all available amusements, Shadow suggests that he marry Baba the Turk, a fairground bearded lady. Tom agrees delightedly and brushes aside Anne, who has followed him to London. After their wedding, Baba proves an infuriatingly ceaseless chatterer until Tom forcibly silences her. Shadow shows Tom a magical machine which turns stones to bread and Tom briefly interests himself in the amelioration of mankind's lot.

But Tom soon loses all his money, and his possessions are put up for auction. After a year and a day, Tom visits a graveyard with Shadow, who reveals that he is the devil incarnate and demands his wages – Tom's soul. He tells Tom that he must now kill himself, but Tom challenges him to a last-minute game of cards, which Tom wins. Shadow is vanquished, but as he descends to hell, he drives Tom into insanity. Anne lovingly visits him in Bedlam and gently lulls him asleep. When he awakes to find himself alone, he dies from grief. The cast assembles to point the moral – 'For idle hands and hearts and minds, the Devil finds a work to do.'

∾ What to listen for

Self-consciously modelled on eighteenth-century operatic style, in which the drama develops through a succession of solo arias, duets, trios and choruses, separated by harpsichord-accompanied recitative and scored for a small orchestra. A Mozartian spirit hovers benignly over the score: *Così fan tutte* is quoted at several points, and the graveyard scene and the audience-addressing epilogue have obvious parallels in *Don Giovanni*, but the influence goes deeper than mere allusion.

Among the many delights of the score are Tom's elegant 'Love, too frequently betrayed', with clarinet obbligato; Anne's coloratura aria 'I go to him', crowned with a difficult, out-of-the-blue ten-beat top C originally interpolated by the first Anne, Elisabeth Schwarzkopf; the exquisitely melancholy Miles Davis trumpet riff which accompanies Anne's arrival in London; the high camp and nonsense patter of Baba the Turk; the comic auction scene; and the wonderful final scene in Bedlam, with its succession of short airs and choruses of which the most beautiful is Anne's lullaby, 'Gently, little boat'.

Stravinsky's setting of Auden's libretto – by turns graceful, quirky and irritatingly mannered – contains several oddly un-English emphases (notably in Baba the Turk's patter). Whether these are indicative of the slightly off-centre, skew-whiff asymmetry of modern neo-classicism or simply an indication that the composer was not a native speaker is debatable.

Tom is a role for lyric tenor, Anne for lyric soprano, Baba for mezzo-soprano, Nick Shadow for bass-baritone; all four are considered a pleasure to sing, and have many distinguished interpreters. However, young, sweet, light, high-lying tenors and sopranos should not be deceived: the music for Tom and Anne requires red-blooded voices which can sing broad phrases over a full orchestra.

Is the opera fifteen minutes too long for its own good? Could both the opening scene and the graveyard scene do with a trim?

❧ In performance

Without doubt, the classic production is the one which originated at Glyndebourne in 1975 (and which subsequently travelled to opera houses all over Europe and the USA), brilliantly designed in cross-hatched black and white by David Hockney. No other design for this opera has ever managed to find such an apt visual match for the neo-classicism of Stravinsky's music. Several productions, such as Peter Mussbach's for Salzburg, have opted to put the opera into modern dress, but the attendant disco-dancing and coke-snorting has become rather predictable. More interesting was the concept of Matthew Warchus for WNO, in which the setting moved forward in historical period from scene to scene; more bizarre was Peter Sellars's idea (for the Châtelet) of locating the opera inside a high-security American prison.

❧ Recordings

CD: Ian Bostridge (Tom); John Eliot Gardiner (cond.).
DG 459 648 2
Video: Felicity Lott (Anne); Bernard Haitink (cond.).
Glyndebourne production. Carlton SL 2008

PART EIGHT

American Opera

The history of American opera is essentially a twentieth-century one. The nation has no grand-opera tradition of its own, although the huge opera houses of New York, Chicago and San Francisco became splendid showcases for great imported singers as well as magnets for those with ambitions to shine in high society.

Through the 1930s and 1940s, a modest form of native 'folk opera' developed. It took as its subject-matter slices of American life, using an unpretentious lyrical idiom that wasn't far from musical comedy and avoiding opera houses for the friendlier, more intimate atmosphere of ordinary theatres. Gershwin's *Porgy and Bess* is the most celebrated example of this school, which also includes Aaron Copland's gentle pastoral *The Tender Land* and Carlisle Floyd's *Susannah* and *Of Mice and Men*, as well as Britten's operetta *Paul Bunyan*, written during his sojourn in the USA, 1939–42.

After the Second World War, American composers became more confident and diverse in their operatic ambitions. Gian Carlo Menotti wrote a hugely successful children's opera for television, *Amahl and the Night Visitors*, and two melodramas which owe much to the verismo school, *The Consul* and *The Medium*. Marc Blitzstein's *Regina* and Samuel Barber's *Vanessa* and *Antony and Cleopatra* are rather grander exercises in a more dignified and conventional style. Leonard Bernstein's one attempt at a full-scale, full-dress opera, *A Quiet Place* (incorporating an earlier one-act comedy, *Trouble in Tahiti*) was not successful. More recent American operas have tended to adapt existing books, plays or films as their subjects – André Previn's *A Streetcar Named Desire* and John Harbison's *The Great Gatsby* among them – but slickly enjoyable and effective as such pieces often are in performance, none of them seems to have established a firm foothold in the repertory.

Younger audiences have been attracted to the more imaginatively daring subjects favoured by the 'minimalist' school. Philip Glass's *Akhnaten* and *Einstein on the Beach* were sensationally successful in the 1970s and 1980s, though their dazzling initial impact seems to have faded fast. More substantial and complex in style is John Adams, whose *Nixon in China* and *The Death of Klinghoffer* rank internationally as two of the most admired operatic scores of recent years.

The American opera scene is enviably rich and active, but generally conservative in tone, with programming dictated by wealthy individual donors. American singers initially found it hard to establish themselves in Europe, but now, helped by the presence of so many great teachers who emigrated from war-related deprivation or persecution to well-paid posts in American conservatoires, they dominate the casts of all the major opera houses.

George Gershwin (1898–1937)
Porgy and Bess

Three acts. First performed 1935.
Libretto by Du Bose Heyward and Ira Gershwin

Initially presented (without much success) as a Broadway
musical, but now rightly accepted as a full-blown operatic
masterpiece, *Porgy and Bess* combines elements of jazz, blues,
and gospel with the classical apparatus of arias, recitatives,
leitmotivs and ensembles – Gershwin hoped that it would
'resemble a combination of the drama and romance of
Carmen and the beauty of *Meistersinger*'.

ᖇ Plot
A black tenement, Catfish Row, in Charleston, South
Carolina, during the 1920s. The stevedore Crown flees after
killing a man in a fight over a crap game. He leaves behind his
wayward girl friend Bess, who moves in with the crippled
Porgy and finds some happiness.

Crown emerges from hiding to claim Bess back, but Porgy
kills him in fury and is arrested by the police. Bess is tricked
by the dope-dealer Sportin' Life into thinking Porgy will
never return and leaves with him for New York. When Porgy
is released from custody uncharged, he sets off on his cart to
find Bess.

ᖇ What to listen for
One of the great tunesmiths of popular song in the inter-war
period, Gershwin surpassed himself in *Porgy and Bess* with
numbers like 'Summertime', 'I got plenty o'nuttin', 'Bess,
you is my woman now', 'I loves you, Porgy', 'It ain't neces-
sarily so' and 'There's a boat dat's leaving soon for New York'
which have passed beyond the opera house and entered the
common musical currency. But these are more than just isolated good tunes – every number grows out of its dramatic

moment, framed by declamatory recitative and integrated with a sequence of motifs linked to individual characters. Although Gershwin spent time in South Carolina soaking up authentic atmosphere and researching indigenous music, jazz fans tend to be sniffy about the results, finding the use of Afro-American elements (such as the liberal use of 'blue' notes and syncopation) ersatz and superficial – Duke Ellington once notoriously excoriated what he called 'Gershwin's lampblack Negroisms' and black activists have taken offence where surely none was intended.

ও In performance

Although *Porgy and Bess* was steadily popular from the early 1940s, it was for many years staged in heavily cut and simplified versions suitable for theatrical runs of eight performances a week. Only in 1976, when Houston Grand Opera gave the first-ever performance of Gershwin's original score did its true operatic stature emerge. It was followed by similarly complete productions in several other major opera houses, notably at Glyndebourne in 1986, where Trevor Nunn was responsible for a colourful yet emotionally hard-hitting staging, also seen at Covent Garden and the Met. The terms of Gershwin's will dictate that *Porgy and Bess* should only be performed by an all-black cast.

ও Recording

CD: Willard White (Porgy); Simon Rattle (cond.). EMI 49568 2

Gian Carlo Menotti (1911–)
The Medium

Two acts. First performed New York, 1946.
Libretto by the composer

Inspired by the young composer's own visit to a seance, and often performed in a double bill with a brief comic curtain-raiser, *The Telephone*. Menotti described it 'as the tragedy of a woman caught between . . . a world of reality she cannot wholly comprehend and a supernatural world in which she cannot believe'.

✎ Plot

The fraudulent Madame Flora prepares her theatrical tricks for a seance with the help of her daughter Monica and mute servant-boy, Toby. A new client, Mrs Nolan wants to be put in touch with her dead daughter. During the seance, Monica duly impersonates the girl, but Madame Flora feels a hand touch her throat and is terrified. She blames the mute Toby, who cannot defend himself from the accusation. Later, Mrs Nolan returns and Madame Flora, now very drunk, confesses she is a fraud. She falls asleep and is awoken by Toby, accidentally making a noise behind a curtain. Madame Flora seizes a revolver and shoots the boy, whom she believes to be a ghost.

✎ What to listen for

Menotti was heavily influenced by Puccini, and the score is couched in an extravagantly dramatic style, interrupted only by Monica's aria, 'Monica, Monica, dance the waltz', and the simple song 'Black Swan', with which Monica soothes her mother's jangled nerves. The music becomes increasingly dissonant as the drama progresses. The opera is orchestrated for fourteen players, including a piano duet.

❧ In performance

One of the most popular post-war operas, once described as an 'operatic film noir', *The Medium* ran for six months on Broadway and was later filmed. Although it has now gone out of fashion, it remains an effective piece of melodrama, with a strong role for the contralto who plays Madame Flora.

❧ Recording

CD: Marie Powers (Flora); Thomas Schippers (cond.).
VAI Audio 1162

Leonard Bernstein (1918–90)
Candide

Two acts. First performed Boston, 1956.
Libretto by Lillian Hellman, revised by Hugh Wheeler
and several other hands

Based on Voltaire's short novel of the same name, this ambitious operetta pre-dates the same composer's hit musical *West Side Story* by a year. At least seven different writers – including Stephen Sondheim – had a hand in the many revisions to the chaotic libretto.

∾ Plot

Mid-eighteenth-century Europe. Candide, an innocent Westphalian youth, is told by his optimistic tutor Pangloss that 'everything is for the best in the best of all possible worlds'. A series of disastrous adventures, which take him all over the world, proves otherwise: his fellow men are rapacious and merciless, and life full of shocks and disappointment. Finally, however, Candide returns home and settles down with Pangloss and his beloved Cunegonde, determined to make his 'garden grow'.

∾ What to listen for

The score of *Candide* may not be profound, but from its scintillating overture, with its Rossini-style crescendo, it is certainly brilliant. The obvious vocal highlight is Cunegonde's 'Glitter and be gay', a witty and dazzling take on coloratura showpieces, but there are also several superb parodies of dance styles, ranging from tango to gavotte, as well as trios, quartets and ensembles of a complexity rare in operetta. Among other numbers, Candide's and Cunegonde's daintily pretty 'O happy we', Candide's elegiac lament, the duet 'We are Women' and the moving final chorus 'Make our Garden Grow' are all outstanding.

✺ In performance

After several substantial revisions, including a 1973 version with a shorter, completely new libretto and some new numbers, Bernstein finally put his imprimatur on the syncretic edition prepared with the help of his pupil John Mauceri and performed and recorded at the Barbican Centre in 1989. But problems remain, and a major revival by the National Theatre in 1999 continued to add, subtract and reorder. It seems unlikely that two productions of *Candide* will ever use quite the same material.

✺ Recording

CD: Jerry Hadley (Candide); Leonard Bernstein (cond.). DG 429 734 2

Carlisle Floyd (1926-)
Susannah

Two acts. First performed Talahassee, 1955.
Libretto by the composer

Floyd ranks among the most steadily popular of modern
American composers. *Susannah* transfers the tale from the
biblical apocrypha of Susannah and the Elders to a rural
Midwest setting, *circa* 1950. It is important to remember that
the opera was written during the era of the McCarthy persecutions – it is contemporary with Arthur Miller's *The Crucible*,
with which it has obvious similarities – and reflects the composer's sympathy for the victims of busybodies, time-servers
and informers.

∾ Plot

In a puritanical mountain village in Tennessee, Susannah
Polk, an innocent orphaned nineteen-year-old brought up by
her brother Sam, is suspected of being sexually wanton.
Despite much disapproval, Bat, a local boy, is courting her.
When Susannah is spotted bathing in a creek used for bap-
tisms, the church Elders accuse her of being devilish, and at a
revivalist meeting the Reverend Blitch urges her to confess
and repent. She refuses, and is cast out of the community. Bat
is forced to bring false evidence against her.

Blitch follows Susannah to her shack outside the village,
where he seduces her, only to discover that she is a virgin.
Stricken with remorse, he tries to defend her without incrim-
inating his own reputation, but nobody believes him. When
Susannah tells Sam what has happened, he kills Blitch. The
villagers assemble to drive Susannah out, but she keeps them
at bay with a shotgun. Driven mad, she slaps Bat across his
face.

❧ What to listen for

There is nothing very complex or innovative about Floyd's score, but it is attractively fluent and communicative. Catchy Appalachian folk-songs, evangelical hymns and square dances are incorporated, and there are some glowingly lyrical arias for the soprano who takes the role of Susannah – music which has attracted several of today's leading American prima donnas, notably Renée Fleming.

❧ In performance

A simple work which requires only a straightforward staging. Originally designed to be performed by university students, it has also been performed in several major opera houses, including the Met, where it has gripped and moved audiences, if not the more exigent critics.

❧ Recording

CD: Cheryl Studer (Susannah); Kent Nagano (cond.).
Virgin 7243 545 03924

Stephen Sondheim (1930–)
Sweeney Todd

Two acts. First performed New York, 1979.
Libretto by Hugh Wheeler

Sondheim's version of the legend of 'the demon barber of Fleet Street' draws on a cod-Victorian melodrama by Christopher Bond, written in 1973. Another Broadway musical which has gravitated towards the opera house and benefits from performers who can sing as well as they can act.

✵ Plot

The demented yet magnificent Sweeney Todd returns to London from long imprisonment, determined to wreak revenge on the Judge who falsely convicted him, raped his wife and now has designs on his daughter Johanna. Todd sets up his barber's shop above a Fleet Street pie-shop owned by the revolting Mrs Lovett, and they set up a gruesome partnership – as Todd uses his razor to slit the throats of all customers, so she cannibalizes the corpses for pie filling. For a while, they are hugely successful – but their nemesis is unimaginably horrible.

✵ What to listen for

In contrast to the black parody of the 'Dies irae' from the Catholic mass and several passages of outright Grand Guignol, Sondheim plays merrily with the styles of Victorian music-hall and Gilbert and Sullivan (notably in Mrs Lovett's 'The Worst Pies in London' and 'By the Sea'). Among the more lyrical numbers, 'Not while I'm around', a duet between Tobias and Mrs Lovett in which the affectionate sentiments are gruesomely undercut by the horror of the situation, stands out. But perhaps the best number in the score is the ironically jolly waltz at the end of Act I in which Todd and Mrs Lovett fantasize over their cannibalistic meat pies.

✤ In performance

In 1984, *Sweeney Todd* was performed at New York City Opera. Since then, it has received several other highly successful opera house productions, one of the most notable being David McVicar's for Opera North. McVicar took Todd seriously, presenting him as a tragic hero consumed with righteous anger at the complacence and self-interest of the Victorian establishment.

✤ Recording

CD: Len Cariou (Sweeney Todd); Angela Lansbury (Mrs Lovett); Paul Gemignani (cond.). RCA 3 379 2

John Adams (1947–)
Nixon in China

Three acts. First performed Houston, 1987.
Libretto by Alice Goodman

Conceived in collaboration with the opera's first director,
Peter Sellars, this has proved one of the most durable and
complex of operas emanating from the 'minimalist' tendency
of modern music, reaching large audiences throughout the
world.

∿ Plot
American President Richard Nixon and his wife Pat arrive in
Beijing on their historic diplomatic mission to Communist
China in 1972. At the airport, they are greeted by the father
of modern China, President Chou En-Lai. Later, Nixon and
his unsympathetic foreign policy expert, Henry Kissinger,
meet Chairman Mao Tse-Tung and discuss the problems of
governing the contemporary world.

Pat Nixon is deeply touched by her tour of the sights of
modern China. At a great state banquet, a revolutionary ballet is presented as entertainment. At its climax, the villainous
Madame Mao exults in Communism's brutal triumph over
counter-revolutionary elements.

On their last night in Beijing, the Nixons, the Maos and
Chou En-Lai reflect in their separate bedrooms on the
course of history and the paths that their lives have taken
through it.

∿ What to listen for
John Adams once wrote that he 'wanted to create a music that
had the energy, drive and ecstasy of minimalism, but which
had much more expressive potential' – this he achieves in
Nixon in China, a work that is both exciting and moving.
Using the basic minimalist device of repeated arpeggios

which modulate harmonically, Adams builds a musical drama which, in the style of baroque opera, focuses as much on the characters' inner meditations (some of them highly complex in their political implications) as on external plot. Highlights include the spectacular opening of the opera, building up to Nixon's arrival, and the magnificent crescendo which accompanies the landing of the aeroplane, followed by Nixon's strikingly syncopated aria, 'News news news'; the comic banquet which concludes Act I; Pat Nixon's visionary reflections on what she sees of China, 'This is prophetic', in Act II, followed by the superb scene in which a performance of the revolutionary ballet *The Red Detachment of Women* is interrupted by a terrified Pat who mistakes theatrical violence for reality. Act II ends with a venomously assertive Queen-of-the-Night style coloratura aria for Madame Mao. Act III is much quieter in tone – like Debussy's *Pelléas et Mélisande*, the opera seems to end with all its questions still wide open.

❧ In performance

Although it has received several other successful stagings, *Nixon in China* must always be deeply bound up with Peter Sellars's original production, which captures, through Adrianne Lobel's designs, the naïve charm and vibrant colours of Chinese poster art. The villains of the piece are Kissinger and Madame Mao, but the libretto adamantly refuses to take sides between capitalist Americans and Communist Chinese, allowing both sides to state their ideological cases with dignity.

The great critic Andrew Porter once pointed out that this must be the only opera in history in which most of the principal characters – the Nixons, Kissinger and Madame Mao – could theoretically have been present at the first performance!

❧ Recording

CD: James Maddalena (Nixon); Edo de Waart (cond.). Nonesuch 7559 79177 2

The Death of Klinghoffer

**Prologue and two acts. First performed Brussels, 1991.
Libretto by Alice Goodman**

Based on events which occurred in 1985, and completed
during the US war against Saddam Hussein's Iraq.

○∾ Plot

Exiled Palestinians sing in counterpoint to a chorus of exiled
Jews. The cruise liner *Achille Lauro* is hijacked by Palestinians
a few miles outside Alexandria and hostages are rounded up.
Leon Klinghoffer, an innocent Jewish tourist in a wheelchair,
is shot dead following an argument between the hijackers.
The captain and the hijackers negotiate, and the ship returns
to Alexandria. Klinghoffer's body is thrown overboard and
the captain tells Mrs Klinghoffer of her husband's death.

○∾ What to listen for

Almost an oratorio in style, much influenced by Bach's
Passions, in which the story proceeds largely through a
sequence of long meditative choruses and arias in which
events are related and then pondered from different perspectives. The score is richer and more complex, but less immediately accessible and entertaining, than that of *Nixon in China*.
The image of the sea constantly laps in undulations through
the music. As well as some tremendous fortissimo choruses
(at the end of Act I, for instance), there are passages of potent
beauty, notably the Act II chorus 'Hagar and the Angel'.
Amplified sound is used at certain points.

○∾ In performance

The inflammatory issue of political terrorism and the refusal
to make predictable condemnations of the Palestinian question has made this opera extremely controversial. The grey,
austere and deliberately unemotional original production by
Peter Sellars avoided any visual distinctions between

Palestinians and Jews, emphasizing the common root of both religions and their shared experience of dispossession. The opera does not have conventionally conceived characters (dancers act out much of the story), but its central figure is the ship's Conradian Captain – neither Jewish nor Palestinian – who stands between passengers and hijackers, unable to control the destiny of his ship.

❧ Recording

CD: James Maddalena (Captain); Kent Nagano (cond.).
Nonesuch 7559 79281 2

Index of Operas

Where an opera is known well in both its original title and its translation, it will appear twice. Operas mentioned in passing appear in italics.

Index of Composers